[handwritten note:] ...leap ...ving in His glorious "Word." As one grandparent to another, Am ; I hope that we see much more of you in the days ahead. With Blessings in Christ. Bob.

101

PORTRAITS OF JESUS

in the

Hebrew Scriptures

101 PORTRAITS OF JESUS IN THE HEBREW SCRIPTURES

© 2008 by Robert C. Beasley

Printed in the United States of America. The typeface is Adobe Garamond Pro.

Editing and cover design by Nat Belz

Cover illustration: Landscape with Ruth and Boaz (detail) by Josef Anton Koch (1768-1839)

ISBN 978-0-9799731-4-7

Library of Congress Cataloging-in-Publication Data • 2007936897

Beasley, Robert C., 1938-

Biblical Studies/Christology

Hendersonville, North Carolina

And beginning with Moses and all the Prophets, [Jesus] explained to them what was said in all the Scriptures concerning himself.

(LUKE 24:27)

"Although the work of redemption was not actually wrought by Christ till after his incarnation, yet the virtue, efficacy, and benefits thereof were communicated unto the elect, in all ages successively from the beginning of the world, in and by those promises, types, and sacrifices, wherein he was revealed, and signified to be the seed of the woman which should bruise the serpent's head; being yesterday and today the same, and forever."

WESTMINSTER CONFESSION OF FAITH, CHAPTER VIII, VI

THE AUTHOR

Bob Beasley lives with his wife, Amy, in the mountains of North Carolina. He is a former entrepreneur and business executive. A native of Tennessee, he spent the majority of his life in San Diego, California. Bob is a graduate of Claremont McKenna College in Claremont, California, and Westminster Theological Seminary in Escondido, California. He has three grown daughters and five grandchildren.

Bob is the author of four books; *The Wisdom of Proverbs*, *Proverbs for Promise-Keeping*, and with Amy, *Wisdom for Women*, all published by Legacy Press of Richmond, Virginia. Additionally, he is the author of *The Commandments of Christ*, published by P&R Publishing of Phillipsburg, New Jersey. Bob is an ordained ruling elder at Trinity Presbyterian Church (PCA) in Asheville, NC.

Contents

DEDICATION

This book is dedicated to the memory of

James Montgomery Boice,
Edmund P. Clowney,
and
Arthur W. Pink

all men who saw in shadows the glory of the
Lord Jesus in the Hebrew Scriptures,
and who now bask in His refulgent glory.

To Him be glory, honor, and power,
both now and forevermore,
amen and amen.

INTRODUCTION

When I came to know Christ as Savior and Lord in 1971, I immediately took a consuming interest in the Bible. For a while, I attended a nearby church in our hometown in California, one that I soon found out had an existential, subjective view of Scripture. They taught that the Bible only *became* God's Word as we come to understand it. For them biblical truth was up to each individual—how each reader responded to it. In other words, their reason trumped God's revelation. The Christian believes that reason is good, but knows that reason is always subordinate to God's Word.

One Palm Sunday, the church planned a parade around town with homemade banners. Since my favorite study was already Jesus in the Old Testament, I made a banner of Zechariah 9:9; *"Rejoice greatly, O Daughter of Zion! Shout, Daughter of Jerusalem! See, your king comes to you, righteous and having salvation, gentle and riding on a donkey, on a colt, the foal of a donkey."* I was amazed that no one seemed to get it: The verse is a clear reference to Jesus' triumphal entry into Jerusalem on "Palm Sunday" prior to His crucifixion. (See Matthew 21, especially verse 5.) This prophetic verse was written hundreds of years before its fulfillment! Did not this verse, and many others like it, speak to the Bible's supernatural origin? Is the Bible not the inerrant Word of God?

The Bible does have a supernatural author. Its origin was not in the minds of mere men, but in the mind of almighty God. One way we know this to be true is that the Bible, although inscribed by many men over thousands of years, has but one central subject—the Lord Jesus Christ, and God's unfolding plan of salvation through Him. If you are willing to search, you will see glimpses of Jesus on every page in every book of the Old Testament—the Hebrew Scriptures. How could this be, apart from these Scriptures being inspired by God?

The final books of the Old Testament were written at least 500 years before Jesus' birth. The first five books of Moses were written at least 1,500 years before that. And yet, one common thread is sewn through them all—Jesus Christ. Imagine for a moment that my great-great-great-grandfather in his journey over the Atlantic to the new world in America had written a book that described me in detail. Although I wouldn't be born for more than a hundred years, his book would describe where and when I would be born, what I would do for a living, what my character and actions would be, my exact name, and so forth. That would be unusual, would it not? Actually, it would be impossible for a mere human. But Jesus was written about thousands of years before His physical appearance on earth.

Following His resurrection, Jesus has a conversation with two of His followers on the road to Emmaus (Luke 24:13-27). The two men are journeying from Jerusalem, and as they walk they talk about the events of the past few days. Jesus walks up to them, but they do not recognize Him. He asks them what they are discussing. One of the men, Cleopas, asks Jesus if he has not heard of Jesus of Nazareth, "a great Prophet of God who was crucified." Why, just this morning is three days since Jesus' death, Cleopas tells him, but when some women went to his tomb, His body was not there. Angels beside the tomb told them Jesus had risen from the grave, Cleopas tells Jesus.

Then Jesus says this to them:

"How foolish you are, and how slow of heart to believe all that the prophets have spoken! Did not the Christ have to suffer these things and then enter his glory?" And beginning with Moses and all the prophets, he explained to them what was said in all the Scriptures concerning himself.

In this short volume I merely scratch the surface of that last verse, *"And beginning with Moses and all the Prophets, he explained to them what was said in all the Scriptures concerning himself."* Ours is a faith established in history.

But Jesus does not jump into the pages of history as a little child in a stable in Bethlehem. His story begins much further back in history than that. In fact, His story goes all the way back to before history on earth began! In a sense, He IS history, as all history is His Story. Jesus is the Creator God, the promised Redeemer, the great Prophet, Priest, and King of the Hebrew Scriptures. He is Yahweh, Jehovah—the great I AM—of the burning bush. He is Immanuel—God with us!

Jesus is pictured in many ways in the Old Testament. He is seen in His mighty acts, such as in Creation. He is the antitype, typified by men like Adam, Melchesidek, and David. Jesus is foreshadowed by furniture, (yes, furniture), rocks, food, doorways, trees, water, boats, colors, animals... in hundreds of ways. His future coming and glory are foretold by men speaking for God about events hundreds, even thousands of years in the future.

Jesus also appears on the pages of the Hebrew Scriptures as the "Angel of the Lord." He visits an incredulous Sarai and Abram with a promise too good to be true. He wrestles with a man named Jacob, changing Jacob's name to "Israel." Like a great novel that gives its readers clues as to what will come about later in the book, the Old Testament is full of allusions to and promises of the kingdom of the coming Messiah who will save His people from their sins. In short, Jesus is revealed everywhere. Only an all-powerful and omniscient God could have conceived it and given it to men to write down in their own words.

Someone asks, "But if Jesus is revealed on every page of the Old Testament, why didn't the Hebrews believe in Him?" The answer is found in Paul's Letter to the Romans chapters 9 through 11. Paul was a Hebrew and persecuted the Church. Later, his spiritual eyes were opened to see the reality of Jesus as the long awaited Messiah—the Christ. It is the same with unbelievers today. Paul writes in 2 Corinthians 4:4, *"The god of this age [Satan] has blinded the minds of unbelievers, so that they cannot see the light of the gospel of the glory of Christ, who is the image of God."*

What happened to the fellows on the road to Emmaus also

happened to Paul on the road to Damascus. It happened to me in 1971. God opened my spiritual eyes so that I could see the reality of who Jesus is. Following their journey to Emmaus we read these words:

> *When he [Jesus] was at the table with them, he took bread, gave thanks, broke it and began to give it to them. Then their eyes were opened and they recognized him, and he disappeared from their sight. They asked each other, "Were not our hearts burning within us while he talked with us on the road and opened the Scriptures to us?"* (Luke 24:30-32).

Jesus says in John 5:24: *"I tell you the truth, whoever hears my word and believes him who sent me has eternal life and will not be condemned; he has crossed over from death to life."*

If you have never received Christ's free gift of salvation by faith alone, you may not be able to see Jesus in the Hebrew Scriptures. This book may not make any sense to you, because your spiritual eyes have not been opened. If this is true of you, I would urge you to lay the book aside for a moment and pray this simple prayer: "Lord, I want to see you. Come into my life and save me from my sins, opening my eyes to the truth of your Word and Gospel. I repent of my unbelief." If you are sincere, Christ will not fail you.

One last housekeeping note. Several places exist in the study where I have emboldened words quoted from the Bible. Those emphases are always mine for clarity's sake. Rather than say that each time one appears, I make that general comment here. Also, I don't have any footnotes in the body of the text. If a page number of an author's book is given, the edition of the book that is referred to will appear in the bibliography.

May God richly bless you as you study His marvelous, inerrant, and all-sufficient Word concerning His Son—our Lord Jesus Christ—and His mission to redeem His people from their sins.

1. JESUS: THE SELF-EXISTENT CREATOR
Genesis 1:1

In the beginning God created the heavens and the earth.

John begins his gospel with these words: "*In the beginning was the Word, and the Word was with God, and the Word was God... Through him all things were made; without him nothing was made that has been made.*" John goes on to say in 1:14, "*The Word became flesh and made his dwelling among us.*" John is speaking of Jesus, testifying to the second person of the Trinity of Father, Son, and Holy Spirit. Jesus, together with the Father and the Spirit, is the Creator of the universe.

The writer to the Hebrews also testifies to this truth. Hebrews 1:1 says, "*...in these last days [God] has spoken to us by his Son, whom he appointed heir of all things, and through whom he made the universe.*" For anything to exist at all, something, (or Someone), must have the power of existence within itself, (or Himself). As John 5:26 testifies, "*For as the Father has life **in himself,** so he has granted the Son to have life **in himself.**" All effects have causes. Without the simple truth of cause and effect, scientific analysis would be impossible. Indeed, knowledge itself would be impossible. The words that are written here are an effect caused in one sense by my fingers hitting my computer's keyboard. You and I are effects as well, contingent creatures caused physically through our natural parents. If we set our peg all the way back to Genesis 1:1, we see that God is the ultimate cause of all that exists. God is the uncaused Causer—the Someone who has the power of eternal self-existence, or **aseity.** Scripture tells us that Jesus Christ is that Someone.

The modern notion that the universe somehow evolved by "chance" over millions or billions of years is astonishingly irrational. After all, "chance" is nothing but the odds of something happening—the odds that a coin will turn up heads 50% of the time it is flipped. The old cliché is applicable here that if you tell a big enough lie, people will begin to believe it. While micro-evolution—change within species—has been observed in the laboratory, macro-evolution—change from one species to another has not, and never will be. Multitudes of people believe the macro-evolution lie for neither scientific nor historical reasons. Their reasons are fundamentally sinful or flow from willful ignorance. They believe macro-evolution—a godless explanation of beginnings—because they want nothing to do with a personal Creator-God. To recognize God as Creator would require personal accountability to Him, and more than anything else, people want autonomy—they want to be a law unto themselves—accountable only to themselves. Desiring autonomy, Adam and Eve gave in to the serpent's challenge and through their sin dumped the whole human race into the sewer we know as human history.

Throughout Genesis 1 and 2, we read that everything the Lord God made He considered *good*. But sin entered the world through the free and sovereign choice of our first father, Adam. Adam rejected the very One who had given him life. Is it any wonder that without God's grace in redemption, we, Adam's children, reject him too?

But the universe's Creator is also the "Re-Creator." Jesus Christ came physically into the world to resurrect a lost and fallen creation. We read in John 3:16, "*For God so loved the world that he gave his one and only Son, that whoever believes in him shall not perish but have eternal life.*" The Creator stands ready to welcome any who would simply put their faith in Him, trusting Christ alone for salvation.

Jesus Christ saves—re-creates—by His Spirit and through His Word, and not by any works that we might do. Salvation is by God's grace alone through faith alone in Christ alone. If you have never put your complete trust in Christ as Lord and Savior, I invite you to do that now. John also says in John 1:14, "*We have seen his glory, ...full of grace and truth.*" For me, "*grace and truth*" are the two greatest words ever. The *truth* is that Jesus Christ is our Creator God. By *grace*, He is also our Savior.

2. Jesus: The Light of the World
Genesis 1:1-5

In the beginning God created the heavens and the earth. Now the earth was formless and empty, darkness was over the surface of the deep, and the Spirit of God was hovering over the waters. And God said, "Let there be light," and there was light. God saw that the light was good, and he separated the light from the darkness. God called the light "day," and the darkness he called "night." And there was evening, and there was morning—the first day.

The first thing we might notice about these verses is that, although we are not given all the specifics about how God created the world, the earth was first characterized by darkness. The Spirit of God hovered over the dark waters. In the same way, the Holy Spirit hovered over the virgin Mary (Luke 1:35). This Holy One, Jesus, who was born of Mary said in John 8:12, "*I am the light of the world. Whoever follows me will never walk in darkness, but will have the light of life.*" So as darkness was separated from light at creation, the darkness of sin is overcome in the birth of Jesus.

Other New Testament writers bear witness to the light of Christ Jesus. Luke records the aged priest Simeon's reaction on seeing Jesus:

*"Simeon took [Jesus] in his arms and praised God, saying: "Sovereign Lord, as you have promised, you now dismiss your servant in peace. For my eyes have seen your salvation, which you have prepared in the sight of all people, a **light for revelation** to the Gentiles and for glory to your people Israel"* (Luke 2:28-32).

The light of Christ is the light of God's special revelation to all mankind. John speaks of John the Baptizer's witness to Jesus' deity. "*In [Jesus] was life, and that life was the light of men. The light shines in the darkness, but the darkness has not understood it...The true light that gives light to every man was coming into the world*" (John 1:4-7). The true light illuminates our spiritual darkness, speaking the truth about our natural condition as sinful enemies of the Creator, while lighting the way to reunion and fellowship with Him.

In John 3:19-21 we read: "*This is the verdict: Light has come into the world, but men loved darkness instead of light because their deeds were evil.*" Mankind's basic problem is that he loves evil—darkness—and doesn't want the truth of his evil exposed. So he suppresses the truth—light—that even the creation itself displays.

> "*The wrath of God is being revealed from heaven against all the godlessness and wickedness of men who suppress the truth by their wickedness, since what may be known about God is plain to them, because God has made it plain to them. For since the creation of the world God's invisible qualities—his eternal power and divine nature—have been clearly seen, being understood from what has been made, so that men are without excuse*" (Romans 1:18-20).

The creation screams the truth of a Creator but men suppress it. What greater responsibility do those have who suppress the truth of His Word?

When I was a child, my parents took our family to the amazing and unforgettable Carlsbad Caverns in New Mexico. Inside the huge cave, the tour guides paused in one of the immense rooms and turned off all the lights that illuminated the various stalagmites and stalactites. I could not see my hands in front of my eyes. The darkness was total. The same black spiritual darkness consumes much of the world today. In Matthew 6:23 Jesus says, "*…if your eyes are bad, your whole body will be full of darkness. If then the light within you is darkness, how great is that darkness!*" Jesus came to bring us out of darkness into the "*true light*" (1 John 2:8). In the same way as the primordial world, the spiritual world is ultimate darkness without Christ.

The gracious provision of physical light at creation is reflected now by God's gracious provision of light for every believer. God says "Let there be light" to countless Christians around the world every day, as they are brought into His family by His grace, and as they grow in the knowledge and image of Jesus through His Spirit and Word.

3. Jesus: The Seed of the Woman
Genesis 3:14-15

So the LORD God said to the serpent, "Because you have done this, 'Cursed are you above all the livestock and all the wild animals! You will crawl on your belly and you will eat dust all the days of your life. And I will put enmity between you and the woman, and between your offspring and hers; he will crush your head, and you will strike his heel'"

Following God's creation of Adam and before he made Eve, He gave this single admonition, *"And the LORD God commanded the man, 'You are free to eat from any tree in the garden; but you must not eat from the tree of the knowledge of good and evil, for when you eat of it you will surely die'"* (Genesis 2:16-17). Under Satan's temptation, Eve ate and gave some to her husband and he also ate. But they didn't die—physically, that is. Nevertheless, something terrible happened. Previously, they walked and talked with God in the Garden in friendship and fellowship. Now, spiritually dead, they hid from God, rejecting His friendship. They were ashamed and attempted to cover their nakedness.

God called for them and said, *"'What is this you have done?'" The woman said, 'The serpent deceived me, and I ate'"* (Genesis 3:13). So God cursed the serpent for leading the couple into sin. He told him that he would crawl on his belly and eat dust, and that something else would happen. The King James Version (KJV) states verse 15 like this: *"And I will put enmity between thee and the woman, and between thy seed and her seed; it shall bruise thy head, and thou shall bruise his heel."* Since through a woman sin entered the world, a woman would one day bring the solution. This woman—the enemy of Satan—is well known to students of history. She is the nation Israel, through whom would come the promised Messiah. From Pharaoh's cruelty of the Hebrew slaves, right up to the present day, this enmity between Satan and "the woman" has been clearly seen. The ultimate "seed of the woman" is none other than the Lord Jesus. *"But when the time had fully come, God sent his Son, born of a woman, born under law…"* (Galatians 4:4).

Isaiah spoke of this woman and her seed in 7:14, *"Therefore the Lord himself will give you a sign: The virgin will be with child and will give birth to a son, and will call him Immanuel."* Ultimately, when *"the time had fully come,"* Jesus would be born of a woman—of a virgin, and she from the house of David. We read these words in Matthew 1:19-24:

> *"...an angel of the Lord appeared to [Joseph] in a dream and said, Joseph son of David, do not be afraid to take Mary home as your wife, because what is conceived in her is from the Holy Spirit. She will give birth to a son, and you are to give him the name Jesus, because he will save his people from their sins."*

Why a virgin? First, the writer to the Hebrews tells us, *"Since the children have flesh and blood,* [Jesus] *too shared in their humanity so that by his death he might destroy him who holds the power of death—that is, the devil…"* (Hebrews 2:14). Our Savior had to be born like any other man, but without the contamination the sin nature that is universally passed from generation to generation through human conjugal union. The technical term for what is handed down is "original sin." Second, Jesus was not only fully man, but fully God. He is the God-man. His true earthly Father had to be the eternal heavenly Father, through the overshadowing of the Virgin Mary by His Spirit.

And who is Satan's "seed" or "offspring"? He is the antichrist. John tells us in 1 John 2:22: *"Who is the liar? It is the man who denies that Jesus is the Christ. Such a man is the antichrist—he denies the Father and the Son."* Jesus is to "crush" the Antichrist's head, even as the Antichrist would "bruise" the heel of Jesus. As the prophet Isaiah said long before Christ went to the Cross, *"But he was pierced for our transgressions, he was crushed for our iniquities; the punishment that brought us peace was upon him, and by his wounds we are healed"* (Isaiah 53:5).

4. JESUS: THE SECOND ADAM
Genesis 3:6

*When the woman saw that the fruit of the tree was good for food and pleas-
ing to the eye, and also desirable for gaining wisdom, she took some and ate
it. She also gave some to her husband, who was with her, and he ate it.*

When God created Adam, but before Eve was created, He gave
the man this simple commandment: ..."*You are free to eat
from any tree in the garden; but you must not eat from the tree
of the knowledge of good and evil, for when you eat of it you will surely die*"
(Genesis 2:16-17). God had created a good man, a man of high intellect
and character, and placed him in an garden environment that was not only
beautiful, but that also filled his every need. In that perfect environment,
Adam chose to commit cosmic rebellion against the One who loved him
and had given him everything he needed. The Bible tells us that when
Adam rebelled against his Creator, the whole world fell under a curse. God
said these things to our first father in Genesis 3:17-19:

*"Because you listened to your wife and ate from the tree about which I
commanded you, 'You must not eat of it,' "Cursed is the ground because
of you; through painful toil you will eat of it all the days of your life.
It will produce thorns and thistles for you, and you will eat the plants
of the field. By the sweat of your brow you will eat your food until you
return to the ground, since from it you were taken; for dust
you are and to dust you will return."*

When I was a youngster, my mom and dad decided to leave Tennessee and move to California. Their decision to do that changed my
life and the lives of my brothers and sisters forever. Somewhere back in
the 1700s, my great-great-great grandfathers made the decision to leave
Europe and immigrate to America. Even though I wasn't around at the
time to cast my vote, I was to come with them, being ultimately born an
American as a consequence of a decision I didn't make. In the same way,

many thousands of years ago, my forefather Adam made the decision to disobey his Creator and I am suffering the consequences of his decision along with every member of the human race who has ever lived, save One. When Adam sinned, I sinned and you sinned and we are all under God's condemnation. All humanity is *in* Adam, in the sense that Adam is the federal head, the representative, of the human race.

Over the course of history, many have scoffed at the idea of a federal headship of the human race. They shove the story of Adam and Eve into the closet of fable, and deride any who would see it as the underpinning of human history. Some of those who scoff have even called themselves Christians. But biblical Christianity rises or falls on the accuracy of the biblical record of Adam. Paul says this in Romans 5:14-16:

> *"Nevertheless, death reigned from the time of Adam...who was a pattern of the one to come... For if the many died by the trespass of the one man, how much more did God's grace and the gift that came by the grace of the one man, Jesus Christ, overflow to the many! Again, the gift of God is not like the result of the one man's sin: The judgment followed one sin and brought condemnation, but the gift followed many trespasses and brought justification."*

In a perfect garden environment, Adam failed to do what God required—to keep one simple command. The Second Adam—our Lord Jesus Christ—came to this earth in squalor and oppression, not in a perfect garden environment. And yet He kept all of God's commandments perfectly. He withstood Satan's attacks and never sinned—not even once. Jesus became the federal head of a new race. Those who have been resurrected to new life by the power of God's Spirit are found to be *in* Christ. By the grace of God, for those who have been resurrected into new life, the curse has been turned into a great blessing.

5. Jesus: Our Gracious Covering
Genesis 3:21

*The LORD God made garments of skin for Adam and
his wife and clothed them.*

Although Adam and Eve did not die physically when they were deceived and ate of the fruit that God had forbidden, their relationship with their Creator was severed. Instead of the joy of walking with Him in the Garden, they suddenly found themselves in conflict. They had belittled God's love, scorned His truth, shunned His majesty, and rejected His authority. Ashamed of their nakedness, they attempted to cover themselves with a patchwork of fig leaves (vs. 7)—the work of their own hands. So it is with all of us who would hide our nakedness from the Creator. We try to use the work of our own hands. We seek to be hidden from God in religion and religious ceremonies, charity balls, helping the poor, nursing the sick, or any one of a thousand "good works." These things can be very worthy pursuits. The problem arises when we think of them as satisfying *in any way* God's demands upon us. God's demands can only be satisfied by God.

So we see in verse 21 that "*The Lord God made garments of skin for Adam and his wife and clothed them.*" Animals had to die. God sacrificed other innocent creatures so that Adam and Eve might be clothed. We see in this verse the first foreshadowing of the principle of substitutionary atonement (covering of sins). It is a principle that will be continued throughout the Old Testament and have its ultimate fulfillment in the sacrifice of the Lord Jesus on Calvary's Cross. Christ had to die as a covering for sin, so that His Church might be clothed in His righteousness. For our "righteousness" is described Isaiah 64:6: *"All of us have become like one who is unclean, and all our righteous acts are like filthy rags..."*

In the book of Leviticus, God laid out the full principle of **substitutionary atonement**. But even in Genesis we see animals being sacrificed for sin. As early as Genesis 4:4 we find Abel bringing an offering to God from his flock. In Genesis 8:20 Noah offers a burnt offering of animals and birds to the Lord following the flood. Abraham does the same, as do Isaac and Jacob. In Leviticus 9:7 we find these words:

"Moses said to Aaron, 'Come to the altar and sacrifice your sin offering and your burnt offering and make atonement for yourself and the people; sacrifice the offering that is for the people and make atonement for them, as the LORD has commanded.'"

The principle of substitutionary atonement is presented throughout the book of Leviticus, and, indeed, the entire Old Testament. But, as the writer to the Hebrews says in 10:11-14:

"Day after day every priest stands and performs his religious duties; again and again he offers the same sacrifices, which can never take away sins. But when this priest, [Jesus], had offered for all time one sacrifice for sins, he sat down at the right hand of God. Since that time he waits for his enemies to be made his footstool, because by one sacrifice he has made perfect forever those who are being made holy."

All that bloody animal sacrifices can do is to remind the Hebrews of the seriousness of their sin and to point them to the coming Messiah (Christ) whose sacrifice alone can truly take away their sins. So, we see here in the earliest pages of God's book a foreshadowing of Christ's substitutionary atonement for the sins of His people. In the Tabernacle in the wilderness, which we will study later in the book, the slaughter and sacrifice of animals is wholesale. Day after day, sheep, goats, steers, and other animals are drained of their blood and placed on the fire of the Altar. They all prefigure the One who is to make one final sacrifice for sin—our Lord and Savior, Jesus.

6. JESUS: OUR TREE OF LIFE
Genesis 3:23-24

So the LORD God banished him from the Garden of Eden to work the ground from which he had been taken. After he drove the man out, he placed on the east side of the Garden of Eden cherubim and a flaming sword flashing back and forth to guard the way to the **tree of life.**

The term "tree of life" is found in three books of the Bible; Genesis (3:9, 3:22, & 3:24), Proverbs (3:18, 11:30, 13:12, & 15:4), and Revelation (2:7, 22:2, 22:14, & 22:19). In Genesis and Revelation—the first and last books of the Bible—the term refers to an actual tree from which fruit comes that, if eaten, brings eternal life. However, in Proverbs, right in the center of the Bible, other concepts such as "wisdom," the "fruit of the righteous," a "longing fulfilled," and a "tongue that brings healing," become trees of life. All of these things may be said of Jesus.

On the Cross, another "tree" in Scripture, our Lord Jesus, became a curse for us. Deuteronomy 21:23 says, *"You must not leave his body on the tree overnight. Be sure to bury him that same day, because anyone who is hung on a tree is under God's curse."* The Apostle Paul picks this up in Galatians 3:13: *"Christ redeemed us from the curse of the law by becoming a curse for us, for it is written: 'Cursed is everyone who is hung on a tree.'"* Going back to Genesis, we remember that another tree was planted in the Garden, the tree of the knowledge of good and evil. Arthur Pink, in *Gleanings in Genesis,* compares and contrasts these two trees, the first of which Adam and Eve ate and were cursed, and the second on which our Lord bore their curse for us. (Much of the following has been abstracted from his book, pages 27-32.)

By way of contrast, Pink notes that the first tree in Eden was planted by God, the second, in Calvary, is planted by man. The first is pleasant to look upon, while the second is hideous and repugnant to the eye. God forbids man to eat of the tree in Eden, while Satan uses all of his cunning to get man to eat of it. In contrast, God calls all people to eat of the tree at Calvary, while Satan uses all of his power to keep people from it. Eating from the first tree brings sin and death, but the second brings life and salvation. Adam steals the fruit of the first tree, bringing condemnation, while the repentant thief at Calvary eats of the fruit of the second and enters Paradise.

Pink compares the two trees. Both trees, he says, are planted in a garden. John 19:41 testifies that, *"At the place where Jesus was crucified, there was a garden…"* Both the first Adam and the last Adam die in a garden. Adam dies spiritually, an estate that brings ultimate physical death, while Jesus dies physically, bringing ultimate spiritual life to all who put their trust in Him. Both trees are "in the midst." The first is in the midst of the Garden of Eden, the second sees Jesus crucified in the midst of sinners. Both trees are trees of the knowledge of good and evil. The first displays sin's vileness, while the second shows God's love and goodness as nowhere else in history.

Finally, Pink compares the fruit of the first forbidden tree with that of the second—the true "tree of life": *"When the woman saw that the fruit of the tree was good for food and pleasing to the eye, and also desirable for gaining wisdom, she took some and ate it. She also gave some to her husband, who was with her, and he ate it"* (Genesis 3:6). Adam and Eve are deceived. The fruit of the first tree may have been pleasing to the eye, but not good for food, nor does it bring wisdom, only separation and death. By contrast, the fruit of Calvary's tree is good for food as we grow in Christ by eating it in study of the Word. It is pleasing to the eye as our eyes are truly opened to the way of eternal life. And, it is fruit that brings ultimate power and wisdom, *"Christ [is] the power of God and the wisdom of God"* (1 Corinthians 1:24).

The tree of life described in Revelation will be ours to eat of for eternity. *"Blessed are those who wash their robes, that they may have the right to the tree of life and may go…into the city."* Jesus is our "Tree of Life."

7. Jesus: The Ark of Our Deliverance
Genesis 6:5-8, 13-14

The LORD saw how great man's wickedness on the earth had become, and that every inclination of the thoughts of his heart was only evil all the time. The LORD was grieved that he had made man on the earth, and his heart was filled with pain. So the LORD said, "I will wipe mankind, whom I have created, from the face of the earth—men and animals, and creatures that move along the ground, and birds of the air—for I am grieved that I have made them." But Noah found favor in the eyes of the LORD... So God said to Noah, "I am going to put an end to all people, for the earth is filled with violence because of them. I am surely going to destroy both them and the earth. So make yourself an ark of cypress wood; make rooms in it and coat it with pitch inside and out."

"How many arks do we find in God's Word?" I sometimes like to ask my Sunday school classes this: The answer is three. First, we have Noah's ark carrying him and his family through the flood. The second usually mentioned is the ark of the covenant and its mercy seat, carried by the Hebrews in the wilderness. The third, and often missed, is the ark of Moses that floats him to safety in the bulrushes (Exodus 2:3). What do all these "arks" have in common? They are all places of refuge for God's people. Truly, the God-man Jesus is our refuge—our heavenly Ark. As the psalmists sing in 46:1-3,

"God is our refuge and strength, an ever-present help in trouble. Therefore we will not fear, though the earth give way and the mountains fall into the heart of the sea, though its waters roar and foam and the mountains quake with their surging."

Again, with Arthur Pink as our guide, (see pages 102-109 of *Gleanings in Genesis*), let us compare the ark of Noah with our Lord Jesus Christ. First, plans for the ark are provided by God well in advance so that Noah and his family and the animals in it will be saved. In the same way, Jesus' arrival on the earth is planned many years in advance. As the prophet Micah says in 5:2, *"But you, Bethlehem Ephrathah, though you are small among the clans of Judah, out of you will come for me one who will be ruler over Israel, whose origins are from of old, from ancient times."* Second, Noah doesn't come up with the idea of a coming universal flood and the need of a big boat to escape it. Both are revealed to him by God. In the same way, our need for a Savior is not our own idea, but shown to us by the special revelation of God—the Bible. Third, the ark is to be made of gopher wood—from trees that have been cut down. This speaks to our Lord's humanity, who *"grew up before him like a tender shoot, and like a root out of dry ground"* (Isaiah 53:2). Daniel 9:26 also speaks of the *"Anointed One [who] will be cut off."*

Fourth, as we have said, Noah's ark "was a refuge from Divine judgment." So also is Jesus a refuge from the wrath to come for all who would simply believe on His name. Fifth, Noah and his family are invited into the ark (Genesis 7:1). In the same way, Jesus' invitation in Matthew 11:28 is, *"Come to me, all you who are weary and burdened, and I will give you rest."* Sixth, the ark is a place of absolute security. So, too, we who are in Christ are eternally secure. Finally, God is faithful to deliver all who had entered the ark back to the earth. Our Lord is also faithful and says to His Father, *"I have not lost one of those you gave me"* (John 18:9).

Other symbols abound: The ark has only one door, so also there is only one way to God, through our Lord Jesus Christ. As He says in John 14:6: *"I am the way and the truth and the life. No one comes to the Father except through me."* Biblical evidence exists that would place the grounding of the ark on Ararat on the same day of the Hebrew calendar that Jesus rose from the tomb. The Word of God is rich and true and beyond the ability of the human mind to fully comprehend, much less write without guidance from heaven. God is its ultimate author, as clearly evidenced by *"many convincing proofs"* (Acts 1:3).

8. Jesus: Our Eternal High Priest
Genesis 14:18-20

Then Melchizedek king of Salem brought out bread and wine. He was priest of God Most High, and he blessed Abram, saying, "Blessed be Abram by God Most High, Creator of heaven and earth. And blessed be God Most High, who delivered your enemies into your hand." Then Abram gave him a tenth of everything.

Following Abraham's rescue of his nephew, Lot, and his defeat of the four kings, a strange man named Melchizedek walks onto the stage. We are told that he was both a king and a priest. He brings bread and wine, elements we use in the Lord's Supper. He blesses Abram, and calls upon God in doing so.

As mentioned in the preface of the book, three central offices are ascribed to the Lord Jesus—Prophet, Priest, and King. Prophets represent God to the people. Priests mediate the people to God, and Kings rule over the people, providing for their needs. In holding two of these offices, Melchizedek is the only character in the Old Testament (other than Moses) to hold more than one. One other detail: Melchizedek's name in the ancient languages means "king of righteousness." We also see that he is "King of Salem." Salem means "peace." He is both "king of righteousness" and "king of peace." Melchizedek is only to be mentioned again in the Old Testament in Psalm 110. What are we to make of him?

The writer of Hebrews has the answer in Hebrews 7:1-3:

"This Melchizedek was king of Salem and priest of God Most High. He met Abraham returning from the defeat of the kings and blessed him, and Abraham gave him a tenth of everything....without beginning of days or end of life, like the Son of God he remains a priest forever"

Notice, first, that the writer to the Hebrews adds more information, specifically that Melchizedek is *without beginning of days or end of life, like the Son of God he remains a priest forever."* He goes on to note that the tithe— (10%)—that Abram paid shows that the patriarch is subordinate to Melchizedek. Because Abram receives the blessing, his subordination is affirmed. Further, the priesthood to be established by God through the tribe of Levi is also subordinate to Melchizedek. The Levitical priesthood, headed by Moses' brother Aaron, is even subordinate to its ancestor, Abraham. The writer says in Hebrews 7:11-16:

> *"If perfection could have been attained through the Levitical priesthood …why was there still need for another priest to come—one in the order of Melchizedek, not in the order of Aaron? … He [Jesus] of whom these things are said belonged to a different tribe [not Levi but Judah], and no one from that tribe has ever served at the altar…And what we have said is even more clear if another priest like Melchizedek appears, one who has become a priest not on the basis of a regulation as to his ancestry but on the basis of the power of an indestructible life. For it is declared:* [in Psalm 110:4]. *"You are a priest forever, in the order of Melchizedek"*

The writer to the Hebrews goes on to speak of this new High Priest; he is unlike the sinful priests of Levi who need to offer sacrifices for their own sins, and who all die. This Priest, Jesus, is sinless and lives forever.

Jesus is both King of righteousness and King of peace. As our great High Priest He lives forever to intercede for us. As our great High Priest, He also gave for us His body and blood, which we commemorate in the Lord's Supper with bread and wine. And, as Micah 5:2 acknowledges, His *"origins are from of old, from ancient times."* He is without beginning, as the Pre-existent Creator of all. Jesus is our Great High Priest after the order of Melchizedek.

9. Jesus: Our Covenant Promise-Keeper
Genesis 15: 7-12, 17

He also said to [Abram], "I am the LORD, who brought you out of Ur of the Chaldeans to give you this land to take possession of it." But Abram said, "O Sovereign LORD, how can I know that I will gain possession of it?" So the LORD said to him, "Bring me a heifer, a goat and a ram, each three years old, along with a dove and a young pigeon." Abram brought all these to him, cut them in two and arranged the halves opposite each other; the birds, however, he did not cut in half. Then birds of prey came down on the carcasses, but Abram drove them away. As the sun was setting, Abram fell into a deep sleep, and a thick and dreadful darkness came over him…When the sun had set and darkness had fallen, a smoking firepot with a blazing torch appeared and passed between the pieces.

To many, this text seems to be one of the strangest in the entire Bible. But I can hardly read it without tears of wonder coming to my eyes. This chapter has to be one of the greatest, if not *the* greatest, chapters in the Bible. In many ways, that is because of verse 6, appearing just prior to our subject text: "*Abram believed the LORD, and he credited it to him as righteousness.*" This verse is a clear announcement of the Gospel of Jesus Christ. We are justified—declared righteous in God's sight—through faith alone and not by any works that we do. In Abraham's case, it is faith in the promise that God will give him a son in his old age and give him the Promised Land for his descendants. But the entire chapter is devoted to God's gracious good news, and the verses I've chosen above illustrate the truth of it perfectly. Let's begin with a short history lesson.

In the ancient middle eastern world, suzerains (kings) ruled vassals—underlings who worked the land. The suzerain was to protect the vassals, and for that protection, the vassals promised to be loyal to the suzerain and give him a portion of the produce of their land. In order to memorialize their oaths of allegiance to the suzerain, the vassals would cut animals in half and sacrifice birds and other smaller animals and set them in a row on two sides so that a path was formed down the middle. Then, the vassals would walk between the pieces. By this process, they were swearing a solemn oath to the suzerain that, "If we do not abide by the oath we have sworn to you, you may do to us what we have done to these animals." It was an oath unto death.

Now, looking at our verses, we notice first that God (the Suzerain of suzerains) orders Abraham (His vassal) to gather up the animals, sacrifice them, cut the larger ones in half, and place the pieces on opposite sides of a path between them. Then, we are told that Abraham *"fell into a deep sleep, and a thick and dreadful darkness came over him."* Then, something really strange happens. *"When the sun had set and darkness had fallen, a smoking firepot with a blazing torch appeared and passed between the pieces."*

The "smoking firepot" and the "blazing torch" are called **theophanies**. They are like the burning bush in Exodus 6. Basically, a theophany is a physical manifestation of God that is either seen or heard, or both. The bottom line is that the Suzerain—God—not His vassal—Abraham—takes the solemn oath of death. Hebrews 6:17-18 says:

> *"...Because God wanted to make the unchanging nature of his purpose very clear to the heirs of what was promised, he confirmed it with an oath. God did this so that, by two unchangeable things [His promise and His oath] in which it is impossible for God to lie, we who have fled to take hold of the hope offered to us may be greatly encouraged."*

The blood oath points to Calvary, where God through our Lord Jesus Christ made the ultimate sacrifice, so that Christians everywhere—Abraham's true descendants according to our simple child-like faith in Christ—are as many as the sands of the seashore or the stars in the sky. Notice that Abram is asleep when the firepot and torch pass between the pieces. Salvation is the sole work of God's grace, not something we do for ourselves. Both regeneration and faith are gifts of God.

10. Jesus: The Infant of Promise
Genesis 21:1-7

Now the LORD was gracious to Sarah as he had said, and the LORD did for Sarah what he had promised. Sarah became pregnant and bore a son to Abraham in his old age, at the very time God had promised him. Abraham gave the name Isaac to the son Sarah bore him. When his son Isaac was eight days old, Abraham circumcised him, as God commanded him. Abraham was a hundred years old when his son Isaac was born to him. Sarah said, ... "Who would have said to Abraham that Sarah would nurse children? Yet I have borne him a son in his old age."

The son that God promises to Abram in Genesis 15 is to come from Abram's own body. But how can that be? Abram and his wife Sarai are both long past the age where she can conceive and bear a child by her husband. But God is faithful to fulfill His promises even when they are seemingly against all hope. Now we find Abraham and Sarah—as they had been renamed by God—joyful over the promised fulfillment. Isaac, a son from their own bodies, is born.

In the same way, another child of promise—the Lord Jesus Christ—will be born according to God's promise and in a manner impossible for the human mind to fully comprehend. The promise of a Savior is first announced by God in the Garden when He tells Adam and Eve, *"And I will put enmity between [Satan] and the woman, and between your offspring and hers; he will crush your head, and you will strike his heel"* (Genesis 3:15). Over and over again in the Hebrew Scriptures the promise is reiterated. In Isaiah 9:6, for instance, a specific promise is made that was written many centuries before its fulfillment. *"For to us a child is born, to us a son is given, and the government will be on his shoulders. And he will be called Wonderful Counselor, Mighty God, Everlasting Father, Prince of Peace."*

It is impossible, in human terms, for a virgin to bear a child. (At least it was for thousands of years before modern science discovered *in vitro* fertilization.) Likewise, it is impossible, also in human terms, for a woman approaching 100 years old, such as Sarah is, to give birth. But for God, nothing is impossible. Our promises are weak and contingent because we are weak and contingent beings. But God is not only sovereign—with the will to do what He has promised—He is also all-powerful. God has the power to do what He says He will do.

The joy that Abraham and Sarah feel as the promise of God to them is fulfilled is a foreshadowing of the joy that will one day be for people everywhere. When Jesus is born in Bethlehem many years after these promises were made of Him, the angels gathered to bear witness to the shepherds. *"...the angel said to them, 'Do not be afraid. I bring you good news of great joy that will be for all the people. Today in the town of David a Savior has been born to you; he is Christ the Lord.'"* (Luke 2:10-11).

This child of promise—Isaac—prefigures Christ in several other ways. But note the name change that God bestows upon Abram and Sarai. You may notice that God basically adds an "h" to their names, changing Abram's name to Abraham and Sarai's name to Sarah. In Hebrew, the term for Spirit is *ruach*, a word pronounced in such a way as to emphasize the "h" sound. In fact, the word is what we would call onomatopoeic—it sounds like something in nature sounds. In this case, *ruach* means wind or spirit and sounds like the wind. Later, in John 3:8 Jesus will make this analogy of the wind to the Spirit of God: *"The wind blows wherever it pleases. You hear its sound, but you cannot tell where it comes from or where it is going. So it is with everyone born of the Spirit."* The added "h" to Abram's and Sarai's names exemplifies a breathing into them of the Spirit of God. The child of promise, Isaac, is a child of the Spirit, picturing our Lord Jesus.

One other word about Abraham's name. "Abram" meant "Daddy" in the ancient language. "Abraham" meant "Big Daddy." Can you imagine the laughter aimed at childless Abraham? It is the same as the scorn often borne by those of us who belong to Christ's Kingdom in "the-already-but-not-yet."

11. Jesus: The Only Son of God
Genesis 22:1, 2

Some time later God tested Abraham. He said to him, "Abraham!" "Here I am," he replied. Then God said, "Take your son, your only son, Isaac, whom you love, and go to the region of Moriah. Sacrifice him there as a burnt offering on one of the mountains I will tell you about."

I suppose someone might object and say, "Lots of couples have only one son. How can you say that these verses make some statement about Jesus?" It is the context in which these verses appear that makes the statement "*your only son*" so rich in meaning for us. As John 3:16 says about Jesus, "*For God so loved the world that he gave his one and only Son, that whoever believes in him shall not perish but have eternal life.*" Notice first that God says, "*Take your son, your only son, Isaac, whom you love…*" One might think that God could have simply said, "Take your son, Isaac…," because, after all, there was another son—Ishmael—from his maidservant, Hagar. But God says it four times. He first says, "*your son,*" then, "*your only son.*" As if that were not clear enough, he adds, "*Isaac,*" then, "*whom you love.*" As the Father speaks from heaven and says of Jesus in Matthew 3:17, "*This is my Son, whom I love; with him I am well pleased.*"

While the word "trinity" does not occur in Scripture, the signature of the triune God—Father, Son, and Holy Spirit—is everywhere present. For instance, in John 15:26 we read these words of Jesus: "*When the Counselor comes, whom I will send to you from the Father, the Spirit of truth who goes out from the Father, he will testify about me.*" Notice, Christ—the Son— is speaking of the Father and the Holy Spirit. There are many like verses in Scripture. The true God of the Christian faith is one God, in three persons. It is a profound mystery, and yet profoundly true.

Down through the ages, even to the present day, there are those who claim to be Christians but deny this biblical truth. One of Christianity's first general councils was held in Nicaea in 358 A.D. A bishop named

Arius claimed that the Son was not equal with the Father, but rather was subordinate. In other words, Arius made Christ a demigod and not the incarnation of the true God. But the council overwhelmingly affirmed Christ to be coequal and coeternal with the Father, stating that he was *homoousias*—of the same substance as the Father.

The Holy Trinity is a mystery, a "sacred secret," to us mere humans. We cannot fully understand it because we are finite creatures, and the Trinity is an infinite reality. It is beyond our full comprehension, but that fact does not deny its reality. Men have complained that the Trinity is a logical fallacy—that God could not be one and three at the same time and in the same circumstance. But we believe that God is one God in substance and yet is in three persons. When Jesus came to earth, He was one person, yet two substances—God and man. This is all perfectly logical, but sublimely mysterious.

Someone says, "Why is this important to us? What difference does it make if God is one person or three persons?" First, it is important because the Bible clearly teaches it. Second, if the Son were not coequal and coeternal with the Father, to worship this demigod would be breaking God's very first commandment: *"You shall have no other gods before me"* (Exodus 20:3). Third, only the infinite and perfectly holy God could take upon Himself the sins of people like you and me, as Jesus did on the Cross. Fourth, if God were not three persons, one of whom became a man, the Cross would have been impossible for Him, in that God cannot die nor completely leave His throne. Finally, and very important, if God were only one person, He would be forced to create something or someone in order to have an object of His love. God would, therefore, be subordinate to His creation in the sense that He was forced to create it. But God is eternally free and does whatever he pleases. He is not forced to do anything. The Father loves His coequal and coeternal only Son. The Holy Spirit who proceeds from the Father and the Son is the manifestation of that love. Beyond that, I can say no more.

12. Jesus: The Sacrifice Provided By God
Genesis 22:3-14

*Early the next morning Abraham got up and saddled his donkey. He took
with him two of his servants and his son Isaac. When he had cut enough
wood for the burnt offering, he set out for the place God had told him
about. On the third day Abraham looked up and saw the place in the
distance. He said to his servants, "Stay here with the donkey while I and
the boy go over there. We will worship and then we will come back to you."
Abraham took the wood for the burnt offering and placed it on his son
Isaac, and he himself carried the fire and the knife. As the two of them went
on together, Isaac spoke up and said to his father Abraham, "Father?" "Yes,
my son?" Abraham replied. "The fire and wood are here," Isaac said, "but
where is the lamb for the burnt offering?" Abraham answered, "God himself
will provide the lamb for the burnt offering, my son." And the two of them
went on together. When they reached the place God had told him about,
Abraham built an altar there and arranged the wood on it. He bound his
son Isaac and laid him on the altar, on top of the wood. Then he reached
out his hand and took the knife to slay his son. But the angel of the LORD
called out to him from heaven, "Abraham! Abraham!" "Here I am," he replied. "Do not lay a hand on the boy," he said. "Do not do anything to him.
Now I know that you fear God, because you have not withheld from me
your son, your only son." Abraham looked up and there in a thicket he saw
a ram caught by its horns. He went over and took the ram and sacrificed
it as a burnt offering instead of his son. So Abraham called that place The
LORD Will Provide. And to this day it is said, "On the
mountain of the LORD it will be provided."*

Of all the portraits of our Lord Jesus in the Old Testament, this
one is perhaps the most striking. In Genesis 15:6 we read that
*"Abram believed the LORD, and he credited it to him as righteous-
ness."* Abraham is saved by faith alone, but here we read that it is not a
faith that stood alone. Abram's faith—his absolute trust—leads to his
obedience—good works that God had for him to do.

Can you imagine how Abram must have trembled at God's command? He must have been very confused by it. Here, after waiting patiently

for years and finally experiencing the joy of Isaac's birth, God now commanded that Isaac be offered as a bloody sacrifice. Abraham must have gone sleepless the night before. And what could he tell his wife, Sarah?

Abraham is really in a difficult situation, but he has no choice but to trust God. The writer to the Hebrews tells us in 11:17-19,

> *By faith Abraham, when God tested him, offered Isaac as a sacrifice. He who had received the promises was about to sacrifice his one and only son, even though God had said to him, "It is through Isaac that your offspring will be reckoned." Abraham reasoned that God could raise the dead, and figuratively speaking, he did receive Isaac back from death.*

Abraham believes in an awesome and powerful God, One who could literally raise the dead. Abraham expects a resurrection.

The mountain on which Isaac is offered is in the range of "Moriah" which literally means, "The Lord will provide." In Genesis 22:14 (above), the exact mountain is called, *"The mountain of the Lord."* Could it be Calvary, near Jerusalem where years later Jesus would be crucified? Many scholars think so. *"Then Jerusalem will be called the City of Truth, and* **the mountain of the Lord** *Almighty will be called the Holy Mountain."* (Zechariah 8:3b).

The scene on top of the mountain takes place between the father and son alone—just as at Golgotha the transaction was solely between God the Father and God the Son. Isaac carries the wood for his burning on his back—just as Jesus later will carry his wooden Cross, the instrument of His death. God stops Abraham's hand from hurting his son, but the Father does not withdraw His hand from Jesus, who is the anti-type of Isaac's experience. Jesus is resurrected on the "third day." Isaac, too, is resurrected, figuratively, on the third day since his journey had begun. Oh, the matchless Word of God and the many infallible proofs that His Word is literally inerrant and sufficient for all our needs.

13. Jesus: Our Access to God
Genesis 28:10-12

Jacob left Beersheba and set out for Haran. When he reached a certain place, he stopped for the night because the sun had set. Taking one of the stones there, he put it under his head and lay down to sleep. He had a dream in which he saw a stairway resting on the earth, with its top reaching to heaven, and the angels of God were ascending and descending on it.

Perhaps you remember the story of Jacob's deceit. He not only tricks his older brother, Esau, out of his birthright, he later deceives his father, Isaac, into giving him Esau's blessing. Fearing mortal reprisal from Esau, Jacob agrees with his mother, Rebekah, that he ought to flee Beersheba and head for his relatives' home in Haran. In these verses we find him on the trail toward Mesopotamia. The Scripture says that he camped for the night in a place called Luz, which Jacob later renamed Bethel. He had only traveled about 10% of the 500 miles of his journey.

As he lies down to sleep with his head propped up on a rock, he has a most mysterious dream. He sees a great stairway or ladder reaching up to heaven. Whatever this "stairway" was, it must have been immense and exceedingly lofty. The Word says that it reached to heaven, and Jacob saw "*the angels of God ascending and descending on it.*" Angels are mentioned often in Genesis, and indeed, in all of Scripture. The New Testament letter to the Hebrews says in 12:22: "*But you have come to Mount Zion, to the heavenly Jerusalem, the city of the living God. You have come to thousands upon thousands of angels in joyful assembly…*" Earlier, in 1:14, the writer tells us that angels are "*ministering spirits sent to serve those who will inherit salvation…*"

What does the presence of the angels on this enormous staircase mean? First, it means that heaven—the "heavenly Jerusalem"—actually exists. Second, it means that heaven is truly interested in the earth. God is invested in His creation. Whatever else it may mean, the stairway's central focus is on God, and His promise to Abram that *"all peoples on earth will be blessed through you and your offspring."* We know that it is through Jesus that the promise will be fulfilled.

But Jacob is not living by faith at the time he receives this promise! In fact, he was fleeing from the results of his sin—the opposite of faith. He shows this in his response to God's promise and reassurance. In verses 20 through 22 a shaken and awestruck Jacob makes this vow:

> *"If God will be with me and will watch over me on this journey I am taking and will give me food to eat and clothes to wear so that I return safely to my father's house, then the LORD will be my God and this stone that I have set up as a pillar will be God's house, and of all that you give me I will give you a tenth."*

Notice that his vow is conditional. If God does all these things for him, then Jacob will submit to Him. That isn't faith; that's bargaining! Jacob begins to negotiate the terms of his trust in God. The point is that Jacob's faith does not precede God's promise. Jacob's salvation depended solely upon God's grace.

God's grace is manifested to us in the person of the same Lord who spoke to Jacob from heaven—the Lord Jesus Christ. He is the central focus of the stairway, as the one Mediator between God and man. In John 1:50-51, after Nathaniel had put his faith in Him, Jesus said,

> *"You believe because I told you I saw you under the fig tree. You shall see greater things than that." He then added, "I tell you the truth, you shall see heaven open, and the angels of God ascending and descending on the Son of Man."*

Jesus is the Mediator of the New Covenant. Through His grace we have access to heaven and eternal life. He is the Father of the living, not the dead. Only Jesus bridges the infinite gap between heaven and earth.

14. Jesus: The Commander in Chief
Genesis 32:24-32

So Jacob was left alone, and a man wrestled with him till daybreak. When the man saw that he could not overpower him, he touched the socket of Jacob's hip so that his hip was wrenched as he wrestled with the man. Then the man said, "Let me go, for it is daybreak." But Jacob replied, "I will not let you go unless you bless me." The man asked him, "What is your name?" "Jacob," he answered. Then the man said, "Your name will no longer be Jacob, but Israel, because you have struggled with God and with men and have overcome." Jacob said, "Please tell me your name." But he replied, "Why do you ask my name?" Then he blessed him there. So Jacob called the place Peniel, saying, "It is because I saw God face to face, and yet my life was spared."

Up to this point of his life, Jacob has been winning life's battles by his own deceit and cunning—using the ways of the world, if you will. He devises a successful, albeit wrongful, strategy for taking his older brother's birthright, then cheats Esau out of his blessing as the first-born. He bests Laban and then runs off with his daughters and a large herd of sheep and goats. But now he is alone. He meets a strange visitor with whom he wrestles until daybreak.

Some commentators have seen these verses as a type of a believer struggling with God in prayer. I believe it's something entirely different: It's to show us that God can't use us until we come to lose our confidence in our own flesh and find it in His strength. In Matthew 10:39, Jesus says, *"Whoever finds his life will lose it, and whoever loses his life for my sake will find it."* Again, in John 15:5 Jesus says, *"I am the vine; you are the branches. If a man remains in me and I in him, he will bear much fruit; apart from me* **you can do nothing**.*"* Jacob is shown that his planning and scheming won't really get him anywhere. He is powerless without God, and only in that realization can true strength surface.

The preincarnate Jesus often appears in the early books of the

Bible as "The angel of the Lord." But here we see that it is a man who wrestled with Jacob. We know that the man is greater than Jacob inasmuch as he subdues Jacob, cripples him, and then he changes Jacob's name to Israel. Finally, the man blesses Jacob. The greater always names the lesser, and also gives the blessing. For instance, parents name children, not vice versa. Next, we're told that Israel *"called the place Peniel, saying, 'It is because I saw God face to face, and yet my life was spared.'"* Who else could this man be but the God-man—our Lord Jesus Christ?

These things are further emphasized by the name Jacob is given— Israel. Many Hebrew names contain the suffix "el," meaning "God." Immanuel means "God with us" (Isa. 7:14 and Matt. 1:23). We might also think of Daniel, which means "God judges." (Note Jacob's blessing of Dan in Genesis 49:16.) In like manner, Israel means "God commands." Jacob is humbled by his failure to subdue the man. He will always be reminded of his weakness by his limp and by his name, "God commands."

Every man and woman who has ever been born on earth has one common characteristic. Each of us wants to be in control. We want to be in command of our own lives. We want to make up our own rules. Only by the grace of God do we come to the true Commander—the Lord Jesus Christ. He says in John 14:15, *"If you love me, you will obey what I command."* Again, in Matthew 5:18-19 Jesus says,

> *"I tell you the truth, until heaven and earth disappear, not the smallest letter, not the least stroke of a pen, will by any means disappear from the Law until everything is accomplished. Anyone who breaks one of the least of these commandments and teaches others to do the same will be called least in the kingdom of heaven, but whoever practices and teaches these commands will be called great in the kingdom of heaven."*

Jesus is our Commander—the One who is in command. Jacob, now renamed Israel, learned the lesson at Peniel. It is a lesson we all need to learn, that Jesus' way is the right way—the best way to live.

15. JESUS: SOLD OUT BY HIS BROTHERS
Genesis 37:23-28

So when Joseph came to his brothers, they stripped him of his robe—the richly ornamented robe he was wearing—and they took him and threw him into the cistern. Now the cistern was empty; there was no water in it. As they sat down to eat their meal, they looked up and saw a caravan of Ishmaelites coming from Gilead. Their camels were loaded with spices, balm and myrrh, and they were on their way to take them down to Egypt. Judah said to his brothers, "What will we gain if we kill our brother and cover up his blood? Come, let's sell him to the Ishmaelites and not lay our hands on him; after all, he is our brother, our own flesh and blood." His brothers agreed. So when the Midianite merchants came by, his brothers pulled Joseph up out of the cistern and sold him for twenty shekels of silver to the Ishmaelites, who took him to Egypt.

This chapter is the first of eight in which we will deal with portraits of Jesus Christ in the life of Joseph. In his book, *Gleanings in Genesis,* Arthur Pink lists 101 portraits of the coming Messiah in Joseph's life alone! In our eight chapters, we'll touch on many of those he lists, dealing mainly with the predominant ones.

Joseph is Jacob's favorite son, being the firstborn of Rachel's children. After Reuben sleeps with Jacob's concubine, Bilhah (Gen. 35:22), his father strips him of his rights as the firstborn and apparently gives those rights to Joseph. Jacob bestows upon his favorite son a richly decorated robe, often described as a *"coat of many colors,"* as in the KJV. The coat is more likely a manager's coat, which reveals Joseph's leadership in the family business. It probably has long sleeves and reaches to the ankles, as opposed to the sleeveless tunics worn by his brothers, who are now mere underlings to their younger brother.

As if Joseph's coat and elevated position were not cause enough for jealousy among his older half-brothers, Genesis 37 tells us about Joseph's odd dreams. The brother's sheaves bowed down to his own. Then Joseph told them of a second dream where not only eleven stars bow down to him, but the moon and sun as well, clearly indicating both his father and mother. Can you imagine how the older brothers must hate his conceit? So, when Joseph comes looking for his brothers who have gone many miles from home searching for pasture for their flocks, they plot to kill him. The oldest, Reuben, talks them into throwing Joseph into a dry cistern. The brothers then sell Joseph into slavery in Egypt. Joseph will be forever changed by the experience.

Jesus, too, is sold out by His brothers. His earthly ministry is characterized in a major way by the opposition and jealousy of His "older brothers"—the established clergy of the day. We read in John 11:47-48 the basic reason for their hatred of Him: *"What are we accomplishing?' they asked....If we let him go on like this, everyone will believe in him, and then the Romans will come and take away both our place and our nation."* They are concerned that their positions vis-à-vis the Roman government will be destroyed because of this young man who performs miracles in their midst.

Jesus Himself describes the situation in a parable found in Mark 12, *"'This is the heir. Come, let's kill him, and the inheritance will be ours.' So they took him and killed him, and threw him out of the vineyard"* (vv. 5-7). Jesus speaks of Himself and the death He will suffer after being sold out by those He came to save.

Joseph and Jesus both love their brothers. Joseph is a shepherd of sheep while Jesus came to shepherd souls. Both men oppose evil and are dearly beloved by their fathers. They are both sent forth on a mission by their fathers. They both foretell their own future glory and sovereignty. They are both the firstborn among their brothers. They both are conspired against by those they loved, insulted, and forsaken. They are each hated without a just cause, and sold by their brothers. But both come forth out of the pit, Joseph into a sojourn in Egypt and ultimate glory on earth; Jesus into eternal glory in heaven and on earth.

16. JESUS: SORELY TEMPTED BUT SINLESS SERVANT
Genesis 39:11-20

One day [Joseph] went into the house to attend to his duties, and none of the household servants was inside. [Potiphar's wife] caught him by his cloak and said, "Come to bed with me!" But he left his cloak in her hand and ran out of the house.

Having been sold into slavery in Egypt, Joseph is probably made to stand naked on a platform where potential buyers check his teeth and physique before bidding. How like Jesus, who is stripped naked and nailed to a cross while soldiers cast lots for His clothes. But the Bible doesn't speak of the slave auction, only that Joseph is sold to a man named Potiphar.

Imagine for a moment being sold into slavery by your family. You are in a foreign country. You don't speak the language and have no friends. Chances are you and I would adopt a victim's mentality, one so prevalent in the world today. We might become anything but a valuable servant. None of that is true of Joseph. Jesus, too, comes *"out of the ivory palaces, into a world of woe."* ("Ivory Palaces" by Henry Barraclough, 1915). The Creator of the universe humbles Himself to be a servant of the world He had made. He lives sinlessly in a sinful world, suffering every minute He is on the earth, living in the midst of a sinful people, yet He does not complain, neither does He sin.

The first Adam is placed in a garden with everything he could possibly want—good food, amiable surroundings, solid work to do, and a wonderful wife. But he isn't satisfied. He wants more. So, he disobeys the only restriction God has placed upon him—he eats of the forbidden fruit. How different for Joseph and for our Lord Jesus, who in terrible circumstances and conditions refuses to give in to temptation. Joseph faces it here in the person of Potiphar's wife. Jesus faced it in the desert, without food or water, (or His family), in an inhospitable environment.

Jesus becomes our second Adam, fulfilling the test of righteousness that our first father fails. Paul speaks of these two Adams in 1Corinthians 15:22:"*For as in Adam all die, so in Christ all will be made alive.*" Joseph, in passing his test, prefigured our Lord as the second Adam.

Before Joseph is falsely accused—as is Jesus at His trial—he makes an amazing statement. He says to Potiphar's wife who attempts to seduce him, *"How then could I do such a wicked thing and sin against God?"* (Genesis 39:9). To be an enslaved man in a foreign country facing this kind of temptation must be terrible. Potiphar's wife has authority over him, so he could easily rationalize his involvement with her. On the other hand, he is a young man, (probably around 25-27 years old), with a normal sex drive. Who would know if he shared her bed? But Joseph fears God. God would know!

Yes, he would be sinning against his master, Potiphar, but much more, it would be an infinite sin against a holy God, because all sins are ultimately against God. Because God is infinite, all sins against Him are infinite. In the same way, during His time of testing in the desert, Jesus invokes the name of God and His Word three times in rejecting Satan's tempting. He says at first, *"It is written: 'Man does not live on bread alone, but on every word that proceeds from the mouth of God.'"* Then, *"It is also written: 'Do not put the Lord your God to the test.'"* Finally, *"Away from me, Satan! For it is written: 'Worship the Lord your God, and serve Him only'"* (Matthew 4:1-10).

Falsely accused, and like Jesus unwilling to offer a defense, Joseph goes to prison. I believe that if Potiphar had really thought Joseph to be guilty, he would have had him executed. Rather, he imprisons Joseph, and thereby saves face. Our Lord's trial also features a judge, Pontius Pilate. Like Potiphar, Pilate wants to keep up appearances and said, *"I find no basis for a charge against this man"* (Luke 23:4). He then sends Jesus to the Cross.

17. Jesus: Numbered Among the Transgressors
Genesis 39:20 and 40:2-3

Joseph's master took him and put him in prison, the place where the king's prisoners were confined...Some time later, the cupbearer and the baker of the king of Egypt offended their master, the king of Egypt. Pharaoh was angry with his two officials, the chief cupbearer and the chief baker, and put them in custody in the house of the captain of the guard, in the same prison where Joseph was confined.

Joseph is cast into prison. And while he is there, he, like Jesus, suffered severely though innocent. Joseph foreshadows the suffering of Christ. While in prison, Joseph, as he had in Potiphar's household, wins the admiration of his jailor who gave him greater and greater responsibilities. So, too, does Jesus win the respect of those who put Him on the cross. As Luke relates in his gospel: *"Jesus called out with a loud voice, 'Father, into your hands I commit my spirit.' When he had said this, he breathed his last. The centurion, seeing what had happened, praised God and said, 'Surely this was a righteous man'"* (Luke 23:46).

Our Lord is crucified between two criminals, one on His left and one on His right. Many years before, Isaiah 53:12 foretells that circumstance:

> *"Therefore I will give him a portion among the great, and he will divide the spoils with the strong, because he poured out his life unto death, and was numbered with the transgressors. For he bore the sin of many, and made intercession for the transgressors."*

Joseph is also thrown in between two men who have been accused of crimes. *"The captain of the guard assigned them to Joseph, and he attended them"* (Gen. 40:4). The cupbearer and the baker have dreams on the same night, and went to Joseph for their interpretation. In the interpretation of both dreams, it is worthwhile to note that Joseph said that each dream was to reach its fulfillment in *"three days"* (vv. 12 and 16). The cupbearer is to receive his freedom in three days. The baker is to be hanged within the same time frame. It is no coincidence that Jesus said to His disciples, *"The Son of Man is going to be betrayed into the hands of men. They will kill him, and after three days he will rise"* (Mark 9:31).

It is also no coincidence that one of the prisoners in Joseph's care is restored to his duties while the other is hanged. This conversation on Golgotha is recorded in Luke 23:39-42:

> *One of the criminals who hung there hurled insults at him: "Aren't you the Christ? Save yourself and us!" But the other criminal rebuked him. "Don't you fear God," he said, "since you are under the same sentence? We are punished justly, for we are getting what our deeds deserve. But this man has done nothing wrong." Then he said, "Jesus,* **remember me** *when you come into your kingdom."*

Our Lord answers the latter man: *"I tell you the truth, today you will be with me in paradise."* So, one of these men, like the baker, meets his destiny in torment, while the other, like the cupbearer, receives pardon.

The transgressor on the cross next to Jesus also says, *"Remember me."* He is known in Church history as St. Didicus. His example is proof of several facts regarding our salvation. First, he is saved at the termination of his life. It is never too late to keep praying for our loved ones who remain unsaved. Second, Didicus is saved without being baptized. We are commanded to be baptized, but the only absolute requirement for our salvation is given in John 3:7 where Jesus says, *"You must be born again."* Third, I believe that Didicus was born from above and that led to his statement of faith. Both regeneration and faith are gifts of God, not something we conjure up on our own. Finally, we know from Jesus' testimony that *"today you will be with me in paradise,"* there is no such thing as "soul sleep." When we die in faith, we are as Paul says in 2 Corinthians 5:8, *"away from the body and at home with the Lord."*

18. Jesus: Revealer of Secret Things
Genesis 41:14-16

*So Pharaoh sent for Joseph, and he was quickly brought from the dungeon.
When he had shaved and changed his clothes, he came before Pharaoh.
Pharaoh said to Joseph, "I had a dream, and no one can interpret it. But I
have heard it said of you that when you hear a dream you can interpret it."
"I cannot do it," Joseph replied to Pharaoh, "but God will give
Pharaoh the answer he desires."*

A verse in the book of Proverbs says, *"The king's heart is in the hand
of the LORD; he directs it like a watercourse wherever he pleases"*
(Proverbs 21:1). It is no coincidence that Pharaoh dreams about
the fat and skinny cows, and the fat and thin shocks of grain. God is behind those dreams to fulfill His purposes on earth. This should come as
no surprise to us. After all, Joseph has had similar dreams, and he correctly
interprets the dreams of the cupbearer and baker. Great literature always
foreshadows events that will occur later on in the book. The Bible is by
far the greatest literature that has ever been written.

From Genesis to Revelation, the Bible is about the foolishness
of the world versus the wisdom of God. (See 1 Corinthians 1:18-31 for
Paul's analysis.) Egypt is a picture of the world. The Egyptians were pagan
idolaters. But God always brings forth a man who fears Him, and who
glorifies His wisdom and His name. God is working all things out to the
ends that He has ordained. Joseph was sold into slavery, then framed and
tossed into prison. Then, like Jesus who would one day be resurrected
physically from the grave, Joseph arises from prison and stands before
Pharaoh to interpret the monarch's dreams. He will then reveal secrets
that God had hidden from the pagan mind.

Jesus is the greatest "revealer of secrets" to have ever walked on
the earth. Indeed, Jesus came to reveal Himself to a lost and dying world.
When He reveals Himself, He reveals the Father, too. Our Lord says in

John 14:9, *"Anyone who has seen me has seen the Father."* He reveals the secrets of the Old Testament—the Hebrew Scriptures. On the road to Emmaus, following His resurrection, Jesus strikes up a conversation with Cleopas and others, during which

> He said to them, *"How foolish you are, and how slow of heart to believe all that the prophets have spoken! Did not the Christ have to suffer these things and then enter his glory?" And beginning with Moses and all the Prophets, he explained to them what was said in all the Scriptures concerning himself* (Luke 24:25-27).

As Joseph reveals future events to Pharaoh, Jesus is to reveal future events to us during His earthly ministry. In Matthew 24, Jesus gives His disciples a glimpse into those things that must come to pass, and just as Joseph warned Pharaoh, Jesus warns His beloved disciples of hazardous days ahead. That chapter begins with these words:

> *Jesus left the temple and was walking away when his disciples came up to him to call his attention to its buildings. "Do you see all these things?" he asked. "I tell you the truth, not one stone here will be left on another; every one will be thrown down"* (vv. 1-2).

This literally happens in AD 70 when the Roman legions under Titus rip the city apart and destroy the Temple to such a degree that not one stone in its superstructure stands upon another. Today, only a portion of its foundation remains—now known as "the wailing wall."

Most importantly, Jesus reveals Himself to be the Savior of the world, and continues to reveal Himself through His Spirit, as day-by-day, people like you and me are added to His kingdom. As we are studying, Jesus' revelation of Himself didn't start with His birth in Bethlehem, but began early in the book of Genesis and continues throughout the Hebrew Scriptures.

19. Jesus: Exalted Among the Gentiles
Genesis 41:41-43

So Pharaoh said to Joseph, "I hereby put you in charge of the whole land of Egypt." Then Pharaoh took his signet ring from his finger and put it on Joseph's finger. He dressed him in robes of fine linen and put a gold chain around his neck. He had him ride in a chariot as his second-in-command, and men shouted before him, "Make way!" Thus he put him in charge of the whole land of Egypt.

As early as the twelfth chapter of Genesis, God promised salvation to all the people of the earth. When He originally blessed Abram and gave him the promises of a land, a people, and His favor, God said:

The LORD had said to Abram, "Leave your country, your people and your father's household and go to the land I will show you. I will make you into a great nation and I will bless you; I will make your name great, and you will be a blessing. I will bless those who bless you, and whoever curses you I will curse; and all peoples on earth will be blessed through you" (Gen. 12:1-3).

The promise of universal blessing through the nation Israel continues throughout the Old Testament. For instance, Psalm 46:10 says, *"Be still, and know that I am God; I will be exalted among the nations, I will be exalted in the earth."* And in Malachi 1:11 we read, *"My name will be great among the nations, from the rising to the setting of the sun. In every place incense and pure offerings will be brought to my name, because my name will be great among the nations,' says the LORD Almighty."*

Jesus came first to His own people, the Jews. When He sent out the twelve in pairs to witness to His coming, He said, *"Do not go among the Gentiles or enter any town of the Samaritans. Go rather to the lost sheep of Israel"* (Matthew 10:5-6). But the mission bore little fruit—His own people rejected Him. In His final commission to His disciples given to us in Matthew 28:18-20, *"...go and make disciples of all nations, baptizing them in the name of the Father and of the Son and of the Holy Spirit..."*

Joseph is rejected and sold into slavery by his own flesh and blood. He proves himself worthy as a slave in Potiphar's household, yet again is rejected and falsely accused. In prison, he yet again is found worthy of honor. Finally, as God has orchestrated the whole sequence of events, Joseph appears before Pharaoh and reveals the secrets of Pharaoh's dreams.

It is well worth noting that Joseph takes no credit for his ability of interpretation. When asked to interpret the dreams, he says in 41:16, *"I cannot do it,"* Joseph replied to Pharaoh, *"but God will give Pharaoh the answer he desires."* How like Jesus who says in John 12:50, *"So whatever I say is just what the Father has told me to say."*

The writer to the Hebrews says of Jesus, our great High Priest, *"Such a high priest meets our need—one who is holy, blameless, pure, set apart from sinners, exalted above the heavens"* (Hebrews 7:26). Jesus has been exalted above the heavens—seated at the right hand of God. Peter writes that Jesus has *"gone into heaven and is at God's right hand—with angels, authorities and powers in submission to him"* (1 Peter 3:22). Joseph, a portrait of Jesus, is himself exalted among the Gentiles, the pagans of a country not his own. Pharaoh said to him in 41:40, *"You shall be in charge of my palace, and all my people are to submit to your orders. Only with respect to the throne will I be greater than you."* In other words, he is to be seated at Pharaoh's right hand. Like Jesus, God has taken Joseph—the lowly, the outcast, the falsely accused—and set him in an exalted place.

Another sense in which Joseph is representative of someone yet unborn is this: He is a portrait of you and me. We believers, too, are to be exalted to the heavenlies as glorified children of God. Joseph's triumph is the triumph of faith. Regardless of your circumstances on this earth, keep your eyes on things above—the glory that shall be ours. This is ours not by anything that we have done. We look only to the blood of Jesus.

20. Jesus: Savior of the World
Genesis 41:56-57

When the famine had spread over the whole country, Joseph opened the storehouses and sold grain to the Egyptians, for the famine was severe throughout Egypt. And all the countries came to Egypt to buy grain from Joseph, because the famine was severe in all the world.

As mentioned earlier, many of the interesting— I should say, astounding—portraits of Jesus in the life of Joseph have come from the pen of Arthur W. Pink in his book, *Gleanings in Genesis*. Here are a few more excerpts from Pink:

In Genesis 41:45, Pharaoh gave the exalted Joseph a new name. *"Pharaoh gave Joseph the name Zaphenath-Paneah…"* Likewise Jesus was given a name in His exaltation. We read in Philippians 2:9-10, *"Therefore God exalted him to the highest place and gave him the name that is above every name, that at the name of Jesus every knee should bow, in heaven and on earth and under the earth…"*

In that same verse in Genesis 41, Joseph was given a wife by Pharaoh: *"and [Pharaoh] gave him Asenath daughter of Potiphera, priest of On, to be his wife."* His wife was a Gentile. In Matthew 22:2, Jesus speaks of a wedding: *"The kingdom of heaven is like a king who prepared a wedding banquet for his son…"* We, both Gentiles and Jews, who have been saved by the blood of Jesus, are the bride of Christ. We read in Revelation 21:2, *"I saw the Holy City, the new Jerusalem, coming down out of heaven from God, prepared as a bride beautifully dressed for her husband…"* Christ is the bridegroom, and we, His bride, are a gift from the Father to Him.

Finally, note in verse 46 of chapter 41 that *"Joseph was thirty years old when he entered the service of Pharaoh."* So in Luke 3:23 we are given this fact about Jesus: *"Now Jesus himself was about thirty years old when he began his ministry."* Joseph and Jesus began their most significant ministries at the same age!

Joseph, in his position as CEO of all Egypt immediately began to make preparations for the coming famine. God had made clear that there would be seven years of plenty, followed by seven years of famine. So Joseph built storehouses for the grain that would be brought forth in the good years, building up a reserve for the lean years ahead. We see in 41:57 above that *"all the countries came to Egypt to buy grain from Joseph, because the famine was severe in all the world."* Even in Palestine the needs were great—so great that Joseph's family also suffered. In verse 55, we read these words: *"When all Egypt began to feel the famine, the people cried to Pharaoh for food. Then Pharaoh told all the Egyptians, 'Go to Joseph and do what he tells you.'"* Joseph held the keys to the storehouse of bread.

Jesus said in John 6:35, *"I am the bread of life. He who comes to me will never go hungry, and he who believes in me will never be thirsty."* We humans face a planet where a real famine exists. Most of us in America may have plenty to eat in the kitchen pantry, but we have a deeper, spiritual hunger that will not be satisfied by any bread but the Bread of Life—Jesus. Just as the whole world came to Joseph in Egypt, we must come to Jesus to get this Bread of Life. As Isaiah says in 55:1, *"Come, all you who are thirsty, come to the waters; and you who have no money, come, buy and eat! Come, buy wine and milk without money and without cost."*

Jesus not only has full authority to distribute this Bread of Life, but just as Joseph, He has unlimited resources. He says in Matthew 11:28, *"Come to me, all you who are weary and burdened, and I will give you rest."* Weary, burdened, hungry…we come to Jesus just as we are. He is the Savior of the world. He is willing and mighty to save.

I may ask you, is Jesus your Savior? If you have been reading these pages and a hunger for God has gripped your soul, don't delay. The table is set and Jesus, like Joseph before him who handed out earthly food to the whole world, invites you to partake of the Bread of Life—the food that gives eternal life.

21. JESUS: A MAN OF TENDER COMPASSION
Genesis 42-45

As he looked about and saw his brother Benjamin, his own mother's son, he asked, "Is this your youngest brother, the one you told me about?" And he said, "God be gracious to you, my son." Deeply moved at the sight of his brother, Joseph hurried out and looked for a place to weep. He went into his private room and wept there (Genesis 43:29,30).

Like the Israelites many centuries later, the Hebrews in Palestine were being driven from the land that God had given them. This time, it was because of famine. Later, the cause would be the Chaldeans, then, ultimately, the Romans in 70 A.D. *Diaspora*—dispersion—is the story of the Jew throughout history. That story begins here in Genesis.

Someone was once asked to prove the truthfulness of the Bible in two words. His words were "The Jew." One of the miracles of the ages has been how the Jewish people have been preserved by God under the most severe persecution and suffering. As Pink says, *"Nothing can account for the unparalleled suffering of this people, but the judgment and discipline of the Lord"* (p. 393).

Paul says in Romans 11:25-27 that it is a mystery:

I do not want you to be ignorant of this mystery, brothers, so that you may not be conceited: Israel has experienced a hardening in part until the full number of the Gentiles has come in. And so all Israel will be saved, as it is written: "The deliverer will come from Zion; he will turn godlessness away from Jacob. And this is my covenant with them when I take away their sins."

Although many Jews, including Paul, came to faith in Jesus in the early days of the Church, the nation itself rejected Jesus as the promised Messiah. That rejection was portrayed for us thousands of years earlier by the brothers' rejection of their brother Joseph—a type of the One to come. Genesis 42 through 45 tell the story of Joseph's dealings with his brothers as they come in search of food. Notice as you read these chapters that Joseph knew his brothers, yet they did not recognize him on their first trip to Egypt. Neither was Jesus known by His brothers at His first appearing. Joseph then punished his siblings by requiring they leave Simeon as a hostage while they returned to Palestine to bring Benjamin back. Notice that Joseph wept as they spoke to one another in 42:24.

The brothers did recognize Joseph the second time they arrived in Egypt, just as the Bible says that Israel will recognize Jesus when He comes again. They are greatly troubled at Joseph's presence, and confess their guilt to him. In the same way, Israel will bow down before the re-fulgent glory of Jesus as He comes to earth again. Joseph then began to weep aloud in 45:1-2. Actually, we read of Joseph weeping seven times in these final chapters of Genesis. (42:24; 43:30; 45:1-2, 15; 46:29; 50:1, and 50:15-17.) He was a man of compassion for his Israelite brothers.

In the same way, Jesus was a man full of compassion for Israel. As Jesus entered the holy city on His way to His destiny on the Cross, Luke recorded His words:

As he approached Jerusalem and saw the city, he wept over it and said, "If you, even you, had only known on this day what would bring you peace— but now it is hidden from your eyes. The days will come upon you when your enemies will build an embankment against you and encircle you and hem you in on every side. They will dash you to the ground, you and the children within your walls. They will not leave one stone on another, because you did not recognize the time of God's coming to you." (Luke 19:41-44).

Earlier, Jesus wept over the grave of His friend Lazarus. But Jesus was to show His greatest compassion at Golgotha, where He died for the sins of people everywhere—of all races, colors, and national origins—the Just for the unjust. Do you recognize Jesus? He is full of tender mercies.

22. JESUS: REVEALER OF GOD'S GRACE
Genesis 45:4-8

*Then Joseph said to his brothers, "Come close to me." When they had done
so, he said, "I am your brother Joseph, the one you sold into Egypt! And
now, do not be distressed and do not be angry with yourselves for selling me
here, because it was to save lives that God sent me ahead of you...But God
sent me ahead of you to preserve for you a remnant on earth and to save
your lives by a great deliverance. So then, it was not you who sent me here,
but God. He made me father to Pharaoh, lord of his entire
household and ruler of all Egypt."*

The brothers came before Joseph twice. Both times they wanted
to pay for the grain they received in their sacks. Both times, as
they were sent back to their father, Israel, they discovered that
their money has been returned to them. In the same way, as Paul tells us
in Romans 9:30-32:

> *What then shall we say? That the Gentiles, who did not pursue righ-
> teousness, have obtained it, a righteousness that is by faith; but Israel,
> who pursued a law of righteousness, has not attained it. Why not?
> Because they pursued it not by faith but as if it were by works. They
> stumbled over the "stumbling stone."*

The *"stumbling stone"* was Jesus. The unbelieving Jews, like most men and
women, stumble over the free gift of God's grace in Jesus Christ. They
want to work for their salvation. But God says we cannot pay anything.
Salvation is by God's grace alone, as Joseph portrayed in giving his brothers their money back.

But greater grace was to be given the sons of Israel in the land of
Egypt. They came before Joseph and the silver cup was found in Benjamin's sack. They trembled with fear, as they stood before the ruler of all
Egypt, one of the most powerful men in the world. Joseph suggested that
they leave Benjamin with him to become his slave. Judah stood up and

offered to remain in his younger brother's place, thereby suggesting the principal of substitutionary atonement. We then read that Joseph could not control himself any longer:

...he cried out, "Have everyone leave my presence!" So there was no one with Joseph when he made himself known to his brothers. And he wept so loudly that the Egyptians heard him, and Pharaoh's household heard about it. Joseph said to his brothers, "I am Joseph! Is my father still living?" But his brothers were not able to answer him, because they were terrified at his presence (Genesis 45:1-3).

Then comes Joseph's most astonishing statement. He releases them from any guilt in the matter of selling him into slavery. He then later explains to them: *"You intended to harm me, but God intended it for good to accomplish what is now being done, the saving of many lives"* (Chapter 50, verse 20). Joseph reveals to them the grace of God. It is one of the greatest and most profound statements in the Bible.

How often do we hear unlearned folks rail against those who sent Jesus to the Cross? Surely, it was the greatest crime that has ever been perpetrated in the history of the world. But it was also the greatest display of the grace of God that has ever occurred. What those who accuse the Jews and the Roman authorities fail to understand is that I, Bob Beasley, sent Jesus to the Cross. If you are saved by His blood, you are guilty of nailing Him to the tree. All who were "there" that awful day intended to harm Jesus... *"but God intended it for good to accomplish what is now being done, the saving of many lives"* (Genesis 50:20).

To provide mercy for his brothers, Joseph could just release them. But he goes beyond mere mercy and provides them with what they really need—grace. He makes full provision for their future, giving them a land—Goshen—where they can live without fear of starving to death over the next five years' famine. Likewise, Jesus gives the kingdom of heaven to those who recognize Him and come to Him in childlike faith. Ours is the God who turns evil into good.

23. JESUS: LION OF THE TRIBE OF JUDAH
Genesis 49:8-12

"Judah, your brothers will praise you; your hand will be on the neck of your enemies; your father's sons will bow down to you. You are a lion's cub, O Judah; you return from the prey, my son. Like a lion he crouches and lies down, like a lioness—who dares to rouse him? The scepter will not depart from Judah, nor the ruler's staff from between his feet, until he comes to whom it belongs and the obedience of the nations is his. He will tether his donkey to a vine, his colt to the choicest branch; he will wash his garments in wine, his robes in the blood of grapes. His eyes will be darker than wine, his teeth whiter than milk."

At the end of the book of Genesis, Israel and his sons and their families have all come into Egypt and settled in Goshen. Now, nearing death, Jacob—Israel—gathered his boys together and gave each his blessing. The first three, Reuben, Simeon, and Levi, draw only the first seven verses of chapter 49 between them, and their "blessings" are more like curses. Reuben had sinned against Jacob in sleeping with his wife Bilhah, and the other two by their extreme vengeance at Shechem. Judah had sinned in his tryst with Tamar, and probably expected the worst. Instead, Israel's blessing was one of triumph for Judah and his descendants.

First, Israel declared that Judah's brothers will bow down to him. Wasn't this Joseph's dream? Yes, but now the preeminence is transferred to Judah's tribe. Interestingly, the next leader of the nation Israel is Moses—a descendant of Levi. Later, the first king of Israel is Saul, of Benjamin. But then the greatest king of Israel takes the throne. David and his descendants form the kingly line in Judah, following the division of Israel. From that kingly line two individuals would ultimately appear upon the scene—a man named Joseph, and a woman named Mary. Mary's son, of course, was Jesus. (See Matthew 1 and Luke 3.) He was to be born in the town of Bethlehem. As we will see later in Chapter 96 regarding Micah 5:2,

Bethlehem is in Judah's portion of the Promised Land of Israel. Jesus, who was to be born there, is the *"Lion of the tribe of Judah"* (Rev. 5:5).

In the next phrase of Israel's prophetic blessing come these words: *"The scepter will not depart from Judah, nor the ruler's staff from between his feet, until he comes to whom it belongs and the obedience of the nations is his."* Later, after David had assumed the throne of Israel, this word of the Lord came to him:

> *"When your days are over and you rest with your fathers, I will raise up your offspring to succeed you, who will come from your own body, and I will establish his kingdom. He is the one who will build a house for my Name, and I will establish the throne of his kingdom forever. I will be his father, and he will be my son..."* (2 Sam. 7:12-14a).

David's son, Solomon, would build the physical Temple in Jerusalem, but this word from God to David clearly spoke of a coming Messiah—Jesus— who would build the true Temple of God—His Church. The *"obedience of the nations"* will be His, and He will reign forever. He will rule not only Israel, but the entire universe of men. Jesus is both the Son of God, and the Son of Man. Although seen only by the eye of faith, Jesus is reigning now from His throne, and will reign forever (Isaiah 9:7).

Jacob's final words in his blessing of Judah concern the abundance of prosperity in the coming reign of this permanent King. Normally, one washes his or her clothing in water. But this coming One will wash His in the *"blood of grapes."* This reminds us of the first miracle that Jesus performed in Cana of Galilee—changing water into wine. Grapes also speak of His death on the Cross and the symbol of wine that Jesus used to speak of His blood shed there.

Three direct prophesies of Jesus exist in Genesis. Genesis 3:15 speaks of His defeat of Satan. Genesis 22:18 tells of the blessing of Abraham flowing out to all the people of the world. Finally, Israel speaks of the One from the tribe of Judah who will rule the world forever.

24. Jesus: Condemned to Die As a Child
Exodus 1:22-2:3

Then Pharaoh gave this order to all his people: "Every boy that is born you must throw into the Nile, but let every girl live." Now a man of the house of Levi married a Levite woman, and she became pregnant and gave birth to a son. When she saw that he was a fine child, she hid him for three months. But when she could hide him no longer, she got a papyrus basket for him and coated it with tar and pitch. Then she placed the child in it and put it among the reeds along the bank of the Nile.

We now leave the book of Genesis and move to Exodus. The Israelites have been in Egypt for over 400 years They have been reduced to slavery, just as God had earlier told Abraham in Genesis 15:13-14:

"Know for certain that your descendants will be strangers in a country not their own, and they will be enslaved and mistreated four hundred years. But I will punish the nation they serve as slaves, and afterward they will come out with great possessions."

Pharaoh worried that the Israelite slaves would become too numerous and overwhelm his kingdom, because according to Exodus 1:7, *"...the Israelites were fruitful and multiplied greatly and became exceedingly numerous, so that the land was filled with them."* He therefore undertook a pogrom—a deliberate massacre—aimed at reducing their number. It was the first in a line of many such campaigns the Jews have suffered throughout history, and continue to suffer.

Pharaoh ordered the Hebrew midwives to kill any male children, but allow the girls to live. That didn't work, so he then ordered that all male children be thrown into the Nile river to drown. Moses was a child so ordered to be murdered. Later we will see Moses as a type of Christ in other respects, but here we see him portraying the baby Jesus even in his infancy. In order to save him, Moses' parents constructed a little "ark"— a boat of reeds and tar, and launched him onto the Nile. (This little boat is also a picture of the Lord Jesus. See "Ark of Deliverance" in chapter 7.)

When Jesus was born, a king—not Pharaoh—reigned, but his worries were similar. Herod learned from a group of wise men from the east that a new "king" has been born in Judea. He worried about a usurper to his throne. After Herod learned from his chief priests and teachers of the law that the Messiah was to be born in Bethlehem, he said to the wise men, *"Go and make a careful search for the child. As soon as you find him, report to me, so that I too may go and worship him"* (Matthew 2:8). So, after the wise men were warned not to return to Herod, and the despot realized he had been outwitted, he began to slaughter all the male children two years old and younger around Bethlehem. The prophet Jeremiah had foreseen the event in 31:15 (As quoted in Matthew 2:18): *"A voice is heard in Ramah, weeping and great mourning, Rachel weeping for her children and refusing to be comforted, because they are no more."*

Joseph was forewarned by an angel of the Lord to flee to Egypt with Mary and the child. He said, *"Get up...take the child and his mother and escape to Egypt. Stay there until I tell you, for Herod is going to search for the child to kill him"* (Matthew 2:13). They stayed there until Herod died and the angel told them it was safe to return. So Joseph and Mary settled in Nazareth, in the district of Galilee.

Moses would grow up to be the most revered leader of the nation Israel. Even today, if a Jew is asked who was the greatest of his people, chances are good that he will answer, "Moses." The author of Hebrews in the New Testament says this of Moses:

For every house is built by someone, but God is the builder of everything. Moses was faithful as a servant in all God's house, testifying to what would be said in the future. But Christ is faithful as a son over God's house. And we are his house, if we hold on to our courage and the hope of which we boast (Hebrews 3:4-6).

25. Jesus: Jehovah—The Great "I Am"
Exodus 3:1-6 & 13-14

*Now Moses was tending the flock of Jethro his father-in-law, the priest
of Midian, and he led the flock to the far side of the desert and came to
Horeb, the mountain of God. There the angel of the LORD appeared to him
in flames of fire from within a bush. Moses saw that though the bush was
on fire it did not burn up. So Moses thought, "I will go over and see this
strange sight—why the bush does not burn up." When the LORD saw that
he had gone over to look, God called to him from within the bush, "Moses!
Moses!" And Moses said, "Here I am." "Do not come any closer," God said.
"Take off your sandals, for the place where you are standing is holy ground."
Then he said, "I am the God of your father, the God of Abraham, the God
of Isaac and the God of Jacob." At this, Moses hid his face, because he was
afraid to look at God...Moses said to God, "Suppose I go to the Israelites
and say to them, 'The God of your fathers has sent me to you,' and they ask
me, 'What is his name?' Then what shall I tell them?" God said to Moses, "I
AM WHO I AM. This is what you are to say to the Israelites:
'I AM has sent me to you.'"*

We saw a "theophany" back in chapter 9 where God appeared
as a smoking firepot and a burning torch. Here, God comes
face to face with Moses, speaking to the frightened Israelite
from a burning bush that is not consumed. Moses asks Him His name.
God answers, *"I AM WHO I AM,"* (or *"I AM THAT I AM."*)

The words *"I AM"* here are *"YHWH"* in the original Hebrew language, in which most of the Old Testament is written. We would say this
word, "Yahweh," in a very guttural way, or more likely, "Jehovah." Jews
might render YHWH as "Adonai" because they have been forbidden to
voice the original pronunciation since about the 3rd century B.C.

What does this "I AM" mean? And how does it link to Jesus? God
is saying that He is the preexistent Creator of the universe, with no beginning and no end. In order to see how the name links to Jesus, let's turn
our attention to a conversation Jesus had with the Pharisees and teachers

of the law that centered on Abraham:

> *[Jesus said], "I tell you the truth, if anyone keeps my word, he will never see death." At this the Jews exclaimed, "Now we know that you are demon-possessed! Abraham died and so did the prophets, yet you say that if anyone keeps your word, he will never taste death." [Jesus said], "Your father Abraham rejoiced at the thought of seeing my day; he saw it and was glad." "You are not yet fifty years old," the Jews said to him, "and you have seen Abraham!" "I tell you the truth," Jesus answered," before Abraham was born, **I am!**" At this, they picked up stones to stone him, but Jesus hid himself, slipping away...* (John 8:51-59).

The *"I am"* Jesus uses here was literally, "Jehovah," or "Yahweh." Jesus is making a direct claim upon eternal preexistence—the claim to be God. Notice that the Jews immediately took up stones to stone Him, which was the method of execution prescribed for blasphemy in Israel. There's no question in their minds that Jesus was using the divine name. Jesus claimed to be the Great "I AM" of the burning bush!

We could go on for pages. Instead, let's look at some other "I AM" statements of our Lord: (Emphasis is always mine.)

> John 6:35: *Then Jesus declared, "I AM the bread of life. He who comes to me will never go hungry, and he who believes in me will never be thirsty."* John 8:12: *"I AM the light of the world. Whoever follows me will never walk in darkness, but will have the light of life."* John 10:7: *I tell you the truth, I AM the gate for the sheep."* John 10:11: *"I AM the good shepherd. The good shepherd lays down his life for the sheep."* John 11:25: *"I AM the resurrection and the life. He who believes in me will live, even though he dies..."* John 14:6: *Jesus answered, "I AM the way and the truth and the life. No one comes to the Father except through me."* John 15:1: *"I AM the true vine, and my Father is the gardener."*

Some have falsely stated that Jesus never really claimed to be God. Nothing could be further from the truth. The Pharisees and teachers of the law knew precisely what He was claiming.

26. Jesus: Conqueror of Satan
Exodus 5-11

Afterward Moses and Aaron went to Pharaoh and said, "This is what the LORD, the God of Israel, says: 'Let my people go, so that they may hold a festival to me in the desert.'" Pharaoh said, "Who is the LORD, that I should obey him and let Israel go? I do not know the LORD and I will not let Israel go" (Exodus 5:1-2).

The fallen angel—Satan—appears on the first pages of holy Scripture, in the Garden with the first couple. Like Jesus, pictures of Satan regularly occur in the Bible. Nimrod, in Genesis 10:8 is one. Pharaoh, king of Egypt is another. Egypt is a picture of the world system, and just as Pharaoh is ruler of Egypt, Satan is the ruler of this world system (See 2 Cor. 4:4, for instance). He is the *"god of this world"* in these verses.

Moses and Aaron have been commissioned by God—who we've just seen is Jesus in the burning bush—to present themselves to Pharaoh and tell him to let the Israelites leave Egypt. God says of Pharaoh in Exodus 9:16, *"I have raised you up for this very purpose, that I might show you my power and that my name might be proclaimed in all the earth."* It is the same with Satan. God allows him to roam because it serves God's purposes in His self-revelation.

The book of Revelation in the New Testament speaks of our Lord conquering Satan by throwing him into the lake of burning sulphur (Revelation 20:10). It is interesting that God also "throws" Pharaoh into a lake to die as well—the Red Sea. In fact, many similarities exist between these chapters in Exodus and Revelation. As you may recall, the 11 plagues that God brings upon Pharaoh and his people in Exodus are the plagues of snakes, water into blood, frogs, gnats, flies, against livestock, boils, hail, locusts, darkness, and finally the deaths of Egypt's firstborn.

Similarly, in the book of Revelation—the "Revelation of Jesus

Christ" to be exact—they appear again. Like Moses and Aaron, two witnesses are promised who will have the power to work miracles in God's name (11:3-6). The beast is also able to work signs and wonders (13:13-16). Once again, water is turned into blood (8:8, 16:4-5). Frogs, conjured up by satanic forces, reappear (16:13). Another plague of locusts appears (9:2-11). Boils from God afflict those who oppose Him (16:2). Hailstones hit the earth once again (8:7). A terrible darkness shall descend upon the earth during those days (16:10). The wicked will harden their hearts, just like Pharaoh (9:20-21). Death will reign on the earth (9:15). Is it a coincidence that John's vision is so much like the history of Israel's journey? I think not.

Like the Israelites who were delivered from Pharaoh's clutches in Exodus, all of God's saints will be delivered from the clutches of Satan. Paul writes in Romans 11:26, *"And so all Israel will be saved, as it is written: 'The deliverer will come from Zion; he will turn godlessness away from Jacob.'"* The Church, of course, is the true Israel. Again, in 1 John 3:8b: *"The reason the Son of God appeared was to destroy the devil's work."*

Some people are eager to attribute Satan with too much power. Many believe that he's a match for God. But the Bible is clear that God controls Satan's every move, and uses him for His own purposes, as we've said above. Nowhere in Scripture is this more clearly seen than in the book of Job. In chapters one and two of that book we have a conversation that took place between God and Satan. Satan accused Job of only trusting in God because of his wealth and good situation. So he proposed a test. God granted Satan the right to attack Job, taking away his wealth and his children, and ultimately his health. Without God's permission, Satan would be powerless. So why does God allow Satan to exist at all? We have the answer in Exodus 9:16, and as quoted by Paul in Romans 9:17, *"For the Scripture says to Pharaoh: 'I raised you up for this very purpose, that I might display my power in you and that my name might be proclaimed in all the earth.'"*

27. JESUS: OUR PASSOVER LAMB
Exodus 12

*Then Moses summoned all the elders of Israel and said to them, "Go at
once and select the animals for your families and slaughter the Passover
lamb. Take a bunch of hyssop, dip it into the blood in the basin and put
some of the blood on the top and on both sides of the doorframe. Not one of
you shall go out the door of his house until morning. When the LORD goes
through the land to strike down the Egyptians, he will see the blood on the
top and sides of the doorframe and will pass over that doorway, and
he will not permit the destroyer to enter your houses and
strike you down"* (Exodus 12:21-23).

Moses and Aaron stood before Pharaoh time and time again.
Each time they displayed the awesome power of God to
perform miracles. Each time God slugged away at Pharaoh
and the Egyptians with all sorts of plagues. Almost every time, Pharaoh
would agree to let the Israelites leave Egypt, only to go back on his word
and keep them in slavery. Finally, God planned one last plague—the
plague on the firstborn.

The Israelites were warned that on a certain evening, the tenth day
of the first month, the Lord would pass over the land of Egypt, slaying
the firstborn, of both men and animals, in every home. In order for their
homes to be spared, they were to sacrifice a lamb, taking some of its blood
and smearing it on the sides and top of the doorframes of their homes.
The lamb was then to be eaten in haste by the family. God ordered that
the Passover feast was to be commemorated continually by the Israelites
after they entered the Promised Land.

We've already seen a sheep sacrificed in chapter 12, where Abraham took his son, Isaac, to Mt. Moriah. Here, another lamb is sacrificed
in protection of God's people. All who faithfully carried out the Lord's
command to slaughter a lamb and place its blood on the doorframes of
their homes, would be spared disaster. The Scripture then says, *"At mid-*

night the LORD struck down all the firstborn in Egypt, from the firstborn of Pharaoh, who sat on the throne, to the firstborn of the prisoner, who was in the dungeon, and the firstborn of all the livestock as well" (Exodus 12:29).

The Last Supper, as it has become known, where Jesus washed the feet of His disciples, was a Passover Feast. These words are from John 13:1: *"It was just before the Passover Feast. Jesus knew that the time had come for him to leave this world and go to the Father."* It is no coincidence that our Lord Jesus was slain on the eve of the Passover, for as Paul says in 1 Corinthians 5:7, *"...Christ, our Passover lamb, has been sacrificed."*

The blood of the lambs in Egypt was to be placed on the horizontal and vertical wooden frames of the door posts. In like manner, Jesus' blood was smeared from His mutilated body on the horizontal and vertical members of the Cross. The original Passover was a time of judgment. All those who put their trust in God's words were spared, and those who did not, suffered the consequences. It is the same at the Cross of Christ. The Cross is the focal point of all history, for on it are the sheep separated from the goats, the regenerate from the reprobate (Matthew 25:32).

On the Cross, the fullness of human depravity echoed the depravity of Pharaoh. Yet the grace of God was shown as never before. Earlier, at that Passover feast in the upper room,

> *While they were eating, Jesus took bread, gave thanks and broke it, and gave it to his disciples, saying, "Take and eat; this is my body." Then he took the cup, gave thanks and offered it to them, saying, "Drink from it, all of you. This is my blood of the covenant, which is poured out for many for the forgiveness of sins"* (Matthew 26:26-28).

We must not be ignorant of these things. Paul said in Acts 17:30 *"In the past God overlooked such ignorance, but now he commands all people everywhere to repent."* Have you trusted the true Passover Lamb—the Lord Jesus Christ?

28. Jesus: Called Out of Egypt
Exodus 12:40-42

*Now the length of time the Israelite people lived in Egypt was 430 years.
At the end of the 430 years, to the very day, all the Lord's divisions left
Egypt. Because the LORD kept vigil that night to bring them out of Egypt,
on this night all the Israelites are to keep vigil to honor the
LORD for the generations to come.*

Previously, in Genesis 15:13, the Lord said to Abraham,

*"Know for certain that your descendants will be strangers in a country
not their own, and they will be enslaved and mistreated four hundred
years. But I will punish the nation they serve as slaves, and afterward
they will come out with great possessions."*

This is exactly what has happened. The Egyptians were so anxious to see the Israelites leave Egypt, that they gave them articles of silver and gold and clothing (Exodus 12:35-36); *"... They plundered the Egyptians."*

The Israelite Exodus from Egypt is one of the most amazing events in the history of the world. Many who study Egyptology doubt its truth, inasmuch as nothing has been found in the ancient Egyptian hieroglyphics to support its veracity. We can understand that, as history has often been distorted by those with something to hide. This awesome defeat of their king and gods was nothing to be proud of—indeed, it was something to forget. One of the reasons to trust the Bible is that it gives us the true story in redemptive history, warts and all. It pulls no punches.

By His mighty hand, God led the people out of Egypt toward the Promised Land. He divided the water of the Red Sea and they walked through on dry land (Exod. 14:21). A verse in Hosea 11:1 speaks of God's call to come out of Egypt. It says, *"When Israel was a child, I loved him, and out of Egypt I called my son."*

That verse in the Old Testament, written many hundreds of years later, speaks to three important events in human history. The first, of course, is as it looks backward to remember the escape of the Israelites from the clutches of Pharaoh. The second historical event of which Hosea 11:1 prophesies is that of Jesus, who, too, was called out of Egypt. It was the call to Joseph in Matthew 2 to take the baby Jesus into Egypt to escape the clutches of the evil Herod. Then, when Herod died, Jesus and his little family was called out of Egypt. The Word of God says;

> So [Joseph] got up, took the child and his mother during the night and left for Egypt, where he stayed until the death of Herod. And so was fulfilled what the Lord had said through the prophet [Hosea]: "Out of Egypt I called my son" (Matthew 2:14-15).

Someone asks, "Where do we read of the third event in history where the verse in Hosea is fulfilled?" Actually, the third event has occurred not once, but millions of times in redemptive history. It occurs each time another man, woman, or child is effectually called to follow Christ. Egypt is a picture of this world and its evil ways. God, in His great love for us, while we were still sinners, calls us "out of Egypt" to Himself (Romans 5:8). We who were in the clutches of Satan, of whom Pharaoh and Herod speak, are by God's grace and power *brought into the glorious freedom of the children of God"* (Rom. 8:21).

An interesting side note to the call to the Israelites to come out of Egypt is found in Psalm 105:37, *"[God] brought out Israel, laden with silver and gold, and from among their tribes no one faltered."* Not only did the Israelites plunder the Egyptians as God had promised in Genesis 15:14, but not one was sickly or infirm in any way. The KJV says, *"...there was not one feeble person among their tribes."* They were in good shape for the journey! So, too, are we who have come out of Egypt, in good shape for the journey as we are fed and led by God's Spirit.

29. JESUS: OUR TRUSTWORTHY GUIDE
Exodus 13:20-22

After leaving Succoth they camped at Etham on the edge of the desert. By day the LORD went ahead of them in a pillar of cloud to guide them on their way and by night in a pillar of fire to give them light, so that they could travel by day or night. Neither the pillar of cloud by day nor the pillar of fire by night left its place in front of the people.

I suppose to be perfectly accurate, the pillar of cloud by day and fire by night that led Israel throughout their entire wilderness experience, is really a picture of the Holy Spirit. Nevertheless, He is called the "Spirit of Christ" in Romans 8:9, and 1 Peter 1:11. Our God is One God. He is manifested in three persons, but one substance, or essence—the Holy Trinity. So, in a way, to speak of the Spirit is to speak also of Christ. Like the burning bush, the pillar, or cloud, was a theophany—a physical manifestation of the living God and preincarnate Messiah.

Just as Christ was one person in two substances—both God and man—the pillar of cloud and fire is believed to be one substance also, but in two manifestations. By day, the pillar led the procession and was a covering from the sun and harsh elements of the desert wilderness. At night, the pillar shone brightly to illuminate the way and the camp. Likewise, the Spirit of God leads the Christian in his daily walk by the Spirit of God. Paul says in Romans 8:14, *"...those who are led by the Spirit of God are sons of God."*

Arthur Pink, in *Gleanings in Exodus*, p. 104, gives five reasons why the pillar was given to Israel. First, that God's great power might continue to be revealed to the people and to the Egyptians. Second, the pillar was to lead Pharaoh and his minions to their deaths in the Red Sea. Third, the pillar led the Israelites—God's Church—to Sinai where the Law might be given them. Fourth, Pink says that it was to organize the nation Israel into a "Church-state," that would enter the Land in strength. Finally, the cloud led the people that they might be *"humbled, tried, and proved"* (Deut. 8:2-3). Above all, the pillar was a clear and unmistakable sign of God's presence with His people. Our transcendent God is also the immanent God. He is both separate from His creation and "with us," through His Spirit and His incarnate Son.

The pillar was a true guide by day and an illumination to the night. The Word of God, in both of its manifestations in Christ, (John 1:1ff) and in the Bible—God's written Word (Hebrews 4:12, for instance)—both lead and illuminate the darkness. Like both Words, God spoke from the cloud. Our God is a God who speaks, unlike mere idols—"Fig Newtons" of the human imagination, as Dr. R.C. Sproul likes to say—who neither speak nor have power.

The pillar of cloud and fire *"brought darkness to the one side (the Egyptians) and light to the other side; so neither went near the other all night long"* (Exodus 14:20). So it is today, as God has called out a people into his wonderful light, but whom the world cannot receive. *"The world cannot accept [Christ's Spirit], because it neither sees him nor knows him"* (John 14:17).

Throughout the entire journey of 40 plus years in the wilderness, the pillar of cloud and fire did not leave the Israelites for one second. Just as the Lord says in Deuteronomy 31:6 (as quoted in Hebrews 13:5); *"... the LORD your God goes with you; he will never leave you nor forsake you."* When the Tabernacle was built and placed in the center of the congregation, *"...the cloud covered the Tent of Meeting, and the glory of the LORD filled the tabernacle"* (Exodus 40:34). Truly, the pillar of cloud and fire was a foreshadowing of the One to come—Immanuel—*"God with us"* (Matt. 1:23).

30. JESUS: OUR RESERVOIR OF LIVING WATER
Exodus 15:22-26

Then Moses led Israel from the Red Sea and they went into the Desert of Shur. For three days they traveled in the desert without finding water. When they came to Marah, they could not drink its water because it was bitter. (That is why the place is called Marah.) So the people grumbled against Moses, saying, "What are we to drink?" Then Moses cried out to the LORD, and the LORD showed him a piece of wood [KJV="a tree"]. He threw it into the water, and the water became sweet.

The Israelites had been led out of Egypt under the mighty hand of Yahweh. He had appeared in the theophany of the pillar of cloud and fire. Yahweh then parted the waters of the Red Sea, so the Israelites could walk through on dry land, while their Egyptian pursuers were drowned when the water closed in on them. Water has basically two meanings in Scripture: Healing, or salvation, and the water of judgment.

Judgment may be seen in the drowning Egyptians, and in those who drowned in the flood of Noah's day. We also may remember how water was used as a medium of judgment in the book of Jonah. While the Egyptians and the antediluvian were judged, their counterparts—the Israelites and Noah—were saved. Jonah was both judged and saved in water. We are commanded to be baptized by water (Acts 2:38 & Matthew 28:19 for instance). While we are not saved by baptism itself, it points to the One who does save us by His grace—the Lord Jesus Christ. He is the Reservoir of Living Water.

In John 4, we are given the account of the meeting of Jesus and the Samaritan woman at the well. Jesus spoke to her of "living water." He said, *"Everyone who drinks this water will be thirsty again, but whoever drinks the water I give him will never thirst. Indeed, the water I give him will become in him a spring of water welling up to eternal life"* (John 4:13-14). Jesus, of course, was referring to Himself. Only Jesus has the power of resurrection—salvation—and judgment. For instance, He says in John 9:39, *"For judgment I have come into this world, so that the blind will see and those who see will become blind."* Only Jesus has the water of salvation for us...or judgment for all those who will not come to Him in faith.

For three days, the Israelites marched in the desert with nothing to drink. Notice that even though God has been leading them, displaying His miraculous power, they complained to Moses. How typical of us in this age of "victimology!" We're ready to blame anyone and everyone for our problems, when, in actuality, it is God with whom we quarrel. This setting of blame on Moses continued throughout the wilderness journey.

When they finally arrived at an oasis in the desert wilderness, the water was bitter! How were they to water themselves and their flocks? So God opened Moses' eyes, and showed him a tree. Moses lifted up the tree and cast it into the water, and the water became sweet and potable. The bitter water represents another point of suffering for the Israelites. Like the young Christian who has been told that if "you come to Jesus, all your earthly problems will be solved," one starts out only to find that following Christ often means suffering and trouble. That was my experience, and probably yours, too. Just as the Israelites found suffering and testing in the wilderness, so we, too, find suffering in our "wilderness"—the world in which we live as wandering pilgrims, as we look *"forward to the city with foundations, whose architect and builder is God"* (Hebrews 11:10). Remember the words of Paul in Philippians 1:29; *"For it has been granted to you on behalf of Christ not only to believe on him, but also to suffer for him..."* We may suffer, but God always sees us through it.

The tree, as we have seen in chapter 6, foreshadows and prefigures Christ. It points to both His humanity and to the Cross on which He died, transforming the bitterness of judgment into the sweetness of salvation for His people. We'll see more of wood as a type of Christ's humanity when we take up the Tabernacle in chapter 34.

31. JESUS: THE BREAD OF HEAVEN
Exodus 16:2-4

In the desert the whole community grumbled against Moses and Aaron. The Israelites said to them, "If only we had died by the Lord's hand in Egypt! There we sat around pots of meat and ate all the food we wanted, but you have brought us out into this desert to starve this entire assembly to death." Then the LORD said to Moses, "I will rain down **bread from heaven** *for you. The people are to go out each day and gather enough for that day. In this way I will test them and see whether they will follow my instructions."*

Jesus said in John 6:35, *"I am the bread of life. He who comes to me will never go hungry, and he who believes in me will never be thirsty."* Again, in Luke 22:19 we read these words as Jesus instituted the Lord's Supper; *"And [Jesus] took bread, gave thanks and broke it, and gave it to them, saying, 'This is my body given for you; do this in remembrance of me.'"* That bread typifies our Lord is so clear in Scripture that it hardly needs any mention. Yet, the sending of the manna in the wilderness is so rich in meaning, two pages can only be a feeble introduction to its content.

Once again, the Israelites grumbled. This time Aaron was included as a target of their anger. Arthur Pink (*Gleanings in Exodus*, p. 131) says of their actions, "A more fearful exhibition of unbelief, ingratitude, and rebellion could scarcely be imagined." So the Lord answered and sent them *"bread from heaven."* It descended upon the Wilderness of Sin from heaven, just as our Lord would come from heaven years later. Paul says, speaking of Jesus as the Second Adam, *"The first man was of the dust of the earth, the second man from heaven"* (1 Cor. 15:47). Manna was the free gift of God. So is our salvation through Jesus Christ's life, death, and resurrection.

The food from heaven was for God's people alone. It began when they were beyond the borders of Egypt and stopped when they entered the Land of Canaan. So it is with Jesus. Our Lord came for "His people." As the angel said to Joseph, *"[Mary] will give birth to a son, and you are* to give him the name Jesus, because he will save his people from their sins" (Matthew 1:21). In the same way, both "breads of heaven" came to a sinful and needy people. As Ephesians 2:3 says; *"All of us also lived among [the reprobate] at one time, gratifying the cravings of our sinful nature and following its desires and thoughts. Like the rest, we were by nature objects of wrath."* We, too, would starve spiritually were it not for Jesus.

The manna was white and sweet. So, too, our Lord is *"holy, blameless, pure, set apart from sinners, exalted above the heavens"* (Hebrews 7:26). In the Transfiguration, *"[Jesus'] clothes became dazzling white, whiter than anyone in the world could bleach them"* (Mark 9:3). We've just seen how the bitter waters of Marah were sweetened by the tree, which spoke of Jesus. The Song of Solomon, where Jesus is pictured throughout, speaks of Him this way: *"His mouth is sweetness itself; he is altogether lovely. This is my lover, this my friend, O daughters of Jerusalem"* (Song 5:16).

Numbers 11:9 tells us, *"When the dew settled on the camp at night, the manna also came down."* The manna came only at night when the camp was asleep. The heavenly food was by God's grace alone, and not by mankind's work. Manna fell upon the dew Jehovah sent, and not the dust of the earth. As quoted in 1 Cor. 15:47 above, fallen humanity is spoken of as "dust" in Scripture. Our Lord came to earth as a little child, sired by the Holy Spirit, lest He be defiled by original sin. So the Manna fell on the dew and not on the dust.

Finally, the coming of the manna is linked in Scripture to the first mention of "the glory of the Lord." In Exodus 16 we read: *"While Aaron was speaking to the whole Israelite community, they looked toward the desert, and there was the glory of the LORD appearing in the cloud"* (Exodus 16:10). In the same way, we read in John 1:14; *"The Word became flesh and made his dwelling among us. We have seen his glory, the glory of the One and Only, who came from the Father, full of grace and truth."* Oh for more space to speak further of these marvelous things.

32. JESUS: THE STRICKEN ROCK
Exodus 17:1-6

The whole Israelite community set out from the Desert of Sin, traveling from place to place as the LORD commanded. They camped at Rephidim, but there was no water for the people to drink. So they quarreled with Moses and said, "Give us water to drink." Moses replied, "Why do you quarrel with me? Why do you put the LORD to the test?"...They said, "Why did you bring us up out of Egypt to make us and our children and livestock die of thirst?" Then Moses cried out to the LORD, "What am I to do with these people? They are almost ready to stone me." The LORD answered Moses, "Walk on ahead of the people. Take with you some of the elders of Israel and take in your hand the staff with which you struck the Nile, and go. I will stand there before you by (KJV = "upon") the rock at Horeb. Strike the rock, and water will come out of it for the people to drink." So Moses did this in the sight of the elders of Israel.

O nce again the Israelites quarreled with Moses. *"Give us water to drink."* God had commanded exactly where they were to camp. Surely the Lord knew there was no water there. How this speaks to our lack of trust in God's leading. One of our greatest failures in the Christian life is to deny God's absolute sovereignty. The Westminster Confession of Faith (III, 1) puts it, *"God from all eternity did, by the most wise and holy counsel of His own will, freely and unchangeably ordain whatsoever comes to pass."* We pay lip service to this fact of Scripture in big things, but not in the details of our lives. Too often we moan and complain of our circumstances.

In response to the Hebrew quarreling, Jehovah instructed Moses to take his rod—the same one he used to strike the Nile—to strike the rock. It is a rod of judgment, and the rock is a picture of Christ and His atoning death on the Cross. The prophet Isaiah says in 53:4: *"Surely he took up our infirmities and carried our sorrows, yet we considered him stricken by God, smitten by him, and afflicted."*

We don't have to question that the rock is a portrait of Jesus because there is an instance in the Bible where we are told specifically that it is. Paul says in 1 Corinthians 10:4: *"[The Israelites] drank the same spiritual drink; for they drank from the spiritual rock that accompanied them,* **and that rock was Christ.***"* In fact, Jehovah is "the Rock" throughout Scripture. David sang of Him in 2 Samuel 22:2: *"He said: 'The LORD is my rock, my fortress and my deliverer...'"* The psalmist cries out, *"Come, let us sing for joy to the LORD; let us shout aloud to the Rock of our salvation"* (Psalms 95:1). And Jesus responds to Peter's understanding of Jesus' godhood with these words: *"...on this rock I will build my church, and the gates of Hades will not overcome it"* (Matthew 16:18).

Moses struck the rock and water gushed forth for the people. We've discussed water earlier as being typical of the Spirit of God—the Spirit of Christ. Acts 2:18 says that the Spirit is to be *"poured out"* upon God's servants—His Church. Just as the Israelites—God's covenant people—all drank from the Rock, so all of God's Church—His covenant people—drink from it, too. There are no "haves and have nots" in the true Church. All partake equally of His Spirit (Romans 8:9).

Later, the prophet Daniel would speak of another rock:

"In the time of those kings, the God of heaven will set up a kingdom that will never be destroyed, nor will it be left to another people. It will crush all those kingdoms and bring them to an end, but it will itself endure forever. This is the meaning of the vision **of the rock** *cut out of a mountain, but not by human hands—a rock that broke the iron, the bronze, the clay, the silver and the gold to pieces"* (Daniel 2:44-45).

Daniel spoke of several kings who would rule on the earth. He described them as part of a statue made of iron, bronze, clay, silver, and gold. The "Rock," not made by human hands, would crush those earthly kingdoms and rule as King forever. Of course, Daniel spoke of our Lord, of whom Isaiah said; *"Of the increase of his government and peace there will be no end"* (Isaiah 9:7).

33. JESUS: OUR LAW GIVER AND LAW KEEPER
Exodus 20:1-17

*And God spoke all these words: "I am the LORD your God, who brought
you out of Egypt, out of the land of slavery. You shall have
no other gods before me..."*

In the Sermon on the Mount, Jesus expanded the meaning of the Ten
Commandments given in Exodus to include even our thought life. As a
part of the Sermon, He said in Matthew 5:17-18;

*"Do not think that I have come to abolish the Law or the Prophets; I have
not come to abolish them but to fulfill them. I tell you the truth, until heav-
en and earth disappear, not the smallest letter, not the least stroke of a pen,
will by any means disappear from the Law until
everything is accomplished."*

Some have made the statement that since Christians have the Holy
Spirit resident within them, no Law is needed. Nothing could be
further from the truth. The Law is still valid today as the day it was
given in the wilderness, and it is applicable to every person on the planet,
to Jew and Gentile, to believer and nonbeliever.

The Law in the wilderness was given for three main reasons. First,
Jehovah—Jesus—established his authority over all that He created and
those He brought forth from Egypt. By the Law, Jehovah revealed to the
people who He was—a holy and altogether righteous God, set apart from
the world and its system. By His Law, He demands this same holiness and
righteousness from all men. Second, Jehovah gave the Law to show men
and women who *they* are—altogether unholy and unrighteous—and to
drive them by this knowledge to seek His forgiveness for their sin. Finally,
the Law was given out of God's perfect love for His people—to show
them the way in this world that was not only pleasing to Him, but a way
that would be free of the entanglements and trouble experienced by law
breakers.

The book of Proverbs in the Old Testament demonstrates this. Proverbs is said to be "the Ten Commandments in shoe leather." In the book, a father seeks to convince his son that to walk in God's ways is to save himself much torment and trouble that accrues to those who follow the "woman Folly" (Proverbs 9:13). Proverbs 3:6 says, *"in all your ways acknowledge him, and he will make your paths straight."* To *"acknowledge"* God is principally to know Him, to love Him, and to keep His commandments. *"Straight paths"* are righteous paths, paths that please God.

Just as Jehovah gave the Ten Commandments out of love for His people and His creation, so love from the people to Jehovah is to keep His commandments. Jesus said in John 14:15, *"If you love me, you will obey what I command."* We read also in 1 John 5:3; *"This is love for God: to obey his commands."* Can you see what Jesus is claiming by His statement? He is the God who gave the Law.

Just as Jesus is the Lawgiver, He is also the only one in the history of humanity who has ever kept the Law, in thought, word, and deed. He is the absolutely holy and altogether righteous God-man. In Hebrews 7, the writer compares Jesus with the priesthood of the Old Testament:

> *"Therefore [Jesus] is able to save completely those who come to God through him, because he always lives to intercede for them. Such a high priest meets our need—**one who is holy, blameless, pure, set apart from sinners,** exalted above the heavens. Unlike the other high priests, he does not need to offer sacrifices day after day, first for his own sins, and then for the sins of the people. He sacrificed for their sins once for all when he offered himself"* (Hebrews 7:23-27).

We are saved through Christ's life of perfect righteousness, and His perfect atoning death and resurrection. We cannot keep the Law of God, so Jesus did it for us. We can only, through His grace, come to Him in saving faith. Then, given wisdom, we can lovingly and gratefully keep His commandments.

34. Jesus: Our Heavenly Tabernacle - I
Exodus 25:8-9

*"Then have them make a sanctuary for me, and I will dwell among them.
Make this tabernacle and all its furnishings* **exactly**
like the pattern I will show you."

J ust as Joseph's life portrayed Jesus Christ to us in so many ways, we now come to one of the most startling and magnificent portraits of Jesus in the entire Hebrew Scriptures. We will spend the next ten chapters dealing with how Jesus is portrayed in this tent in the wilderness. The Tabernacle is described from Exodus 25 to chapter 40, minus an important detour in chapters 32-34. In the New Testament, the Tabernacle is primarily spoken of in Hebrews. In Hebrews 8:5, the writer said,

> [The Aaronic priests] serve at a sanctuary that is a copy and shadow of what is in heaven. This is why Moses was warned when he was about to build the tabernacle: "See to it that you make everything according to the pattern shown you on the mountain.

He goes on to say in Hebrews 9:11-12,

> When Christ came as high priest of the good things that are already here, he went through the greater and more perfect tabernacle that is not man-made, that is to say, not a part of this creation. He did not enter by means of the blood of goats and calves; but he entered the Most Holy Place once for all by his own blood, having obtained eternal redemption.

More ink in Scripture is given to the Tabernacle, its description and construction, than any other single topic, save Jesus. Why? Because it is a visual representation to God's people of Jesus, of heaven, and of His plan of salvation. Among many other things, He reveals to us that a Mediator is needed for sinners to approach Him. God shows us that atoning blood is necessary to justify the unjust. And, God uses the Tabernacle to reveal Himself as both transcendent—separate above His people—and immanent—dwelling in the midst of His people. No other "god" of man's imagination has both of those qualities.

Adolph Saphir says,

> *"...the Tabernacle is a type, a visible illustration, of that heavenly place in which God has His dwelling. In the second place, the Tabernacle is a type of Jesus Christ, who is the meeting place between God and Man. And in the third place, the Tabernacle is a type of Christ in the Church—of the communion with Jesus of all believers."*

The first of Saphir's anti-types is found in Hebrews 9:23-24, and in 9:11-12 as quoted above. But it is the second and third anti-types—Christ as Mediator between God and man, and Christ among His people—that shall be our focus.

John 1:14 says of Jesus: *"The Word became flesh and made his dwelling among us."* Literally, the Greek reads, *"The Word flesh became, and tabernacled among us."* No mere man designed the salvation that is ours in Christ, nor sired the baby born in Bethlehem. In the same way, no mere man designed the Tabernacle in the wilderness. The pattern was God's.

Jesus came to this earth in human flesh to dwell among His people and to have communion with us. Revelation 21:3 says, *"And I heard a loud voice from the throne saying, 'Now the dwelling of God is with men, and he will live with them. They will be his people, and God himself will be with them and be their God.'"* So also the Tabernacle, like Jesus, was a "tent of meeting" between God and man.

The Tabernacle was temporary. Later, the Temple in Jerusalem would be a more permanent dwelling place for God in Israel. The Tabernacle pointed to Christ in His earthly, priestly, ministry, while the Temple speak of Christ's eternal reign as King of Kings over His Church.

35. Jesus: Our Heavenly Tabernacle - II
Exodus 25:8-9

"Then have them make a sanctuary for me, and I will dwell among them.
Make this tabernacle and all its furnishings exactly
like the pattern I will show you."

The Tabernacle was placed in the center of God's people as they camped around it (Numbers 1:50). In the same way, Jesus said in Matthew 18:20: *"For where two or three are gathered together in my name, there am I in the midst of them"* (KJV). In it, sacrifices of animals were made, typifying the ultimate sacrifice of Jesus on the Cross of Calvary.

This "tent of meeting" was also where the Levitical priesthood received its daily food. Likewise, we believers are priests of Christ (1 Peter 2:5) and receive our daily bread from our Bread of Life (John 6:35). There was but a single door to the Tabernacle, as there is but one way to enter the Kingdom of God. As Jesus said in John 10:9, *"I am the door..."* Or again in John 14:6: *"I am the way and the truth and the life. No one comes to the Father except through me."*

That solitary door was placed on the east side of the Tabernacle, directly in front of the tribe of Judah's camping place (Numbers 2:3 with Exodus 27:12-17). This arrangement meant that anyone entering the Tabernacle had to do so through the tribe of Judah. Jesus was to come from the tribe of Judah as we have seen in our Chapter 23. He is the *"Lion of the tribe of Judah, the Root of David,"* as spoken of Him in Revelation 5:5.

The Tabernacle area was completely enclosed by a high curtain held up by silver poles and bases. The curtain created an outer courtyard of approximately 75 feet in width by 150 feet in depth. Upon entering this courtyard by the single gate, a visitor encountered first a bronze altar, which we will discuss in Chapter 43. Moving on, he would see the bronze

Laver (Chapter 44). In the center of the courtyard stood a large tent, 15 feet wide by 45 feet long and 15 feet tall. Its two rooms were the outer "Holy Place," and the inner "Holy of Holies."

The planning and construction of the Tabernacle covers Exodus 25-31, plus chapters 35 through 40. They are bridged by the tragic story of the Golden Calf and its aftermath. The first section deals with God giving Moses the exact parameters of the Tabernacle's construction, furniture, and priestly garments. The Tabernacle was designed in heaven. Then, in the final six chapters, we are given the account of the actual construction on earth. We learn in chapter 31:

> *Then the LORD said to Moses, "See, I have chosen Bezalel son of Uri, the son of Hur, of the tribe of Judah, and I have filled him with the Spirit of God, with skill, ability and knowledge in all kinds of crafts—to make artistic designs for work in gold, silver and bronze..."* (Exod. 31:1-4).

We have here a wonderful picture of the Spirit of God bringing the Tabernacle into being. It should be no stretch for us to understand that the Tabernacle represents our Lord Jesus, who from all eternity was in covenant with the Father to redeem the human race, and who was born into this world by the power of the Holy Spirit.

In the bridge chapters of Exodus 32 through 34 is the truth about fallen humans. You may recall that Moses has gone to the top of Mt. Sinai to meet with God and to receive His commandments. Meanwhile, the people grow restless and pressure Aaron into fashioning a golden calf out of their earrings. They bow down to the calf and worship it, working themselves into a frenzy. We too are idol makers. While God in His grace prepares a great salvation for us, we are not satisfied. We want to do it ourselves. We want a Golden Calf. We want an idol we can control, one created in our own image. Unless God's Spirit brings us to faith, we want nothing to do with a Holy God and His holy commandments.

36. Jesus: The Ark of Our Redemption
Exodus 25:10-11

"Have them make a chest of acacia wood—two and a half cubits long, a cubit and a half wide, and a cubit and a half high. Overlay it with pure gold, both inside and out, and make a gold molding around it."

The very first article described by God in the pattern for the Tabernacle was a big box. It was approximately four feet long by two and a half feet deep and wide. It was the central article of furniture in the Holy of Holies. God described the specifications for the Ark first because it was to be the most important part of the Tabernacle. The Ark was to be where God was to reside among His people.

It was to be made of *shittim* wood—a type of acacia tree found in the arid desert. This acacia—now known as *acacia seyal*—is a hardwood that is not subject to decay nor decomposition. This wood formed the superstructure for the Ark, and speaks of Christ's humanity. In his stunning prophecy of our Lord Jesus, Isaiah equates this wood with Him: *"He grew up before him like a tender shoot, and like a root out of dry ground"* (Isaiah 53:2). Like the acacia wood, neither was Jesus subject to decay (Acts 2:27 with Psalm 16:10).

The Ark was to be covered with gold, which speaks of the deity of our Lord. While the wood created the configuration of the enclosure, the gold covered the wood completely. And so it was and is presently. A man was born in Bethlehem, and He resides bodily in heaven today, seated in majesty at God's right hand. The Ark is a portrait of the God-Man—our Lord Jesus Christ. He is the union of the divine and the human—entirely divine, yet entirely human.

What was to be placed in the Ark? We have already discussed two of the articles—a jar or bowl of manna, (Chapter 31), and the two tablets of the Law (Chapter 33). We will discuss the third article—Aaron's rod that budded—in more detail below and later in the book.

The manna was contained in a golden jar (Hebrews 9:4). Of course, the manna depicts Jesus as the Bread of Heaven. As Jesus said in John 6:41: *"I am the bread that came down from heaven."* The two tablets of the Law speak of Christ's righteousness, and His ability to keep every commandment perfectly. Remember, these tablets are the second tablets that Jehovah had Moses engrave. The first set—inscribed by God Himself—was destroyed by Moses after he came down from the mountain and saw the people in great sin with their Golden Calf idol. The broken tablets speak to our unrighteousness and need for a Savior—who is Jesus.

Aaron's rod was covered not only with buds, but had *"blossomed and produced almonds"* (Numbers 17:8). It speaks to resurrection and renewal. It had been just an old dead rod, yet it represented Aaron's authority as high priest, an authority that Korah and his followers questioned. Out of its deadness, it was resurrected. Of course, this speaks of our Lord who rose again and of those who trust in Him.

These things, then, set forth Jesus' three offices—Prophet, Priest, and King. The tablets of the Law indicate the Prophet. Prophets speak the words of God to the people. Aaron's rod shows Jesus' role as Priest. Priests mediate between the people and God. Jesus as High Priest would suffer death for His people, but would rise again, so that they might have eternal life. Finally, manna foreshadows Jesus' office as King. Kings find out what their people need and get it for them. By His wonderful providence, Jesus provides for all our needs.

The Ark was the only piece of furniture from the Tabernacle that was transferred into Solomon's Temple when it was built in Jerusalem. It is called many things in Scripture, but its principal name in Exodus is "The Ark of the Testimony." It is a wonderful testimonial to the person of Jesus Christ.

37. Jesus: The Covering for Our Sin
Exodus 25:17-22

"Make an atonement cover of pure gold—two and a half cubits long and a cubit and a half wide. And make two cherubim out of hammered gold at the ends of the cover. Make one cherub on one end and the second cherub on the other; make the cherubim of one piece with the cover, at the two ends. The cherubim are to have their wings spread upward, overshadowing the cover with them. The cherubim are to face each other, looking toward the cover. Place the cover on top of the ark and put in the ark the Testimony, which I will give you. There, above the cover between the two cherubim that are over the ark of the Testimony, I will meet with you and give you all my commands for the Israelites."

The Ark of the Testimony was covered with a solid gold lid, known commonly as the "Mercy-seat" (See the KJV, for instance). The NIV, as in verse 17 above, calls it the *"atonement cover."* The Hebrew word is *kapporeth,* which is translated with the Greek word *ilasterion* in Hebrews 9:5, (also in the Septuagint, the Greek translation of the Old Testament). *Ilasterion* means a place of propitiation or appeasement. It was upon this covering that the blood of animals was sprinkled once a year as an atoning sacrifice for the sins of the people (Hebrews 9:7). This golden slab, hidden in the Holy of Holies of the Tabernacle, represented God's mercy to His people.

The cover had the same horizontal dimensions as the Ark. It was hammered out all in one piece with two cherubim facing each other, each with his wings spread upward. This is the second time cherubim are mentioned in the Bible. In Genesis 3:24, we read these words; *"After he drove [Adam] out, he placed on the east side of the Garden of Eden cherubim and a flaming sword flashing back and forth to guard the way to the tree of life."* In other places of Scripture, we see cherubim associated with God's throne and His glory. They represent for us God's judgment and divine authority. (See 1 Samuel 4:4 and Ezekiel 10, for instance.) They speak of God's holiness versus man's depravity, and guard His holiness.

Here in a solid gold cover, we have a picture of God's judgment and His mercy joined together. Where else in the history of redemption do we see God's mercy and judgment coincide in one place—in one event? Only at the Cross. The judgment of the Father was poured out on the Son to satisfy His justice, so that His Church might receive mercy.

Inside the Ark, as we have seen, lay the two stone tablets on which were carved the Law of God by Moses' hand. The Mercy-seat hid them from view, just as God's mercy in Christ hides us from the judgment of our sins against that same Law. In 1 Samuel 6 we have the story of the Ark being returned from its captivity in the hands of the Philistines:

> *God struck down some of the [Israelite] men of Beth Shemesh, putting seventy of them to death because they had looked into the ark of the LORD...*
> *the men of Beth Shemesh asked, "Who can stand in the*
> *presence of the LORD, this holy God?"* (1 Samuel 6:19-20).

The men had exposed themselves to the judgment of the Law. By removing the atoning cover, they separated mercy from judgment and suffered the consequences.

The Mercy-seat was the only seat in the Tabernacle. On it, God sat enthroned in the midst of His people (2 Samuel 6:2). It was hidden from view in the Holy of Holies, a place where God met with the people only through the high priest. In the same way, our great High Priest—Jesus—sits at the throne of grace in heaven, seen only by the eye of faith.

Finally, the Mercy-seat was a place of communion between God and His people, through their mediator. God said in Exodus 25:22, as quoted above, *"There, above the cover between the two cherubim that are over the ark of the Testimony, I will meet with you and give you all my commands for the Israelites."* God spoke to His people. He guided them in the wilderness experience. In the same way, our Lord Jesus speaks to us through His Word, and guides us by His Spirit. May He have mercy upon us.

38. Jesus: Our Communion With God
Exodus 25:23-30

"Make a table of acacia wood—two cubits long, a cubit wide and a cubit and a half high. Overlay it with pure gold and make a gold molding around it. Also make around it a rim a handbreadth wide and put a gold molding on the rim...Put the bread of the Presence on this table to be before me at all times."

While the Ark stood behind the Veil in the Holy of Holies, the Table stood with the Lampstand and the Altar of Incense in the Holy Place, just outside. The Table was the same height as the Ark, and was also constructed of acacia wood with an overlayment of pure gold. As in the Ark, the wood and gold speak of Jesus' perfect humanity and deity: two natures in one person without confusion. The Table speaks of communion and fellowship, just as 1 Corinthians 10:21 says, *"You cannot drink the cup of the Lord and the cup of demons too; you cannot have a part in both the Lord's table and the table of demons."* In other words, you can't have communion or fellowship with Christ and Satan, too.

When we are called to the Lord's Supper in our worship times, we think of being invited to the Lord's Table. It is the place where we remember Christ's sacrifice for us, and grow in grace as we partake of spiritual food—the bread and wine. In the same way, the Table in the Holy Place held the *"Bread of the Presence."* It was made of pure, refined, unleavened flour. (Leviticus 24:5). This "showbread" was to be baked into twelve loaves of equal size and placed upon the table in two equal rows of six each. It was to remain before the Lord for a period of seven days, replaced each Sabbath. Then, it could be taken away and eaten by the priests of Levi.

No wine was on the Table in the Holy Place. Wine in the Lord's Supper points back to the blood of Christ, which we have seen earlier, is portrayed in the Tabernacle by the sprinkling of animal blood on the Mercy-seat on the Day of Atonement. But bread was laid out on the

Table, and that bread clearly points to our Lord, who said in John 6:35, *"I am the Bread of Life..."* Notice in Exodus 25:25, above, that a rim was to be fashioned around the Table. It was to be a *"handbreadth wide"*—the width of the human hand. It kept the bread from falling off of the Table, and speaks of our eternal security in Christ who says, *"Never will I leave you; never will I forsake you"* (Hebrews 13:5).

The twelve loaves of bread speak of God's covenant people. Although the twelve tribes were of different sizes and had different assignments and roles, the loaves are the same size, weight, and quality. This tells us that "the ground is level at the foot of the Cross." All God's people are equal in His sight. The loaves are also laid out in two rows of six. None of the tribes had greater standing than the others. All were equally near God's heart. As Paul says in 1 Corinthians 10:17: *"Because there is one loaf, we, who are many, are one body, for we all partake of the one loaf."*

Perhaps it seems to you that I've mixed up my metaphors. I say on the one hand that the bread stands for Christ, and then I turn around and say that the bread on the Table speaks of His covenant people. Which is it? It is both. Have you heard the secular saying, "You are what you eat?" While that statement should be rightly questioned in the physical world, it is true in the spiritual realm. To be like Christ should be every Christian's goal. In order to grow to be like Jesus, we must feed upon Him, by ingesting His Word and His Supper. We already have the down payment of our goal. As Paul says in 2 Cor. 5:17: *"Therefore, if anyone is in Christ, he is a new creation; the old has gone, the new has come!"*

God said, *"Put the bread of the Presence on this table to be before me at all times"* (Exodus 25:30). This speaks to God accepting us eternally, because of the Father's delight in His Son, through whom He sees us. Oh, the wonderful riches of the Word of God, and of our salvation only by His grace!

39. Jesus: The Light of the Christian Life
Exodus 25:31-39

"Make a lampstand of pure gold and hammer it out, base and shaft; its flowerlike cups, buds and blossoms shall be of one piece with it. Six branches are to extend from the sides of the lampstand—three on one side and three on the other. Three cups shaped like almond flowers with buds and blossoms are to be on one branch, three on the next branch, and the same for all six branches extending from the lampstand. And on the lampstand there are to be four cups shaped like almond flowers with buds and blossoms. One bud shall be under the first pair of branches extending from the lampstand, a second bud under the second pair, and a third bud under the third pair— six branches in all. The buds and branches shall all be of one piece with the lampstand, hammered out of pure gold. Then make its seven lamps and set them up on it so that they light the space in front of it. Its wick trimmers and trays are to be of pure gold. A talent of pure gold is to be used for the lampstand and all these accessories."

The King James Version of the Bible, and some other transla-
tions, wrongly calls the Lampstand a "candlestick." There were
no candles in the Tabernacle, as we are told definitively that oil
would be the fuel burned to bring light to the Holy Place (Leviticus 24:2).
The Lampstand was one of three objects in the Holy Place—the others
being the Table of Showbread, which we've just discussed, and the Altar
of Incense. The room was separated by a veil from the Holy of Holies,
and was the place where the Levites served daily.

Notice first that we are given no measurements for the Lampstand.
It was to be hammered out of a talent of pure gold—about 120 pounds.
Again, gold speaks to us of Jesus' divinity as "fully God and fully man."
It must have been very large, as it was situated opposite the Table. It was
to shed its light upon the Table. While the Table and its bread shows us
Jesus as the meat of our faith—the Person we feed upon for sustenance
and growth—the Lampstand portrays Christ as the source of strength for
our faith, as He gives us light for the journey. The Altar of Incense speaks

of Christ's intercessory work for us in Heaven. We feed on Jesus, receive light through His Word, and grace through His intercession for us.

While Jesus is truly the *"Light of the World"* (John 8:12), the light from the Lampstand is more like that described in Proverbs 4:18-19: *"The path of the righteous is like the first gleam of dawn, shining ever brighter till the full light of day. But the way of the wicked is like deep darkness; they do not know what makes them stumble."* The Lamps were to be lit at night (Exodus 27:21) to give light to the darkness of the Holy Place. The light emitted also speaks of our own time, between the first and second advents, when Christ, through His Spirit, helps His people in their daily walk with Him.

The Lampstand had seven bowls, or cups into which oil was placed and lit to emit light. In Scripture, oil often portrays the Holy Spirit. Jesus told the parable of the ten virgins in Matthew 25. In it, five of the women failed to bring oil to the wedding feast. *"But while they were on their way to buy the oil, the bridegroom arrived. The virgins who were ready went in with him to the wedding banquet. And the door was shut"* (Matthew 25:10). The Spirit of Christ is spoken of in the oil and in the light.

Like Aaron's rod that budded, flowered, and bore fruit, so also the Lampstand had buds, blossoms, and fruit—almonds. As in the rod inside the Ark, the Lampstand speaks of Jesus' resurrection, and of our sanctification in Christ. In our immaturity we bud, then blossom, and ultimately bear mature fruit to the glory of God.

Notice, finally, that the talent of gold is beaten into the shape God has ordained. To hammer an intricate shape as the shape of a *menorah* took God-given skill. It speaks of the beating that our Lord took in His death, ordained in eternity. His face was marred beyond recognition, but as Paul has told us, *"For God, who said, 'Let light shine out of darkness,' made his light shine in our hearts to give us the light of the knowledge of the glory of God in the face of Christ"* (2 Corinthians 4:6).

40. Jesus: The Righteous King of Heaven
Exodus 26:1-3

"Make the tabernacle with ten curtains of finely twisted linen and blue, purple and scarlet yarn, with cherubim worked into them by a skilled craftsman. All the curtains are to be the same size—twenty-eight cubits long and four cubits wide. Join five of the curtains together, and do the same with the other five."

As described earlier, the Tabernacle in the Wilderness was a structure that could be dismantled, moved, and set up again. It pictured the earthly reign of Jesus, as opposed to His eternal reign, which was to be portrayed in the later Temple in Jerusalem. Its structure was formed with boards made of acacia wood, and covered with four different materials for its roof and sides. The first covering, that which could only be seen from the inside, was made of fine, white linen, with cherubim embroidered into it of blue, purple, and scarlet yarn. We will discuss the other, outer coverings, in the next chapter.

In Mark 9:3, we read of Jesus' transfiguration on the Mount of Olives: *"His clothes became dazzling white, whiter than anyone in the world could bleach them."* Again, in Revelation 7:14 we learn of the Tribulation saints who *"have washed their robes and made them white in the blood of the Lamb."* White speaks of righteousness, and here it speaks of Jesus and His life of sinless perfection, thereby fulfilling the Law and becoming our perfect Savior. His perfection of holiness was imputed to His Church on the Cross, just as also our sin was imputed to Him. As Paul says in 2 Corinthians 5:21: *"God made him who had no sin to be sin for us, so that in him we might become the righteousness of God."*

That the white linen covering was only seen by Jehovah's priests was no accident. It is the same today. Only God's people have a real appreciation for Jesus' perfections. When we assemble to worship, it is Jesus whom we see and praise in sermon, hymn, prayer, and sacrament. Those who have not received God's saving grace in their lives see none of it and will have nothing to do with the Savior. For as Paul says in 2 Corinthians 4:4: *"The god of this age has blinded the minds of unbelievers, so that they cannot see the light of the gospel of the glory of Christ, who is the image of God."*

On the Mercy Seat the cherubim were fashioned out of pure gold. They speak of God's righteous judgment. On the inner covering of the Tabernacle, they are incorporated into the fine, white linen with blue, purple, and scarlet yarn. Blue portrays heaven. Its only natural to look to the sky above and see its cerulean purity. *"Moses and Aaron, Nadab and Abihu, and the seventy elders of Israel went up and saw the God of Israel. Under his feet was something like a pavement made of sapphire, clear as the sky itself"* (Exod. 24:9-10). Sapphires are a brilliant, deep azure blue color.

Purple is the color of royalty. It is made by mixing red and blue. We read in John 19:1-2: *"Then Pilate took Jesus and had him flogged. The soldiers twisted together a crown of thorns and put it on his head. They clothed him in a purple robe..."* Jesus descended from the kingly line of David, King of Israel. He was, and is, *"THE KING OF THE JEWS"* (Mark 15:26).

Red, or scarlet, pictures Jesus' suffering while on earth. It is, of course, the color of blood. Christ's blood is the precious substance that is the elemental foundation of our salvation. *"For you know that it was not with perishable things such as silver or gold that you were redeemed..., but with the precious blood of Christ, a lamb without blemish or defect"* (1 Peter 1:18-19). In the upper room, Jesus celebrated the Passover, the first Lord's Supper, with His disciples. *"Then he took the cup, gave thanks and offered it to them, saying, 'Drink from it, all of you. This is my blood of the covenant, which is poured out for many for the forgiveness of sins'"* (Matt. 26:27-28).

As the priests looked up at the ceiling above, they were overshadowed by the wings of the cherubim. This is a picture of Jesus' care for His Church. As the Psalmist says in 17:8: *"Keep me as the apple of your eye; hide me in the shadow of your wings..."*

41. JESUS: OUR UNSIGHTLY SACRIFICE FOR SIN
Exodus 26:7-14

"Make curtains of goat hair for the tent over the tabernacle—eleven alto-gether...Make for the tent a covering of ram skins dyed red, and over that a covering of hides of sea cows."

As we have just seen, the inner white linen curtain portrays Jesus in His earthly righteousness and holiness, and as King of Heaven, whose blood atoned for the sins of His people. But what of these other three coverings, of goat hair, and ram skins, and hides of "sea cows?" Let us examine each covering from the outer to the inmost.

The outer covering has sometimes been rendered "badger skins," or "sea cows" as here in the NIV. The animal was perhaps a porpoise, whose skin would have been impervious to the desert sand and winds and the occasional thunder shower. It was a material that was probably used for shoes and could have been found in the region of the Nile. It was the only covering visible from the outside. As they were bleached by the sun, the skins became unsightly. How opposite they were from the beautiful inner curtains of fine linen.

The skins portray Jesus in His humanity. We read in Isaiah 53:2: *"[Jesus] had no beauty or majesty to attract us to him, nothing in his appear-ance that we should desire him."* Again, Isaiah says in 52:14: *"Just as there were many who were appalled at him—his appearance was so disfigured beyond that of any man and his form marred beyond human likeness..."* On Calvary, Jesus was scourged with whips, bloodied by a crown of thorns, and suffered ultimate humiliation and shame. This is the way the world sees Jesus. They pay Him lip service, but His name is often a curse word. His person and His people are the subjects of ridicule. He is unattractive, unless the Spirit of God intervenes. Only then, when we are drawn into His fellowship, can we see the beauty and majesty of our Lord.

The ram skins are a portrait of Jesus as our sacrificial substitute who died in our place on the Cross. From the earliest pages of Genesis we see this principle. After Adam and Eve sinned and tried to cover themselves with leaves, God provided a covering of animal skins. Thereafter, animals sacrificed for human sin pointed to our ultimate substitute—the Lord Jesus Christ—who *"was delivered over to death for our sins and was raised to life for our justification"* (Romans 4:25). These ram skins covering the Tabernacle were also dyed red. We are reminded that only in Christ's shed blood do we have salvation. *"[Jesus] did not enter [heaven] by means of the blood of goats and calves; but he entered the Most Holy Place once for all by his own blood, having obtained eternal redemption"* (Hebrews 9:12). The author of Hebrews goes on to say that believers share in the efficacy of His blood.

The inner covering, just above the linen curtains, were fashioned of goats' hair. The goat is seen often in the Old Testament, typically as a picture of sin. In Leviticus 16:8-9, we read these words: *"[Aaron] is to cast lots for the two goats—one lot for the LORD and the other for the scapegoat. Aaron shall bring the goat whose lot falls to the LORD and sacrifice it for a sin offering."* We shall examine the "scapegoat" in detail in a coming chapter. Notice, now, that the first goat is to be sacrificed as a "sin offering." The goats' skins are a portrait of Jesus as our sin offering—the One who has taken our sin upon Himself. Isaiah 53:6 tells us; *"We all, like sheep, have gone astray, each of us has turned to his own way; and the LORD has laid on him the iniquity of us all."*

Before His crucifixion, Jesus prayed, *"Father, if you are willing, take this cup from me; yet not my will, but yours be done"* (Luke 22:42). What was this "cup" but the sin He was to bear on behalf of His people? The Father would turn His back on His Son, because He could not look upon sin. As we have quoted earlier, *"God made him who had no sin to be sin for us, so that in him we might become the righteousness of God"* (2 Corinthians 5:21). May Jesus be praised!

42. Jesus: Our Entrance to the Throne of God
Exodus 26:31-33

*"Make a curtain of blue, purple and scarlet yarn and finely twisted linen,
with cherubim worked into it by a skilled craftsman. Hang it with gold
hooks on four posts of acacia wood overlaid with gold and standing on four
silver bases. Hang the curtain from the clasps and place the ark of the Testimony behind the curtain. The curtain will separate the
Holy Place from the Most Holy Place."*

This veil, or curtain, separated the Holy Place from the Holy of
Holies, where the Ark of the Covenant resided. Only the High
Priest was allowed to enter the Most Holy Place through this veil,
and then only once a year on the Day of Atonement (Hebrews 9:7). Again,
we see cherubim embroidered on the veil, symbolizing their guardianship
of God's holiness. Unlike the curtain that separated the Outer Court from
the Holy Place, which invited the priests into fellowship with God, this
veil was designed to restrict, to separate, and to protect.

The veil was made of the same material as the covering seen from
inside the Holy Place. It was of fine white linen, and speaks of the person
of Jesus, who was sinless and perfectly righteous. The colors of yarn that
created the cherubim are also the same—blue, purple, and scarlet. Remember that blue speaks of heaven, purple of royalty, and scarlet of Jesus'
blood. The veil is a picture of Christ's earthly body and heavenly, eternal
kingship.

When the Temple was constructed by King Solomon in Jerusalem, it was built in basically the same pattern as the Tabernacle. A Holy
Place was separated from the Holy of Holies by a huge curtain. Some
have said that the veil in the Temple was four inches thick. On the Cross,
*"...when Jesus had cried out again in a loud voice, he gave up his spirit. At
that moment the curtain of the temple was torn in two from top to bottom"*
(Matthew 27:51). The Most Holy Place, where all were forbidden entry
save the High Priest, and him only once a year, was opened by the broken

body and shed blood of Jesus. Notice that the veil was torn from top to bottom. No man tore this curtain. It was torn by the hand of God, just as surely as was Jesus' life taken from Him. *"No one takes [my life] from me, but I lay it down of my own accord. I have authority to lay it down and authority to take it up again"* (John 10:18).

Early tradition speaks of the Temple priests' attempts to sew the curtain back together after its rending at the death of our Lord. Such an action would speak clearly of mankind's attempts to justify himself through his own works. But we are told over and over again in Scripture that our works are but *"filthy rags"* (Isaiah 64:6, Philippians 3:9, for instance). We are saved only through faith, and that only by the grace of God (Ephesians 2:8-9). As Paul says in Titus 3:4-5: *"But when the kindness and love of God our Savior appeared, he saved us, not because of righteous things we had done, but because of his mercy. He saved us through the washing of rebirth and renewal by the Holy Spirit…"*

The curtain in the Tabernacle shows us the great gulf that exists between God—One altogether holy and righteous—and a depraved humanity. Over against the beauty of the fine white linen of the veil, we are the filthy rags of Isaiah 64:6.

Finally, we don't have to imagine that the Tabernacle veil outside the Most Holy Place is a portrait of Jesus' body, broken for us on Calvary. We are told so in Hebrews 10:19-22:

> *Therefore, brothers, since we have confidence to enter the Most Holy Place by the blood of Jesus, by a new and living way opened for us* **through the curtain, that is, his body,** *and since we have a great priest over the house of God, let us draw near to God with a sincere heart in full assurance of faith, having our hearts sprinkled to cleanse us from a guilty conscience and having our bodies washed with pure water.*

43. JESUS: HIS CROSS—OUR SACRIFICIAL ALTAR
Exodus 27:1-8

"Build an altar of acacia wood, three cubits high; it is to be square, five cubits long and five cubits wide. Make a horn at each of the four corners, so that the horns and the altar are of one piece, and overlay the altar with bronze. Make all its utensils of bronze—its pots to remove the ashes, and its shovels, sprinkling bowls, meat forks and firepans. Make a grating for it, a bronze network, and make a bronze ring at each of the four corners of the network. Put it under the ledge of the altar so that it is halfway up the altar...Make the altar hollow, out of boards. It is to be made just as you were shown on the mountain."

When a priest entered the Outer Courtyard, through the only Gate, the first article of furniture he encountered was the Brazen Altar. On it, the substitutionary sacrifices of animals were carried on day and night without ceasing. It is difficult for us to imagine the scene. Bleating sheep and goats, along with braying cattle slaughtered in front of the Altar. Their blood was spilled out on the sand, and their bodies then consumed as they were laid upon the blazing fire. Why? Why would God demand such a terrible slaughter? I'll tell you why. To show the Hebrews, and us, the awful seriousness of human sin, and to provide the way for a solution to it.

The way into the Tabernacle had to go by the Brazen Altar. For anyone to enter into fellowship with a holy God, the way must lead by the Cross of Jesus Christ, where our Lord shed His precious blood for the sins of people throughout the whole world (1 John 2:2). The Altar foreshadowed the Cross.

The Altar was constructed of acacia wood, a desert hardwood that was not subject to deterioration. We've already seen Jesus' humanity in this wood. The Altar was covered with bronze. Bronze represents judgment in Scripture, as does the continuing fire of the Altar. Bronze is made by combining copper and tin, and is an ancient metal alloy, as opposed to its more modern counterpart—brass. You may recall these verses of judgment in (Leviticus 26:18-19 where Jehovah says: *"If after all this you will not listen to me, I will punish you for your sins seven times over. I will break down your stubborn pride and make the sky above you like iron and the ground beneath you like bronze."*

The Altar was designed by God with four horns, one on each of its four corners. These horns speak of power and mercy. You may recall the "horns" described in the books of Daniel and Revelation that speak of power. And, of course, we read of men like *"Adonijah, in fear of Solomon, [who] went and took hold of the horns of the altar"* (1 Kings 1:50). On the horns of the Altar, one could find mercy. In what other place in Scripture do we find this combination? I can think of none, other than the Gospel of our Lord. Remember Paul's words in Romans 1:16: *"I am not ashamed of the gospel, because it is the power of God for the salvation of everyone who believes: first for the Jew, then for the Gentile."* The Altar speaks of the grace of God that comes in power through His Gospel. Placed as they were on all corners, the horns looked out to all "corners" of the world. So also, God's grace is available to all people everywhere, not just to the people of Israel.

That the continuing fire on the Brazen Altar speaks of judgment needs little explanation. Fire went out and consumed Aaron's sons, Nadab and Abihu, because of their sin against God (Lev. 10:1-3). And, of course, Jesus spoke often of *"hell, where the fire never goes out"* (Mark 9:43).

The bloody sacrifices were a horrible sight. So, too, the awful Cross on which our Savior died for the sins of His people. As Paul says unequivocally in Romans 5:8-9: *"But God demonstrates his own love for us in this: While we were still sinners, Christ died for us. Since we have now been justified by his blood, how much more shall we be saved from God's wrath through him!"* Have you been *"justified by His blood?"* "Were you there when they crucified my Lord?" Did He die for you? Come to Him in simple childlike faith. Faith is the evidence that He did (Hebrews 12:1).

44. JESUS: THE WATER OF OUR CLEANSING
Exodus 30:18-21

"Make a bronze basin, with its bronze stand, for washing. Place it between the Tent of Meeting and the altar, and put water in it. Aaron and his sons are to wash their hands and feet with water from it. Whenever they enter the Tent of Meeting, they shall wash with water so that they will not die. Also, when they approach the altar to minister by presenting an offering made to the LORD by fire, they shall wash their hands and feet so that they will not die. This is to be a lasting ordinance for Aaron and his descendants for the generations to come."

Just before the priest would enter the Tabernacle building from the Outer Court, he encountered the Laver, or Wash-basin. Like the Brazen Altar, which he had just passed, the Laver was constructed of bronze. Interestingly, we are told in Exodus 38:8 that *"They made the bronze basin and its bronze stand from the mirrors of the women who served at the entrance to the Tent of Meeting."* Bronze accepted a mirror-like polishing. That same mirrored finish was to be retained in the Laver itself.

As the Brazen Altar represents the Cross of Christ as the only way of salvation, so the Laver represents the cleansing obtained by the Word of Christ. It represents the sanctification of each believer. The priests were to wash their hands and their feet prior to entering the Tabernacle. The washing of the hands indicates cleanliness for our service in the Kingdom; washing the feet, cleanliness for our walk with Christ.

The priests of the Old Testament ministered before the Lord, and on behalf of others. We also are called to be priests. As we read in Revelation 1:5-6, *"...To him who loves us and has freed us from our sins by his blood, and has made us to be a kingdom and priests to serve his God and Father—to him be glory and power for ever and ever! Amen."* We are to walk before Him and serve Him in humble obedience to His Word.

Christ is the Word of God (John 1:1), and His is the Word of Christ—the Bible. Our very salvation—the new birth that brings faith—

comes from His Word, as Paul tells us; *"...faith comes from hearing the message, and the message is heard through the word of Christ"* (Romans 10:17). Peter also says, *"For you have been born again, not of perishable seed, but of imperishable, through the living and enduring word of God"* (1 Peter 1:23).

Likewise, we are washed by Christ's Word. The Psalmist says in Psalm 119:9; *"How can a young man keep his way pure? By living according to your word."* Jesus echoes this truth in John 15:3; *"You are already clean because of the word I have spoken to you."* Indeed, we are washed by Christ's Word. Paul says, *"Husbands, love your wives, just as Christ loved the church and gave himself up for her to make her holy, cleansing her by the washing with water through the word..."* (Ephesians 5:25-26).

Looking into the large washbasin, the priests saw their reflection in its mirrored surface, thereby viewing their defilement and consequent need for cleansing. Likewise, we view ourselves over against the mirror of Christ's Word and are able to see our sin and shortcomings. A non-Christian friend of mine once asked me why I read the Bible over and over again. Wasn't once sufficient? I replied that one reason I read it was to be made aware of how far short I fell of God's standard of perfection. Another was to see in it Christ's righteousness, graciously imputed to me on the Cross.

Here is an extremely important lesson: As a priest entered the outer courtyard through the single entrance, he first had to encounter the sacrificial Altar with its continuing fire. As in the previous chapter, the Altar represents Christ's Cross. It was only *after* passing the altar that he would come to the cleansing water in the Laver. The true Gospel of Jesus Christ is that before you can get cleaned up, you must come first to the Cross. Many today confuse justification and sanctification. Both are works of the Holy Spirit in us, but sanctification—cleansing—always follows justification. Justification is the free gift of God through faith in His Son and His atoning work on Calvary's Cross.

45. JESUS: TYPIFIED IN THE LIFE OF MOSES - I
Deuteronomy 18:17-18

*The LORD said to [Moses]: "...I will raise up for them a prophet like you
from among their brothers; I will put my words in his mouth,
and he will tell them everything I command him."*

Once again, I am indebted to Arthur Pink for his insights into the foreshadowing of Jesus in the life of Moses, much like he saw in the life of Joseph (*Gleanings in Exodus*, pp. 379-384). He writes of 75 parallels between Moses and Jesus, but says "the subject is well-nigh exhaustless" (p. 384). The principle comparison is that, in the entire Bible, only Moses and Jesus occupy the three offices: prophet, priest, and king. The author of Hebrews draws a prominent comparison as both are presented as mediators between God and His people when he says in 3:2:

[Jesus] was faithful to the one who appointed him, just as Moses was faithful in all God's house...Moses was faithful as a servant in all God's house, testifying to what would be said in the future. But Christ is faithful as a son over God's house. And we are his house, if we hold on to our courage and the hope of which we boast.

We've already compared Moses' brush with death as a baby with that of Jesus back in chapter 24. Like Jesus, Moses was of the house of Israel, and was born in a time when Israel was in bondage. Moses was adopted by Pharaoh's daughter, while Jesus, being sired by the Holy Spirit, was adopted by Joseph. Both, as in chapter 28 above, were called out of Egypt. Each one had compassion on Israel, and knew from his early days that he had a mission to deliver his people from their slavery (Acts 7:25, Hebrews 11:24-26). Each renounced the glory and riches of a royal throne for a wilderness (Philippians 2:6-7). As Moses was rejected by the very people he was hoping to save (Acts 7:16-17), so also Jesus was rejected by the people He came to save.

Both Moses and Jesus were shepherds. Moses watched over his father-in-law's flocks in Midian. Likewise, Jesus said in John 10:16: *"I have other sheep that are not of this sheep pen. I must bring them also. They too will listen to my voice, and there shall be one flock and one shepherd."* Both were "sent ones"—apostles—commissioned by God: Jesus before the creation of the world (1 Peter 1:20), and Moses at the burning bush.

Both Jesus and Moses performed mighty miracles. Moses appeared before Pharaoh and sent miraculous plagues upon Egypt, the Red Sea parted, and bitter water was made sweet. Jesus turned water into wine, cured diseases and raised the dead. By their miracles, each authenticated their authority from God. Of course, both delivered their people from slavery. Moses delivered Israel from Egyptian slavery, and Jesus delivered His Church from slavery to Satan. Both assumed headship of the Church. We're told in 1 Corinthians 10:1: *"[The Israelites] were all baptized into Moses in the cloud and in the sea."* Christians are *"...baptized into Christ Jesus"* (Romans 6:3). Later, Moses' authority would be challenged (Numbers 16:3). Jesus was continually challenged by the leaders of His day.

Both Moses and Jesus were physically threatened by stoning—the method of public execution in Israel. In Exodus 17:4 *"...Moses cried out to the LORD, 'What am I to do with these people? They are almost ready to stone me.'"* In Jesus' day, *"[the people] picked up stones to stone him, but Jesus hid himself, slipping away from the temple grounds"* (John 8:59). Both Jesus and Moses loved their people and felt great sorrow at their rejection. And yet, both prayed for those who persecuted them, forgiving them. *"When they hurled their insults at [Jesus], he did not retaliate; when he suffered, he made no threats..."* (1 Peter 2:23). Likewise, Moses prayed for the healing of his backslidden people (Numbers 12:13). [Continued]

46. JESUS: TYPIFIED IN THE LIFE OF MOSES - II
Hebrews 3:5-6

Moses was faithful as a servant in all God's house, testifying to what would be said in the future. But Christ is faithful as a son over God's house. And we are his house, if we hold on to our courage and the hope of which we boast.

Continuing our discussion of Moses and Jesus, we read in Numbers 12:3: *"Now Moses was a very humble man, more humble than anyone else on the face of the earth."* Of Jesus we read in Philippians 2:6-7: *"Who, being in very nature God, did not consider equality with God something to be grasped, but made himself nothing, taking the very nature of a servant, being made in human likeness."* Both were examples of extreme humility. Both were also faithful in all they did. As mentioned before, both were priests of God. We read in Leviticus 8:15: *"Moses slaughtered the bull and took some of the blood, and with his finger he put it on all the horns of the altar to purify the altar..."* (See also Psalm 99:6 and Hebrews 9:14). They were also kings. While Jesus still reigns eternally over His Church and His creation, Moses ruled over the Israelites in the wilderness.

As mentioned in the last chapter, both Jesus and Moses were prophets and mediators between God and man. (Compare Deuteronomy 5:5 with 1 Timothy 2:5). Both Jesus and Moses were the initiators of a covenant. Moses initiated the Mosaic covenant of Exodus 20 and following, while Jesus introduced the new, better, covenant of His blood (Matthew 26:28 with Hebrews 8:6). Moses appointed 12 men to send into the land of Gentiles, so also Jesus appointed the twelve disciples to *"go and make disciples of all nations, baptizing them in the name of the Father and of the Son and of the Holy Spirit"* (Matthew 28:19). Each also appointed seventy men, Moses in Numbers 11:24: *"He brought together seventy of their elders and had them stand around the Tent."* Jesus *"...appointed seventy-two others and sent them two by two ahead of him to every town and place where he was about to go"* (Luke 10:1).

Both Jesus and Moses had intimate communion with God. They each brought the Law of God to their people. Moses, of course, brought down from the mountain ten commandments inscribed on tablets of stone by God, and gave the nation Israel its ceremonial and civil laws. Jesus, on the other hand, expanded the Law of Moses in the Sermon on the Mount and other places, and fulfilled the entire Law of Moses to the uttermost. Both fasted, Moses in Exodus 34:29, and Jesus in Matthew 4:2. We read this in Exodus 34:29-30:

> *When Moses came down from Mount Sinai with the two tablets of the Testimony in his hands, he was not aware that his face was radiant because he had spoken with the LORD. When Aaron and all the Israelites saw Moses, his face was radiant, and they were afraid to come near him.*

Later, on another high mountain, *"There [Jesus] was transfigured before them. His face shone like the sun, and his clothes became as white as the light"* (Matthew 17:2). Jesus' disciples also were terrified on the mount. And just who appeared there with them? *"Just then there appeared before them Moses and Elijah, talking with Jesus"* (Matthew 17:3). Moses appeared a second time in Scripture, just as Jesus will appear a second time to put an end to the sin and turmoil of this earth (Acts 1:11).

Moses washed his brothers (Leviticus 8:6), just as Jesus would one day wash His disciples (John 13:5). Both were perfectly obedient to the Father. *"Moses did everything just as the LORD commanded him"* (Exodus 40:16). Jesus said in John 8:29: *"I always do what pleases [the Father]."* Finally, both Moses and Jesus died for the sake of their brothers (Psalm 106:32 and Deuteronomy 3:26), giving them an inheritance of a better place to call their own (Joshua 1:14 with Ephesians 1:11). Could all of this be coincidence? No. In God's wonderful Word, we witness His miraculous power and truth.

47. Jesus: Our Scapegoat
Leviticus 16:8-10

"Aaron is to offer the bull for his own sin offering to make atonement for himself and his household. Then he is to take the two goats and present them before the LORD at the entrance to the Tent of Meeting. He is to cast lots for the two goats—one lot for the LORD and the other for the scapegoat. Aaron shall bring the goat whose lot falls to the LORD and sacrifice it for a sin offering. But the goat chosen by lot as the scapegoat shall be presented alive before the LORD to be used for making atonement by sending it into the desert as a scapegoat."

Once a year, on the Day of Atonement, one of the offerings made for the sins of the people involved two goats. Lots were cast to see which goat would be slaughtered as a sin offering to Yahweh, and which would be taken out to the far wilderness and released. (We don't know what the "lot" looked like, only that it was a device used for determining choice. See John 19:24 where the soldiers cast lots for Jesus' clothing.) The first goat represents Jesus' death on the Cross, while the second, called the "scapegoat," represents the fact that Jesus' atoning death carried his people's sins away. Psalms 103:12 says; *"...as far as the east is from the west, so far has he removed our transgressions from us."*

Both goats were actually one offering. The goat to be sacrificed was slain by Aaron the high priest, and its blood sprinkled on the altar. After this, we read of the scapegoat:

He is to lay both hands on the head of the live goat and confess over it all the wickedness and rebellion of the Israelites—all their sins—and put them on the goat's head. He shall send the goat away into the desert in the care of a man appointed for the task. The goat will carry on itself all their sins to a solitary place; and the man shall release it in the desert (Leviticus 16:21-22).

The laying on of Aaron's hands here represents the transference of Israel's sins upon an innocent goat. Later in Israel's history, the prophet Isaiah wrote of the scapegoat, looking forward to the coming of Him who would be its fulfillment. *"We all, like sheep, have gone astray, each of us has turned to his own way; and the LORD has laid on him the iniquity of us all"* (Isaiah 53:6). And again in Isaiah 53:12 we see Jesus as this sin offering: *"...he poured out his life unto death, and was numbered with the transgressors. For he bore the sin of many, and made intercession for the transgressors."*

A man had to lead the scapegoat far into the wilderness, there releasing the animal. When the man returned to the camp, he had to *"wash his clothes and bathe himself with water; afterward he may come into the camp"* (Leviticus 16:26). The slightest transgression that the animal bore was not welcome back in the camp. Any remnants of sin had to be removed from the goat's attendant. This reminds us of Hebrews 10:17 which says, *"... Their sins and lawless acts I will remember no more."*

Following its demise, the slain goat was to be taken outside the encampment, and there burned. Leviticus 16:27 tells us: *"The bull and the goat for the sin offerings, whose blood was brought into the Most Holy Place to make atonement, must be taken outside the camp; their hides, flesh and offal are to be burned up."* Therefore, both goats wound up outside the camp. Likewise, *"...Jesus also suffered outside the city gate to make the people holy through his own blood."* The author of Hebrews then adds, *"Let us, then, go to him outside the camp, bearing the disgrace he bore"* (Hebrews 13:12-13).

Jesus was the scapegoat for our sins—the innocent for the sinful. *"God made him who had no sin to be sin for us, so that in him we might become the righteousness of God"* (2 Corinthians 5:21). What can we add but, "Hallelujah, what a Savior!"

48. Jesus: We Live Because of His Blood
Leviticus 17:8-14

"'Any Israelite or any alien living among them who eats any blood—I will set my face against that person who eats blood and will cut him off from his people. For the life of a creature is in the blood, and I have given it to you to make atonement for yourselves on the altar; it is the blood that makes atonement for one's life. Therefore I say to the Israelites, 'None of you may eat blood, nor may an alien living among you eat blood. Any Israelite or any alien living among you who hunts any animal or bird that may be eaten must drain out the blood and cover it with earth, because the life of every creature is its blood. That is why I have said to the Israelites, 'You must not eat the blood of any creature, because the life of every creature is its blood; anyone who eats it must be cut off.'"

Perhaps you have had friends or loved ones who have been in an accident, or endured an operation where blood was needed to replace their own. If we lose too much blood, or if our blood is allowed to become overly contaminated, we will die, because as the verses above tell us, *"the life of every creature is its blood..."*

For the ancient Hebrew, as well as modern Jews, the blood of animals and people was sacred. The verses above make that abundantly clear. If a Hebrew ate blood, the penalty was for him to be *"cut off from his people"* (Lev. 18:8, above). He was to be executed. In Acts 15:23-29, we have a letter from Paul and Barnabas to the Gentile believers in Antioch, regarding Jewish dietary restrictions for the Christian. They mention only four to be continued, and among them the eating of blood is forbidden.

Can you imagine, then, what the reaction of the people was when they heard Jesus say, *"I tell you the truth, unless you eat the flesh of the Son of Man and drink his blood, you have no life in you"* (John 6:53)? We are told that many of His disciples at that time were offended and left Jesus. (John 6:59-66). What could He have possibly meant? We have the answer in Matthew 26:27-28: *"Then he took the cup, gave thanks and offered it to* them, saying, "'Drink from it, all of you. This is my blood of the covenant, which is poured out for many for the forgiveness of sins.'" The blood He was speaking of was the wine of the Lord's Supper that commemorates the blood of Christ, shed on the Cross for His Church.

Many metaphors might be drawn from the blood that brings physical life, and Jesus' spiritual blood that brings eternal life. For instance, natural blood brings oxygen to our cells, nourishing the body. In the same way, Jesus' blood (taken in the Lord's Supper) nourishes us spiritually. Further, John says in 1 John 1:7: *But if we walk in the light, as he is in the light, we have fellowship with one another, and the blood of Jesus, his Son, purifies us from all sin."* Jesus' blood purifies us just as natural blood carries waste materials from the cells of the body and cleanses them through the kidneys and liver.

Perhaps the clearest verses regarding how blood in the Old Testament reaches its fulfillment in Jesus' blood are in Hebrews chapter 9:

> *The blood of goats and bulls and the ashes of a heifer sprinkled on those who are ceremonially unclean sanctify them so that they are outwardly clean. How much more, then, will the blood of Christ, who through the eternal Spirit offered himself unblemished to God, cleanse our consciences from acts that lead to death, so that we may serve the living God!* (vv.13-14). *[Moses] said, "This is the blood of the covenant, which God has commanded you to keep"… In fact, the law requires that nearly everything be cleansed with blood, and without the shedding of blood there is no forgiveness* (vv. 20 & 22).

William Cowper wrote this immortal hymn in 1771: *"There is a fountain filled with blood, drawn from Immanuel's veins; and sinners, plunged beneath that flood, lose all their guilty stains."* The blood of Christ is the most precious element that ever existed. Have you been plunged beneath its flood?

49. JESUS: SACRIFICED ONLY ONCE FOR SIN
Numbers 20:7-12

*The LORD said to Moses, "Take the staff, and you and your brother Aaron gather the assembly together. **Speak to that rock** before their eyes and it will pour out its water. You will bring water out of the rock for the community so they and their livestock can drink." So Moses took the staff from the Lord's presence, just as he commanded him. He and Aaron gathered the assembly together in front of the rock and Moses said to them, "Listen, you rebels, must we bring you water out of this rock?" Then Moses raised his arm and **struck the rock twice** with his staff. Water gushed out, and the community and their livestock drank. But the LORD said to Moses and Aaron, "Because you did not trust in me enough to honor me as holy in the sight of the Israelites, you will not bring this community into the land I give them."*

I n the New Testament, Paul wrote these words to the church in Corinth: *[The Hebrews in the wilderness] all ate the same spiritual food and drank the same spiritual drink; for they drank from the spiritual rock that accompanied them,* **and that rock was Christ**" (1 Cor.10:1-4).

We have again a specific parallel between the Old Testament type—the rock in the desert that brought forth water—and its antitype Christ—*The* Rock who brings forth "the water of life." We looked briefly at another, similar rock in chapter 32. There, Moses was instructed by God to strike the rock and water would gush forth. Moses' rod at that earlier time was his rod of judgment with which he struck the Nile and performed God's miracles in front of Pharaoh and his magicians. On that occasion, given to us in Exodus 17:1-7, Moses struck the rock only once and water for the people flowed out of it. The striking of the rock cries out about God's judgment poured out on Jesus on the Cross.

In this instance, God instructed Moses to *speak* to this rock and water would flow from it. For some reason, unlike the earlier rock in Exodus, Moses just had to strike this rock with his priestly staff! He struck it not just once, but twice. Moses disobeyed God by striking the rock and not merely speaking to it. Then, to compound the sin, he hit it twice. Because of his sin, God relieved Moses of his future command of the Israelites.

Moses was not to strike this rock in the wilderness because a rock had already been struck. No need existed to do it again. That's why God told Moses to put on his priestly or prophetic hat and speak to this rock, not strike it. In the same way, the writer to the Hebrews in the New Testament tells us this about Jesus' sacrifice of Himself:

> *Nor did he enter heaven to offer himself again and again, the way the high priest enters the Most Holy Place every year with blood that is not his own. Then Christ would have had to suffer many times since the creation of the world. But now he has appeared once for all at the end of the ages to do away with sin by the sacrifice of himself. Just as man is destined to die once, and after that to face judgment, so* **Christ was sacrificed once** *to take away the sins of many people; and he will appear a second time, not to bear sin, but to bring salvation to those who are waiting for him* (Hebrews 9:25-28).

To claim that Christ needs to be sacrificed again and again, rather than once for all time, devalues Christ's once for all sacrifice for His people. To call Jesus down time and again to shed his precious blood disparages the complete and final efficacy of the Cross.

The Reformers abbreviated their teaching in what has become known as the five "solas." Sola is the Latin word meaning "alone." They said that we are saved by grace alone (Sola Gratia), through faith alone (Sola Fide), in Christ alone (Solus Christus). We know this through the Scripture alone (Sola Scriptura), and because of this, all glory is to God alone (Soli Deo Gloria). Jesus paid it all. He was struck but once for our salvation. To strike Him again is to bring contempt upon His perfect work.

50. JESUS: OUR GREAT PHYSICIAN
Numbers 21:8-9

The LORD said to Moses, "Make a snake and put it up on a pole; anyone who is bitten can look at it and live." So Moses made a bronze snake and put it up on a pole. Then when anyone was bitten by a snake and looked at the bronze snake, he lived.

The Israelites had just destroyed the Canaanites after praying to the Lord for a victory over them. After that, they set out toward the Red Sea. As they traveled, they complained about the Lord's provision again:

...they spoke against God... and said, 'Why have you brought us up out of Egypt to die in the desert? There is no bread! There is no water! And we detest this miserable food!' Then the LORD sent venomous snakes among them; they bit the people and many Israelites died. The people came to Moses and said, "We sinned when we spoke against the LORD and against you. Pray that the LORD will take the snakes away from us." So Moses prayed for the people (Numbers 21:4-7).

A snake seems a strange way to picture Christ. One normally thinks of a serpent as indicative of Satan. And even stranger is that He uses a bronze image of a snake to heal poisonous snakebites. Maybe even stranger still, the text tells us that *"many Israelites died"* merely because they complained.

But in the New Testament, Jesus says, *"Just as Moses lifted up the snake in the desert, so the Son of Man must be lifted up, that everyone who believes in him may have eternal life"* (John 3:14-15). The context of those verses is where Jesus speaks with Nicodemus, a Pharisee of the ruling council. During the course of their conversation, Jesus says, *"I tell you the truth, no one can see the kingdom of God unless he is born again"* (John 3:3). Then, after speaking of the bronze snake, Jesus says, *"For God so loved the world that he gave his one and only Son, that whoever believes in him shall not perish but have eternal life"* (John 3:16).

This story in Numbers 21 gives us the reason Jesus had to die on the Cross. First, we need to understand the utter heinousness of sin—any sin. Here, the people merely complain about the food. Complaining against God is something we modern people do frequently. Does this deserve death under the fangs of a serpent? Yes. Paul says in Romans 6:23, *"For the wages of sin is death..."* Again, he says in 3:23, *"for all have sinned and fall short of the glory of God."* This is every person's situation. All have sinned, just like the Israelites. What can be done about it?

Notice that the solution to the Israelite problem with all those venomous snakes is not to stomp on them, or somehow kill them. Nothing in their power can provide a solution. But in His grace, God provides the cure. Some of the Israelites must have been incredulous! "What, just look up at a bronze snake on a pole and be saved? How ridiculous!" they may have argued. People today are just as incredulous regarding the Gospel. But we shouldn't be surprised. As Paul says in 1 Corinthians 1:18, *"For the message of the cross is foolishness to those who are perishing, but to us who are being saved it is the power of God."* And as Jesus reveals in John 3:14-15, that just as the bronze snake was lifted up, so He, too, would be lifted up (on a Cross) *"that everyone who believes in him may have eternal life"* (John 3:16).

God provides our salvation, from beginning to end. Like the Israelites, we are powerless to escape His just punishment. As Paul also writes,

> *You see, at just the right time, when we were still powerless, Christ died for the ungodly. Very rarely will anyone die for a righteous man, though for a good man someone might possibly dare to die. But God demonstrates his own love for us in this: While we were still sinners, Christ died for us* (Romans 5:6-8).

What about you? Are you trying to stomp on the snakes of sin in your life? Are you counting on your "good works" to get to heaven? Or are you looking only to the Cross of Christ? Look only unto the Savior—Jesus.

51. JESUS: PORTRAYED IN AARON'S ROD
Numbers 17:6-8

So Moses spoke to the Israelites, and their leaders gave him twelve staffs, one for the leader of each of their ancestral tribes, and Aaron's staff was among them. Moses placed the staffs before the LORD in the Tent of the Testimony. The next day Moses entered the Tent of the Testimony and saw that Aaron's staff, which represented the house of Levi, had not only sprouted but had budded, blossomed and produced almonds.

Numbers 16 gives us the story of Korah, Dathan, Abiram, and their followers. Two hundred fifty men rose up and challenged the leadership of Moses and Aaron. The Lord destroyed the three ringleaders and their families by opening up the earth beneath their tents, burying them alive. God then consumed the 247 others with fire from heaven. Angry because of what the Lord had done, the entire assembly rose up against Moses and Aaron, and God sent a plague among them, killing 14,700 before Aaron burned incense as an atonement for them.

Then God had leaders from each of the twelve tribes appear before Him with their rods, or staffs. Each was to write his name upon his own rod. The name of Aaron was inscribed on the rod of the tribe of Levi. The rest of the story is in the verses above. Aaron's rod, *"had not only sprouted but had budded, blossomed and produced almonds."* The remaining eleven rods were not changed, thereby revealing God's choice of Aaron as the High Priest. Only *he* had the right to enter the Holy of Holies to make atonement for the sins of the people.

As God chose Aaron to minister before Him, so also Jesus was the One chosen by God to be His great High Priest. The writer to the Hebrews speaks of Jesus in 5:4, *"No one takes this honor [high priest] upon himself; he must be called by God, just as Aaron was."* The wood of Aaron's rod speaks not only of Jesus' humanity, as we have seen earlier, but also of His Cross, where Jesus shed His precious blood for the Church. Aaron's rod, along with the other eleven, was placed overnight in the Tent of the Testimony—the Tabernacle. Likewise, Jesus was placed in a tomb following His death on the Cross. In the morning, when Moses went in to bring out the twelve rods, only Aaron's rod *"had budded, blossomed and produced almonds."* Like Jesus would be many years later, Aaron's dead rod had been resurrected to new, fruit-bearing life. It points to our resurrected Lord who *"...has indeed been raised from the dead, the first fruits of those who have fallen asleep"* (1 Corinthians 15:20).

Yahweh then instructed Moses, *"'Put back Aaron's staff in front of the Testimony, to be kept as a sign to the rebellious. This will put an end to their grumbling against me, so that they will not die.' Moses did just as the LORD commanded him"* (Numbers 17:10-11). Aaron's rod that budded spoke of the authority and judgment of God. It was a warning that it was a dangerous matter to approach God without a mediator. We are reminded of Jesus in His mediatorial role as our great High Priest in the heavenly Tabernacle:

> *[The Levitical priests] serve at a sanctuary that is a copy and shadow of what is in heaven. This is why Moses was warned when he was about to build the tabernacle: 'See to it that you make everything according to the pattern shown you on the mountain.' But the ministry Jesus has received is as superior to theirs as the covenant of which he is mediator is superior to the old one, and it is founded on better promises* (Hebrews 8:5-6).

Inside the Ark of the Covenant, Aaron's rod spoke of Christ's high priestly role, just as the jar of manna spoke of His kingly role, and the tablets of the law His role as Prophet.

One verse in the Old Testament stands out when I think of Jesus' rod. It is in the 23rd Psalm, verse 4: *"Even though I walk through the valley of the shadow of death, I will fear no evil, for you are with me; your rod and your staff, they comfort me."* Christ's rod is for the backs of the wicked (Isaiah 11:4). But for His own, His rod is a comfort and a delight.

52. JESUS: OUR HIDING PLACE
Numbers 35:6-34

Six of the towns you give the Levites will be cities of refuge, to which a person who has killed someone may flee (Numbers 35:6).

One of the most interesting facets of God's economy for the nation Israel is the six cities He established as "cities of refuge." They were positioned throughout the Land, set high on hills, so that anyone who lived in Israel was within a day's journey of at least one of the cities, and could see it from a distance. The penalty for murder in Israel was death (Genesis 9:6). The executioner was to be a close relative of the deceased and was called "the avenger of blood" (Numbers 35:19-27). This avenger was to pursue the perpetrator and kill him with impunity. However, if the accused could reach one of these cities of refuge before he was caught by the avenger, he could live there until receiving a fair trial. If found innocent, he was to live in the city where he found refuge until the death of the high priest, at which time he was free to return to his home (Joshua 20:2-6).

These cities speak of the refuge we have found in Christ. Jesus says in Matthew 11:28; *"Come to me, all you who are weary and burdened, and I will give you rest."* Again, in Romans 6:23, Paul says: *"For the wages of sin is death, but the gift of God is eternal life in Christ Jesus our Lord."* Our rest in Christ has many facets, but foremost is our rest from the fear of death (Hebrews 2:15). The writer to the Hebrews speaks of fleeing toward the great hope we have in Christ (Hebrews 6:18), much like the accused in ancient Israel fled toward a city of refuge where he found hope.

The cities of refuge were situated at high elevations, where one fleeing could find them easily. They were also widely known. So it is with Christ. He is not hidden from our view, but is present in His Word, the most widely printed book in the history of the world. Churches that bear His name are everywhere, as are Christian books, radio and television programs, web sites, and other sources.

The gates to the cities of refuge were always open. So it is with Jesus. Anyone can come to Him for refuge. People of every race and nationality are invited. One of the charges leveled against God's Church is that we are exclusivistic. Nothing could—or should—be further from the truth. God says, *"Come, all you who are thirsty, come to the waters; and you who have no money, come, buy and eat! Come, buy wine and milk without money and without cost"* (Isaiah 55:1). Another misconception is that one must work his way into God's favor with good deeds. But as Paul says in Ephesians 2:8; *"For it is by grace you have been saved, through faith—and this [faith] not from yourselves, it is the gift of God—not by works, so that no one can boast."* God's Gospel of grace extends to all people without distinction.

While in a city of refuge awaiting trial or release, fugitives were fed and clothed by the Levites of the city. In the same way, Jesus says, *"... He who comes to me will never go hungry, and he who believes in me will never be thirsty"* (John 6:35). And, like a city of refuge, the only place of refuge for the accused in Israel, Jesus alone is the way to salvation. He said in John 14:6, *"I am the way and the truth and the life. No one comes to the Father except through me."* Again, in John 10:9, *"I am the gate; whoever enters through me will be saved..."* Jesus is the only refuge for murderers.

Someone says, "I'm not a murderer! Why do I need Jesus?" Unlike the cities of refuge, anyone guilty of the slightest sin against God is under His wrath unless he or she flees to Jesus. God is not just our place of refuge, he is also the "avenger of blood." And, *"...all have sinned and fall short of the glory of God"* (Romans 3:23). We who have fled to Jesus for our great hope, helped to murder Him, by placing Him on the Cross. But there, by His grace, His blood atoned for our every sin (Ephesians 1:7). Unlike the high priest, who was subject to death, our great High Priest—Jesus—lives forever. We who have fled to Him are declared innocent by God, and will live and reign with Him eternally.

53. Jesus: Commander of the Lord's Army
Joshua 5:13-15

Now when Joshua was near Jericho, he looked up and saw a man standing in front of him with a drawn sword in his hand. Joshua went up to him and asked, "Are you for us or for our enemies?" "Neither," he replied, "but as commander of the army of the LORD I have now come." Then Joshua fell facedown to the ground in reverence, and asked him, "What message does my Lord have for his servant?" The commander of the LORD's army replied, "Take off your sandals, for the place where you are standing is holy." And Joshua did so.

We now leave the five books of Moses and enter the Land of promise with Joshua now leading the people of Israel. Moses had died in the wilderness. The Israelites crossed over the Jordan River when the swollen river stopped flowing at a place upstream. As at the crossing of the Red Sea, the people crossed on dry ground, this time with the Ark of the Testimony leading the way (Joshua 3:14-17). Camping at Gilgal, the people ate the produce of the Land for the first time, and the manna stopped.

Joshua must have left the camp to make a reconnaissance of the situation the people were to face at Jericho. Its high walls were undoubtedly worrisome to the commander, as his people had no battering rams, tall ladders, or modern artillery to breach them. All they had were simple hand weapons. How were they to conquer the city?

As Joshua drew near to Jericho, all of a sudden a man stood in front of him with a drawn sword in his hand, seemingly ready for battle. But whose side was this man on? Joshua walked up to him and asked him the same question. *"Are you for us or our enemies?"* The man replied, *"Neither, but as the commander of the army of the LORD I have now come."*

During World War I (and many other wars fought on this earth) both sides claimed that God was on their side. "If God is on our side, how can we possibly lose?" We sinners want God to be our "ace in the hole," that hidden trump card that will make our worldly success certain. But God is nobody's secret trump card, and He says so here.

Joshua had no right to claim God was on his side. Instead, Joshua needed to understand that he was there to serve God's purposes. The battle is the Lord's and we must be faithful to His leadership, submit entirely to His authority, and rest in His strength and sovereignty.

Joshua fell prostrate to the ground in reverence. He was commanded to take off his sandals as a gesture of submission and respectful worship. Recall Moses at the burning bush where Jehovah said, *"Do not come any closer, take off your sandals, for the place where you are standing is holy ground"* (Exodus 3:5). Jehovah—the preincarnate Christ—was there at Jericho. We have already discussed theophanies—visual and audial manifestations of God. We have here a Christophany: a real manifestation of, the One and only God who reveals God (John 1:18).

How do we know this to be true? Why couldn't the man be an angel? For one thing the Man claims to be the Supreme Commander of the LORD's Army. No mere angel makes such a claim. Angels are contingent creatures, *"ministering spirits sent to serve those who will inherit salvation"* (Hebrews 1:14). Also, Joshua recognized Him to be the LORD Jehovah and fell at His feet in worship. The man would not have accepted worship from Joshua if He had not been Jehovah. Remember Paul and Barnabas in Acts 14:8-14, when the people of Lystra wanted to worship them as gods, they tore their clothes and shouted they were but mere men. Only God is worthy of worship (Exodus 20:2-3).

Finally, we know that this man is the pre-incarnate Christ because the plan of attack He dictates is one that will give God all the glory. It is a plan that no mere man would devise. By faith, Joshua leads the Israelites around Jericho for six days, and on the seventh...well, you know the rest of the story. The walls *"came a-tumblin' down."*

54. JESUS: THE LORD OF THE UNIVERSE
Joshua 10:12-14

On the day the LORD gave the Amorites over to Israel, Joshua said to the LORD in the presence of Israel: "O sun, stand still over Gibeon, O moon, over the Valley of Aijalon." So the sun stood still, and the moon stopped, till the nation avenged itself on its enemies, as it is written in the Book of Jashar. The sun stopped in the middle of the sky and delayed going down about a full day. There has never been a day like it before or since, a day when the LORD listened to a man. Surely the LORD was fighting for Israel!

These verses are among the most controversial in the Word of God. They have been cited as a proof text for geocentricity, that the earth is at the center of the universe. Other critics have called them a later addition to the book of Joshua, and an impossible miracle, even for God. Well, we don't have room to get involved in all the controversy. I simply believe that the Bible is inerrant, and that these verses record what really happened on the strangest and longest day in human history.

The writer to the Hebrews states in chapter 1, verse 3a, *"The Son [Jesus] is the radiance of God's glory and the exact representation of his being,* **sustaining all things by his powerful word.** "Jesus, in His earthly ministry, showed that He had the power to control the elements. In John 2:1-11, at the wedding in Cana, Jesus turned water into fine wine. Think about that for a second.

To produce great wine, one must ordinarily plant grape vines and wait at least three years for the first harvest, all the while pruning and fertilizing and watering the vines. Great wines are generally made from grape vines that have been in existence for much longer than three years, however. One must also be blessed with excellent weather and sunshine. But let's assume we get a great vintage year. Then we need to pick our crop, crush the grapes, ferment the juice with a quality yeast, add clarifiers and other refining agents, and then let it sit in oak casks for at least another year. Jesus did all that in a matter of seconds at Cana.

Jesus also performed other physical miracles such as calming the tempestuous waters (Mark 4:35-41), taking a stroll on top of the sea, (Mark 6:47-50), and feeding the five thousand (plus women and children) in Mark 6:37-44. He also raised the dead such as Lazarus in John 11:34-46, and was Himself resurrected in a new body from the grave. Could stopping the earth's rotation for a while be too difficult for the One who created it? I think not.

Today, naturalism, or materialism, forms the basis for much of what passes for secular philosophy. A materialist claims that the world works according to set laws, and that nothing happens outside their boundaries. In the first half of the 20th century, a philosophy of materialism called "Logical Positivism" was in vogue. It claimed that unless one could see, taste, touch, hear, or smell something, it didn't exist. So much for God. Knowledge for the Positivist was based solely on his senses. Then, somebody asked about their formula. Can you see, taste, touch, hear, or smell the notion that knowledge comes only from the senses? Of course not. So, the whole system fell of its own weight.

To claim that there's no gold in Alaska, one needs to dig up the entire state to prove it. Negative statements such as, "There is no such thing as a miracle," are impossible to prove. A materialist would have to be omniscient, like the very God he is dismissing.

One other word about these verses. The Bible uses anthropomorphic language—man-centered language. For instance, Ecclesiastes 1:5 says, *"The sun rises and the sun sets, and hurries back to where it rises."* We say the same thing, all the while knowing that the sun rises because the earth rotates on its axis as it moves around the sun. These verses were never a proof text for the sun moving around the earth. They are proof, however, that Jesus, who is now *"sustaining all things by his powerful word"* (Hebrews 1:3b), can stop the earth's rotation any time He wants.

55. Jesus: Foreshadowed by Samson
Judges 13-16

*A certain man of Zorah, named Manoah, from the clan of the Danites,
had a wife who was sterile and remained childless. The angel of the LORD
appeared to her and said, "You are sterile and childless, but you are going
to conceive and have a son. Now see to it that you drink no wine or other
fermented drink and that you do not eat anything unclean, because you will
conceive and give birth to a son. No razor may be used on his head, because
the boy is to be a Nazarite, set apart to God from birth, and
he will begin the deliverance of Israel from the hands
of the Philistines" (Judges 13:2-5).*

We must tread carefully here, as much has been written about the story of Samson alluding to things in the future that has been, in my mind, fanciful allegorizing. Allegorizing differs from the typology or foreshadowing we have been studying, in that it projects actions of characters in a story to be symbols of some other abstract meaning. For instance, the story of Samson might be taken as a warning for men to watch out for the wiles of the opposite sex. Or, conversely, it could be cautioning women to beware of very strong men. Anything goes in allegorizing!

Typology, on the other hand, takes the story of a figure from an earlier time as a "type" that prefigures or foreshadows some person or event that actually comes along later in history, that is its "anti-type." In the medieval church, much interpretation was allegorical, as it was even by some early church fathers. The Reformers rightly rejected this kind of allegorical interpretation.

Samson is one of the most enigmatic characters in redemptive history. It's almost as if he's a born loser, rather than a Christ figure! But there are some similarities that bear study. First, in the above verses we learn that Samson's coming birth was announced by the Angel of the LORD. The Angel is a Christophany—a manifestation of the preincarnate Christ—as we have seen in earlier chapters. (Note Judges 13:22 where Manoah cried out, "*We are doomed to die! We have seen God!*") But it is His announcement that is in view. Only four other children are announced in Scripture by an angel: Isaac, Samuel, John the Baptizer, and Jesus. Manoah's wife, like Sarai and Hannah, foreshadowed Mary.

Samson's name meant "light," and speaks to us of Jesus' being the "light of the world." He is to be a Nazarite, one set aside to serve the Lord. In that sense he is more like John the Baptizer, also set apart as a Nazarite. But Samson's attributes were more Christ-like. He had superhuman strength as the Spirit of the Lord was upon him, and he performed miraculous feats using it. As he approached Timnah, he was attacked by a roaring lion, which he quickly killed. How similar to Jesus who defeated Satan, that *"roaring lion looking for someone to devour"* (1 Peter 5:8).

Samson left his parents, forsaking their appeals for him to marry someone in Israel, and sought foreign women to marry. In like manner, Jesus left His home in heaven to seek a bride for Himself from the uncircumcised Gentiles. Samson fell in love with a Philistine woman, (Philistine means "one who crawls in the dust"), and became engaged. She turned against him out of fear of man. So, he went to a prostitute, then encountered Delilah and fell in love once again. You know the rest of the story. She finally got him to tell her the secret of his strength. He was captured and blinded by his Philistine captors.

Meanwhile, Samson's hair grew back and he recovered his strength. As I write this, I can see in my mind's eye Victor Mature in the 1950s version of "Samson and Delilah" standing between the two main columns of the pagan temple, his arms outstretched like Jesus on the Cross, as he takes the temple down upon himself and all around him.

Whatever else we may think of Samson, his life is honored by God in chapter 11 of the New Testament book of Hebrews, often called the Bible's "Hall of Faith" (Hebrews 11:32).

56. Jesus: Our Kinsman-Redeemer
The Book of Ruth

When Boaz had finished eating and drinking and was in good spirits, he went over to lie down at the far end of the grain pile. Ruth approached quietly, uncovered his feet and lay down. In the middle of the night something startled the man, and he turned and discovered a woman lying at his feet. "Who are you?" he asked. "I am your servant Ruth," she said. "Spread the corner of your garment over me, since you are a kinsman-redeemer" (Ruth 3:7-9).

The Book of Ruth is a wonderful love story that depicts our salvation in Christ in many ways. Ruth was a Moabitess, a Gentile, who married a son of Naomi, a Jewess who had gone with her husband and two sons into Moab to escape the ravages of famine in her own land. Moabites descended from Lot following his drunken tryst with his oldest daughter. They were a cursed Gentile people. Under the Mosaic law, *"No Ammonite or Moabite or any of his descendants may enter the assembly of the LORD, even down to the tenth generation"* (Deuteronomy 23:3).

Ruth's husband, Mahlon, along with Naomi's other son and her husband, Elimelech, died in Moab. Rather than stay with her own people, Ruth followed Naomi back to Israel, saying, *"Where you go I will go, and where you stay I will stay. Your people will be my people and your God my God"* (Ruth 1:16). In Israel, Ruth began to glean from the fields of Boaz, a member of Elimelech's clan. He cared for her and when the proper time came, Naomi guided Ruth to the situation that is described in the verses above. However, before he is free to marry Ruth and redeem Elimelech's property, Boaz must deal with a closer relative. He does so favorably and the two are married.

The term "kinsman-redeemer" is a tautology—it describes exactly what his relationship and role is to be. First, he is to be of the same family—a kinsman. Like Boaz, Jesus is our close relative. He became part of the family of man. Hebrews 2:17 says, *"[Jesus] had to be made like his brothers in every way, in order that he might become a merciful and faithful high priest in service to God, and that he might make atonement for the sins of the people."* Second, the kinsman-redeemer's duty was to redeem his deceased relative's property, and to marry his widow. *"If brothers are living together and one of them dies without a son,...Her husband's brother shall take her and marry her and fulfill the duty of a brother-in-law to her"* (Deuteronomy 25:5). In the same way, our great Kinsman-Redeemer will marry His bride, the Church, and will one day redeem the earth from its curse.

The kinsman-redeemer also bought relatives their freedom who had been enslaved or incarcerated because of debts they owed but could not pay. We, too, have been bought out of slavery to Satan, and set free from the burden of the debt of sin through our Redeemer's blood alone. Boaz married Ruth not because of any obligation, but because he loved her. In the same way, *"...Christ loved the church and gave himself up for her"* (Ephesians 5:25). Our great Kinsman-Redeemer planned from all eternity to save His people from their sins. So also did Boaz create a plan to approach the closer relative and bring about his marriage to Ruth.

Now God provided a glorious destiny for Ruth in his household: Boaz took Ruth to be his bride. He has also provided a glorious destiny in heaven for His bride, the Church. Our God is the God of happy endings. Famine forced Naomi and her family into Moab, where her husband and two sons died. But out of this tragedy, God shaped a wonderful future for Naomi, as she held in her arms Ruth's child, Obed. He was to be the father of Jesse, the father of David the king.

All this took place in Bethlehem of Judah. Centuries later, another child—Jesus—would be born there, a descendant of the kinsman-redeemer, Boaz, and his bride, the Gentile Moabitess, Ruth. Oh, the wonders of God's Word and His plan for our eternal salvation!

57. Jesus: Foreshadowed by King David
1 Samuel 16:12-13

*So he sent and had him brought in. He was ruddy, with a fine appearance
and handsome features. Then the LORD said, "Rise and anoint him; he is
the one." So Samuel took the horn of oil and anointed him in the presence
of his brothers, and from that day on the Spirit of the LORD came
upon David in power. Samuel then went to Ramah.*

The New Testament begins with these words, *"A record of the geneal-
ogy of Jesus Christ the son of David, the son of Abraham"* (Matthew
1:1). Not only is our Lord foreshadowed by David's life, the great
king of Israel is Jesus' forefather. These following words are part of what is
called "The Davidic Covenant" from 2 Samuel 7:11-16 which God spoke
to David through the prophet Nathan:

*"'The LORD declares to you that the LORD himself will establish a house
for you: When your days are over and you rest with your fathers, I will
raise up your offspring to succeed you, who will come from your own
body, and I will establish his kingdom. He is the one who will build a
house for my Name, and I will establish the throne of his kingdom forever. ...Your house and your kingdom will endure forever before me; your
throne will be established forever.'"*

God speaks here of both David's son Solomon, and of His greater Son—
our Lord Jesus Christ, whose *"throne will be established forever."* Christ is
the Son of David, and yet, He is David's Lord (Matthew 22:41-46).

David's foreshadowing of Jesus began shortly after David was
anointed king in our subject text of 1 Samuel 16, above. Once again
Israel was at war with the Philistines. On the field of battle, a nine-foot
tall giant named Goliath challenged the Israelites to send out a man to
fight him. Goliath boasted that the winner of the match would decide
the battle for both armies. The youth David, visiting the battle site while
bringing food for his older brothers, heard the challenge and talked King
Saul into letting him fight the brute. *"Then [David] took his staff in his*

hand, chose five smooth stones from the stream, put them in the pouch of his shepherd's bag and, with his sling in his hand, approached the Philistine" (1 Samuel 17:40). As he approached Goliath, *"David said to the Philistine, 'You come against me with sword and spear and javelin, but I come against you in the name of the LORD Almighty, the God of the armies of Israel, whom you have defied'"* (1 Samuel 17:45). With one smooth stone imbedded in his forehead, the giant slumped to the ground. The Philistine army then turned and ran.

Goliath foreshadows the anti-Christ Satan, who also defies the army of the Lord. The little stone in Goliath's head calls to mind the name that Jesus gave to Simon son of Jonah—*Cephas,* or Peter, which means "little stone" (Matthew 16:18). But the one who saved the day and slew the enemy was David, forefather and foreshadower of the victorious One to come who has defeated Satan. David was a shepherd, and wrote of Him who is our great Shepherd (Psalm 23). He also wrote many distinct messianic prophesies in the Psalms, some of which we will see later on in this study. As a shepherd, David killed lions when they threatened his sheep. So Jesus also protects those in His care. Not one of His sheep will be lost (Matthew 18:13-14).

David was pursued and persecuted by a jealous King Saul, while Jesus was pursued and persecuted by the leaders of Israel in His day. David endured the wilderness of Israel, just as did Jesus centuries later. Jesus said, *"Do not suppose that I have come to bring peace to the earth. I did not come to bring peace, but a sword"* (Matthew 10:34). Jesus divides families and communities with His Gospel message. David drew a physical sword in his day, protecting the people of God from their enemies. King David ruled the people in justice and equity, just as King Jesus rules from His throne in heaven. While David's rule over Israel was only temporary, Jesus will rule His people in truth and mercy for all eternity.

58. JESUS: OUR FRIEND OF FRIENDS
1 Samuel 18:1-4

After David had finished talking with Saul, Jonathan became one in spirit with David, and he loved him as himself... And Jonathan made a covenant with David because he loved him as himself. Jonathan took off the robe he was wearing and gave it to David, along with his tunic, and even his sword, his bow and his belt.

The friendship between Jonathan and David is the closest and most devoted in all of God's Word. One thinks of the exemplary friendships of Ruth and her mother-in-law, Naomi, or between Mary and her cousin, Elizabeth. But this friendship exceeds those in important ways.

Jonathan was King Saul's son, and heir to the throne of Israel. Throughout the Bible, we see the envy of kings and princes against anyone who might be the slightest threat to their reign. Abimelech, in Judges 9:5, murdered his seventy brothers just before receiving his crown. In 2 Kings 10:7, followers of King Jehu slaughtered seventy princes of Ahab's family. We have read of Herod and his jealous rage on hearing of a king being born in Bethlehem. But Jonathan is different. Not only does he befriend the man whom his father envies and will seek to murder, he loves David "as himself." What's going on here?

In Leviticus 19:18, God gave this command: *"Do not seek revenge or bear a grudge against one of your people, but love your neighbor as yourself. I am the LORD."* In Matthew 22:37-40, Jesus reinforced the absolute primacy of this decree over all of the rest of the Law regarding earthly relationships. Jonathan's love for David reflects obedience to this command like no other, save the Lord Jesus Himself. Notice that he becomes "one in spirit" with David and makes a covenant with him. Their friendship is not based on, "What have you done for me lately?" Instead, it is based on a solemn oath of covenant loyalty.

I believe that Jonathan knows that the salvation of Israel will come through David's kingly line. In order for that to happen, he has to get out of the way. Notice that he gives David his robe. A prince's robe speaks of his claim upon the throne. He gives David his right to be king! Then he gives David his sword, his bow, and his belt. (In ancient times, the surrender of the sword usually meant death for the surrendering king.) Jonathan hands over not only the throne, but his very life, knowing that his covenant with David will probably mean his own death. He is willing to die that his friend might ascend to the throne.

To love someone as yourself, you must stake your own joy in the joy of the loved one. When our Savior came to this earth He gave up His throne in heaven. He also was willing to die so that His Church might find joy. Paul writes in Philippians 2:5-8:

> *Your attitude should be the same as that of Christ Jesus: Who, being in very nature God, did not consider equality with God something to be grasped, but made himself nothing, taking the very nature of a servant, being made in human likeness. And being found in appearance as a man, he humbled himself and became obedient to death—even death on a cross!*

In the same way that Jonathan makes a covenant with David, Jesus makes a covenant with His friends—the Church. His is an eternal covenant that will make His friends to be kings, ruling with Him forever. Jesus said in John 15:13: *"Greater love has no one than this, that he lay down his life for his friends."* Imagine! The King of the universe loves you and me as Himself, and was willing to come to earth as a servant and die for us! The King of Kings has become our Friend of Friends.

We humans want to be king, to sit on the throne of our own lives. But, like Jonathan, we need to get out of the way. Have you forsaken the throne of your own life? Unlike Saul, who sought foolishly to hang on to his kingdom, Jonathan shows us that the only way to be a true king and servant of the people is to relinquish your throne to Jesus.

59. JESUS: FORESHADOWED BY ELIJAH
1 Kings 17:1ff

Some time later the son of the woman who owned the house became ill. He grew worse and worse, and finally stopped breathing. She said to Elijah, "What do you have against me, man of God? Did you come to remind me of my sin and kill my son?" "Give me your son," Elijah replied. He took him from her arms, carried him to the upper room where he was staying, and laid him on his bed. Then he cried out to the LORD, "O LORD my God, have you brought tragedy also upon this widow I am staying with, by causing her son to die?" Then he stretched himself out on the boy three times and cried to the LORD, "O LORD my God, let this boy's life return to him!" The LORD heard Elijah's cry, and the boy's life returned to him, and he lived (1 Kings 17:17-22).

God ordained Elijah the Tishbite as a prophet. Elijah lived during the reign of one of the most infamous kings in Israel's history—Ahab—and his villainous wife—Jezebel. Like Jesus, whom he foreshadowed, Elijah was a prophet strong in word and in deed. He performed amazing miracles like the one above, as he raised the widow's son from the dead. Jesus would perform this miracle three times in the gospels, ending with the raising of Lazarus in John 11:43-44.

Ahab and Jezebel remind us of Herod and his wicked queen, Herodias, of Jesus' time. Just as Elijah was pursued and persecuted by the brutal monarchs of his day, so Jesus was forced to flee to Egypt with His parents under Herod's death threat. Angels warned Elijah, hiding in Sinai, and Jesus' family, hiding in Egypt, to flee (1 Kings 18:5-8 with Matthew 2:13-14).

Elijah spoke and the rain in Israel ceased (1 Kings 17:1f). In the same way, Jesus exhibited amazing control of the elements of nature as He changed the water into wine at the wedding in Cana (John 2:1f); walked on the Sea of Galilee (Matthew 14:25-33); and calmed the furious storm (Matthew 8:24-27). Elijah also showed miraculous power dealing with storms (1 Kings 18:43-45). Both Elijah and Jesus revealed God's sovereign power over the natural world that He created.

Another similarity in Elijah's and Jesus' control over the natural world lay in their ability to miraculously multiply food to satisfy the hungry. In 1 Kings 17:12-14 we read this conversation between Elijah and the widow of Zarephath:

> *She replied, "I don't have any bread—only a handful of flour in a jar and a little oil in a jug. I am gathering a few sticks to take home and make a meal for myself and my son, that we may eat it—and die." Elijah said to her, "Don't be afraid. Go home and do as you have said...For this is what the LORD, the God of Israel, says: 'The jar of flour will not be used up and the jug of oil will not run dry until the day the LORD gives rain on the land."*

It happened just as Elijah said it would. In a more open and much larger way, Jesus turned five loaves and two fish into a meal that satisfied the hunger of five thousand men and probably twice that number of women and children (Matthew 14:15-21). Twelve baskets full of leftovers were gathered up. On another occasion, our Lord fed four thousand men plus women and children with but a few loaves and fish (Matthew 15:32-38).

Both Jesus and Elijah demonstrated great power against the false prophets and teachers of the day. Elijah brought down fire from heaven to burn up the Lord's sacrifice when Baal failed to show up for his priests. Jesus caused false, evil spirits to come out of those men and women they had inhabited, and was able to read the minds of the false teachers—the scribes and Pharisees who regularly pestered him.

Finally, both Elijah and Jesus were taken up into heaven bodily. Elijah went up in a whirlwind in view of Elisha, his disciple (2 Kings 2:11), while the Lord ascended to heaven in full view of His disciples (Acts 1:1-11).

60. Jesus: Foreshadowed by Elisha
1 Kings 19:16f

*When Elisha reached the house, there was the boy lying dead on his couch.
He went in, shut the door on the two of them and prayed to the LORD.
Then he got on the bed and lay upon the boy, mouth to mouth, eyes to eyes,
hands to hands. As he stretched himself out upon him, the boy's body grew
warm. Elisha turned away and walked back and forth in the room and
then got on the bed and stretched out upon him once more. The boy sneezed
seven times and opened his eyes. Elisha summoned Gehazi and said, "Call
the Shunammite." And he did. When she came, he said,
"Take your son"* (2 Kings 4:32-36).

Elisha, Elijah's protege, also prefigured the Lord Jesus Christ. He
was given a double portion of Elijah's spirit. Elisha confirmed
the gift as he struck the Jordan with Elijah's cloak, and the waters
piled up on the right and on the left. He then crossed over on dry ground
(2 Kings 2:9-14). The parallels between Elisha and Elijah are striking,
although Elisha's many acts seem even more miraculous.

Like Elijah, and Jesus—the One to whom they both pointed—
Elisha showed God-given power over natural laws. In 2 Kings 4:1-7, Elisha
miraculously increased the olive oil supply of a widow until there was
enough to pay her debts. His thoughtful consideration of her need, and
the miraculous way in which he opened his ministry, cannot but remind
us of Jesus' miracle at Cana, where He turned mere water into fine wine.
Later, in 2 Kings 4:42-44, Elisha multiplied 20 loaves of barley bread and
some grain to feed 100 men. Like the meals by which Jesus would later
feed thousands, food was left over after everyone was full.

Jesus went around healing the sick, the blind and the lame. In the
same way, Elisha cleansed the leper Naaman of his disease (2 Kings 5).
Elisha also cleansed the spring at Jericho (2 Kings 2:18-22). On another
occasion, Elisha miraculously purified a poisonous stew (2 Kings 4:38-41).
He enabled the Shunammite woman to conceive, even though her husband

was old (2 Kings 4:12-17). We're not told so, but the Bible's silence on the subject would lead us to believe that the pregnancy was miraculous, like that of Sarah, Hannah, and Mary. Later, the child died. We have the story in the subject verses, above. Like Elijah before him and Jesus who followed, Elisha raised the dead child to life. Amazingly, the Bible also records the story of a man being raised to life merely by touching the dead bones of Elisha (2 Kings 13:21). Frightened by some raiders from Moab, some Israelites who were burying a man suddenly threw his body into Elisha's tomb. The dead man came to life and stood on his feet.

Jesus would later prophesy about many future events. For instance, He foretold the destruction of the Temple in Jerusalem in Matthew 24. Our Lord also spoke of His own death and resurrection (John 2:19-21). In like manner, Elisha foretold future events, events which actually occurred during his lifetime or shortly thereafter. For instance, in 2 Kings 3:17-20, Elisha predicted that water would fill the land, even though the people would see neither wind nor rain. In the same chapter 3, Elisha predicted that Joram, son of Ahab, would defeat Moab. It happened just as he said it would. In 2 Kings 7:1-2, Elisha predicted the end of the Aramean siege that had choked the city of Samaria. Later, his accurate pictures of future events foresaw that Hazael would become king of Aram (2 Kings 8:7-15); that Jehu would destroy the house of Ahab (2 Kings 9:7); and that dogs would eat the body of Jezebel at Jezreel (2 Kings 9:10).

Of course, one of the things that the Old Testament prophets of God did was to foretell future events. They also revealed the Word of God to the people. Our Lord is the great Prophet, who revealed God as no other prophet before Him. Yet all of the prophets spoke of Jesus in their words and actions. Later on in this volume, we will have opportunity to see many of their predictions come true in the life of one solitary man: Jesus the Christ.

61. JESUS: OUR MIGHTY WARRIOR
2 Kings 18:19-19:37

[God said] "I will defend this city and save it, for my sake and for the sake of David my servant." That night the **angel of the LORD** *went out and put to death a hundred and eighty-five thousand men in the Assyrian camp. When the people got up the next morning—there were all the dead bodies! So Sennacherib king of Assyria broke camp and withdrew. He returned to Nineveh and stayed there* (2 Kings 19:34-36).

Manifestations of the "Angel of the LORD" occur in many places in the Old Testament. (We find the phrase 65 times in 61 verses.) We saw Him speaking to Samson's mother in chapter 56. We saw Him standing before Joshua at Jericho (Chapter 54). Back in Exodus 3, He spoke to Moses out of a burning bush (Chapter 25), and in Genesis 32, He wrestled with Jacob at Peniel (Chapter 14). We claimed that the "Angel of the LORD" was none other than the pre-incarnate Christ. We called His appearance a "Christophany."

Before we speak of the pre-incarnate Christ slaying 185,000 soldiers in these verses—a fact that some may think out of character for the Babe of Bethlehem—consider more proof that this Angel was truly a manifestation of the pre-existent Jesus. Two points are to be made. The first is that those viewing the Angel of the Lord are afraid of dying. The second is that the Scripture itself testifies to the Angel being God.

In Exodus 33:20, God tells Moses in no uncertain terms that, *"you cannot see my face, for no one may see me and live."* In Judges 6:12-14 we read of an encounter between Gideon and the Angel. *"When the* **angel of the LORD** *appeared to Gideon, he said, "The LORD is with you, mighty warrior."* Then, in verse 14, in the same conversation, *"The* **LORD** *turned to him and said, "Go in the strength you have and save Israel out of Midian's hand. Am I not sending you?"* A few verses later, in 22 and 23, *"When Gideon realized that it was the angel of the LORD, he exclaimed, 'Ah, Sovereign LORD! I have* *seen the angel of the LORD face to face!' But the LORD said to him, 'Peace! Do not be afraid. You are not going to die.'"*

This same concern about death after seeing the Angel of the LORD—the actual LORD—is seen in Judges 13:22. Samson's father said: *"We are doomed to die!...We have seen God!"* When Moses saw the burning bush, *"There the **angel of the LORD** [Yahweh] appeared to him in flames of fire from within a bush"* (Exodus 3:2). Immediately thereafter, we read these words:

> When the LORD saw that he had gone over to look, **God** called to him from within the bush, "Moses! Moses!" And Moses said, "Here I am." "Do not come any closer, God said. "Take off your sandals, for the place where you are standing is holy ground." Then he said, "I am the God of your father, the God of Abraham, the God of Isaac and the God of Jacob." At this, Moses hid his face, because he was afraid to look at God (Exodus 3: 4-6).

It is very clear to me that the Angel of the Lord is none other than God Himself, in the person of the pre-incarnate Christ.

Finally, let's look at this mighty Warrior Angel who went through the Assyrian camp and destroyed the army. He is a portrait of Jesus, not Jesus in His first appearance, but in His second. We read these words in Revelation 19:11-16:

> I saw heaven standing open and there before me was a white horse, whose rider is called Faithful and True. With justice he judges and makes war. His eyes are like blazing fire, and on his head are many crowns. He has a name written on him that no one knows but he himself. He is dressed in a robe dipped in blood, and his name is the Word of God...Out of his mouth comes a sharp sword with which to strike down the nations. "He will rule them with an iron scepter." He treads the winepress of the fury of the wrath of God Almighty.
> On his robe and on his thigh he has this name written:
> KING OF KINGS AND LORD OF LORDS.

62. Jesus: Our Living Redeemer
Job 19:23-27

"Oh, that my words were recorded, that they were written on a scroll, that they were inscribed with an iron tool on lead, or engraved in rock forever! I know that my Redeemer lives, and that in the end he will stand upon the earth. And after my skin has been destroyed, yet in my flesh I will see God; I myself will see him with my own eyes—I, and not another. How my heart yearns within me!"

The Book of Job is an ancient writing. Some believe it is the oldest book of the Hebrew Scriptures. In it, we are introduced to a man of great faith in God. He is given over to Satan for scourging, as Satan has challenged God that Job will renounce his faith if his children, his belongings, and his health are taken from him. Job has to endure all these things, plus the shallow and useless words of his friends—Eliphaz, Bildad, and Zophar—who falsely claim that Job must have sinned greatly to deserve such treatment from God.

We read the words of Job 19:23-27, above, in that context. Job longs for his Redeemer. Like Ruth, Job needs a kinsman-redeemer. In these verses, however, Job isn't looking for a close relative in the next county to restore him. Rich cousin Vinny from Cleveland can't help him. Rather, he is looking, by faith, for the living God.

Notice, first, in the above verses from Job, that Job's plea is that his words would be recorded—inscribed for all time. Oh, the permanence and endurance of the eternal Word of God! Job's plea was answered. We don't know who inscribed Job's words, but we know that we can trust God for bringing them to us intact through the ages.

Now, behold the Redeemer for whom Job longed! First, Job's Redeemer is divine. Job has lost his children, his wealth, and, if you listen to his wife and so-called friends, his integrity. He is a broken man. Only the living God can help. Second, Job's Redeemer **is** alive. His God is not like Baal, or Ashtoreth, or Ra, or Buddha, or Allah, dead figments of the human imagination. Job's God is the Creator and Sustainer of the universe. He is the God who IS! Job's God is the omniscient and omnipotent sovereign Ruler of His creation.

Third, Job's Redeemer is personal. He is not some ethereal spiritual being who is unknowable or unreachable. Job's Redeemer is not so much a part of every rock and tree and bird that He has no interest in Job's situation, or cannot communicate with Job, hearing His longings and his prayers. Job's God is both transcendent above His creation, yet personally involved in it.

Finally, by the eye of faith, Job sees his Redeemer with an actual body. But, someone says, "God has no body! God is a Spirit!" But Job says, *"I know that my Redeemer lives, and that in the end he will stand upon the earth."* Job says that he will see God, face to face! Job longed for what we Christians long for—the Beatific Vision. John speaks of this vision in 1 John 3:2-3:

> *Dear friends, now we are children of God, and what we will be has not yet been made known. But we know that when [Jesus] appears, we shall be like him, for we shall see him as he is. Everyone who has this hope in him purifies himself, just as He is pure.*

Job's Redeemer is the same as yours and mine, dear reader. He is the Lord Jesus Christ, who will one day stand again on the surface of this planet, recognized as Job's Redeemer. Paul writes these words:

> *For the Lord himself will come down from heaven, with a loud command, with the voice of the archangel and with the trumpet call of God, and the dead in Christ will rise first. After that, we who are still alive and are left will be caught up together with them in the clouds to meet the Lord in the air. And so we will be with the Lord forever*
> (1 Thessalonians 4:16-17).

63. Jesus: A Tree Planted by Streams of Water
Psalm 1

Blessed is the man who does not walk in the counsel of the wicked or stand in the way of sinners or sit in the seat of mockers. But his delight is in the law of the LORD, and on his law he meditates day and night. He is like a tree planted by streams of water, which yields its fruit in season and whose leaf does not wither. Whatever he does prospers. Not so the wicked! They are like chaff that the wind blows away. Therefore the wicked will not stand in the judgment, nor sinners in the assembly of the righteous. For the LORD watches over the way of the righteous, but the way of the wicked will perish.

If you are familiar with the Book of Proverbs, this first Psalm is similar to many verses in that book. It contains what is called, "antithetical parallelism." That's a fancy term that simply means the Psalm portrays a contrast between two types of people—the "righteous" and the "wicked." In Proverbs, or the Bible, you won't find any "semi-righteous" or "sort-of-wicked" people. Only two camps exist—the righteous and the wicked.

All men and women, by virtue of their being in Adam, begin life in the wicked camp (Romans 5:19). Some remain there forever. Only one man was ever born righteous. Only one lived a perfectly righteous life. He is Jesus, the God-Man. Those who join Him in the righteous camp are His invited ones, chosen not because they were righteous in any way, but because they were wicked in every way and needed a Savior.

The first two Psalms serve as an introduction to the book of Psalms. They provide keys to the rest of the book. It is a book principally about Jesus Christ and His righteousness, about His offices as Prophet, Priest, and King, and about His Church and His Kingdom. It is the song and prayer book of the Church.

The first Psalm starts with the words, *"Blessed is the man..."* Does that sound familiar? It is a simple indicative statement that reminds us of Jesus' Beatitudes of Matthew 5:3-12. It isn't a subjunctive phrase that might be saying, "If you'll do these things you will be blessed." Neither is it an imperative that commands us to do these things or else! It is a simple declarative statement telling us what is true. Who is this man? Of course He is our Lord. But he is also everyone who has come to Him in simple childlike faith, trusting in Jesus' provision for his every need. We are only joined to the righteous camp by faith in the blood of Jesus that cleanses us from all sin, and in no other way.

We who are "in Christ" are "blessed men and women" because of who we are in Christ. We will delight in His Word—summarized in verse 2 by "the law." We will avoid the "counsel of the wicked," trusting rather in the counsel of Christ's Word. We are firmly planted in Christ, like a tree. Jesus compared the righteous and the wicked in Matthew 7:17-20:

> *Likewise every good tree bears good fruit, but a bad tree bears bad fruit. A good tree cannot bear bad fruit, and a bad tree cannot bear good fruit. Every tree that does not bear good fruit is cut down and thrown into the fire. Thus, by their fruit you will recognize them.*

Any fruit we bear is because we are attached to the "root"—our Lord. Jesus said in John 15:5: *"I am the vine; you are the branches. If a man remains in me and I in him, he will bear much fruit; apart from me you can do nothing."* Whatever we do will prosper (v. 3b). *"And we know that in all things God works for the good of those who love him, who have been called according to his purpose"* (Romans 8:28).

"Not so the wicked! They are like chaff that the wind blows away" (v. 4). John the Baptist spoke of Jesus in His role as Judge: *"His winnowing fork is in his hand to clear his threshing floor and to gather the wheat into his barn, but he will burn up the chaff with unquenchable fire"* (Luke 3:17). Again, we see the two camps. This time they are spoken of as "wheat" and "chaff." We are not in the wheat camp by what we do. We are there only by the grace of God, operating in the world effectually through the power of the Holy Spirit, and by the medium of the shed blood of Jesus Christ.

64. JESUS: THE ANOINTED SON
Psalm 2

*"I have installed my King on Zion, my holy hill." I will proclaim the decree
of the LORD: He said to me, "You are my Son; today I have become your
Father. Ask of me, and I will make the nations your inheritance, the ends of
the earth your possession. You will rule them with an iron scepter ; you will
dash them to pieces like pottery." Therefore, you kings, be wise; be warned,
you rulers of the earth. Serve the LORD with fear and rejoice with trembling. Kiss the Son, lest he be angry and you be destroyed in your way, for
his wrath can flare up in a moment. Blessed are all who
take refuge in him"* (Psalms 2:6-12).

The first three verses of the Psalm show us the world's adverse
reaction to a Holy God and to His Anointed One. Unless God
changes our hearts in the new birth, we sinners want no part
of a God who sees and will judge our evil deeds. Kings and rulers also
gather against the one true God. We saw it in Jesus' day with the Herods
and Caesars. We see it in our day throughout the world, as many world
leaders reject Him.

But the Lord in heaven laughs at them. He knows that the wicked
know the truth of Him, but suppress the truth in their unrighteousness
(Romans 1:18-20). God has installed his King on Zion—Jesus, King of
the Jews. When Pilate asked, *"Are you the king of the Jews?"* Jesus responded,
"Yes, it is as you say" (Mark 15:2). His is an eternal kingdom, and He rules
today over His creation (Hebrews 1:2 & 8).

Some have claimed that this Psalm had its ultimate fulfillment in
King David, and not in Jesus Christ. While rejecting this view, we must
also be aware that David's life foreshadowed that of Jesus, (Chapter 58),
and much of this Psalm and others had a partial fulfillment during his
leadership of Israel. But only Jesus' kingdom stretches to the *"ends of the
earth."* The writer to the Hebrews makes it clear that the *"Son"* in verse 7
of our subject text is the Lord Jesus. He quotes Psalm 2:7 in 1:5, saying,

"For to which of the angels did God ever say, 'You are my Son; today I have become your Father?" In Luke's gospel, we read these words spoken to Mary by the angel:

> *You will be with child and give birth to a son, and you are to give him the name Jesus.* **He will be great and will be called the Son of the Most High.** *The Lord God will give him the throne of his father David, and he will reign over the house of Jacob forever; his kingdom will never end* (Luke 1:31-33).

While David was also a son of God, as are all who have come to Christ in saving faith (Galatians 3:26), only one Son, the Lord Jesus, is the *"only begotten of the Father, full of grace and truth."* (John 1:14, KJV).

Verse 8 of our subject verses says, *"Ask of me, and I will make the nations your inheritance..."* In John 17:4-24, His great high-priestly prayer for the Church, Jesus claims that inheritance. In the almost 2,000 years since His resurrection, people of all families, tribes, and nations have become His inheritance. More than that, He has inherited all things. He rules the nations *"with an iron scepter."* We only see Him now through the eye of faith, but one day, He will come again and *"will dash them to pieces like pottery."* (Revelation 2:27 & 12:5).

Finally, in verses 10 through 12 of Psalm 2, the kings and rulers of the earth are warned to *"serve the Lord with fear...kiss the Son, lest he be angry..."* It is a warning to obey Him before it is too late. Our Lord Jesus came to this earth as a little helpless child, but He will one day return in great power. Jesus speaks of that day in Mark 13:26: *"At that time men will see the Son of Man coming in clouds with great power and glory."* For those with whom Christ is angry in that day, only doom and destruction await. But for those who have simply clung to Him by faith, Psalm 2 closes with this benediction: *"Blessed are all who take refuge in him."*

65. JESUS: THE SON OF MAN
Psalm 8

*"O LORD, our Lord, how majestic is your name in all the earth! You have set your glory above the heavens. From the lips of children and infants you have ordained praise because of your enemies, to silence the foe and the avenger. When I consider your heavens, the work of your fingers, the moon and the stars, which you have set in place, what is man that you are mindful of him, **the son of man** that you care for him? You made him a little lower than the heavenly beings and crowned him with glory and honor. You made him ruler over the works of your hands; you put everything under his feet: all flocks and herds, and the beasts of the field, the birds of the air, and the fish of the sea, all that swim the paths of the seas. O LORD, our Lord, how majestic is your name in all the earth!"*

The phrase "son of man" occurs 186 times in the Bible, 100 times in the Old Testament, (92 of which are in Ezekiel), and 86 times in the New. This is the first time the phrase occurs in the Bible. Of the places we see it in the New Testament, 82 times it is used by Jesus to describe Himself. For instance, the first place we see the phrase is in Matthew 8:20: *Jesus [said], 'Foxes have holes and birds of the air have nests, but the **Son of Man** has no place to lay his head.'"* Again, in Matthew 9:1-7, this conversation occurred:

> *Some men brought to [Jesus] a paralytic, lying on a mat. When Jesus saw their faith, he said to the paralytic, "Take heart, son; your sins are forgiven." At this, some of the teachers of the law said to themselves, "This fellow is blaspheming!" Knowing their thoughts, Jesus said, "Why do you entertain evil thoughts in your hearts? Which is easier: to say, 'Your sins are forgiven,' or to say, 'Get up and walk'?* **But so that you may know that the Son of Man has authority on earth to forgive sins. . . ."** *Then he said to the paralytic, "Get up, take your mat and go home." And the man got up and went home.*

By claiming to have authority to forgive sins, Jesus was claiming to be God incarnate!

The title "Son of Man" is by far Jesus' favorite title for Himself. "But why?" someone asks. "Wouldn't 'Son of God' be more appropriate?" Perhaps the writer to the Hebrews can supply the answer. He says in 2:5-9, quoting our subject verses;

> *It is not to angels that he has subjected the world to come, about which we are speaking. But there is a place where someone has testified:* **"What is man that you are mindful of him, the son of man that you care for him? You made him a little lower than the angels; you crowned him with glory and honor and put everything under his feet."** *In putting everything under him, God left nothing that is not subject to him. Yet at present we do not see everything subject to him. But we see Jesus, who was made a little lower than the angels, now crowned with glory and honor because he suffered death, so that by the grace of God he might taste death for everyone.*

I've emboldened the quote from Psalm 8:4-5. Many heretics through the centuries have used these verses (along with Philippians 2:6-7), in an attempt to prove that Jesus wasn't equal with God, but merely an angelic being or demigod. But we should understand Jesus' becoming "lower than the angels" only during the limited time that He became a man in His incarnation, *"so that by the grace of God he might taste death for everyone."*

Hebrews 2:17 clarifies this in saying, *"For this reason he had to be made like his brothers in every way, in order that he might become a merciful and faithful high priest in service to God, and that he might make atonement for the sins of the people."* In other words, Jesus had to become a real human in order to shed His real, human blood. So, He is both Son of Man, and Son of God. Jesus is the God-Man.

One other brief comment on Psalm 8:2a, which reads, *"From the lips of children and infants you have ordained praise ... "* Praised by the little children in the Temple, Jesus applied this verse to Himself in Matthew 21:16, as the religious leaders confront Him again.

66. Jesus: The Resurrected Savior
Psalm 16

"I have set the LORD always before me. Because he is at my right hand, I will not be shaken. Therefore my heart is glad and my tongue rejoices; my body also will rest secure, because you will not abandon me to the grave, nor will you let your Holy One see decay. You have made known to me the path of life; you will fill me with joy in your presence, with eternal pleasures at your right hand" (Psalms 16:8-11).

Little is said in the Old Testament of eternal life. In fact, the Sadducees, or chief priests of Jesus' day, didn't believe in the resurrection of the dead. Paul, a Pharisee prior to His conversion, did believe in resurrection, but his evidence in the Hebrew Scriptures was scanty. He said in addressing the Sanhedrin in Acts 23:6, *"My brothers, I am a Pharisee, the son of a Pharisee. I stand on trial because of my hope in the resurrection of the dead."* That reopened debate between the two sects.

In Psalm 16, however, we have a presentation of not only David's hope in his own resurrection from the grave, but by the leading of God's Spirit, an insight into the bodily resurrection of Jesus—God's "Holy One." At the beginning of Psalm 16, David exhorts God to *"Keep me safe, O God, for in you I take refuge."* Ordinarily, we might think it's just David asking to be kept safe during a battle, or from an assassin in his court. Certainly, there is that element, but as we read on, we find that he is speaking about an eternal safety. He says to the Lord in verse 2: *"You are my Lord, apart from you I have no good thing."* I believe David is saying, "Lord, I come to you having no good thing in me, only that I seek refuge eternally in you." He has heard and has believed the Gospel—that salvation is by faith alone in Christ alone.

Am I imagining things? I don't think so. In verse 5 he says that God has made his *"lot secure."* Then in verse 6, he speaks of his *"delightful inheritance."* Notice that it is God who has made David's *"lot secure,"* and no good work of his own doing. The word *"inheritance"* speaks of receiving something in the will of a relative or a friend. Hebrews 9:17 says, *"because a will is in force only when somebody has died; it never takes effect while the one who made it is living."* In Psalm 16:9-10a, David confirms that the security of which he speaks looks forward to when his body is in the grave. He says, *"Therefore my heart is glad and my tongue rejoices; my body also will rest secure, because you will not abandon me to the grave..."*

David's faith wasn't just that God would let him see old age and die in reasonable comfort, but that he would be resurrected bodily. He says to God in verse 11, *"You have made known to me the path of life; you will fill me with joy in your presence, with eternal pleasures at your right hand."* What is this *"path of life"* that David speaks of here? I submit that it is the Gospel. Did David know Jesus by name? Probably not. But he was saved just as we are today, by simply trusting in God's promises (Genesis 15:6).

David must have been given some insight into what would be in the future, that God's *"Holy One"* would come to the earth and die. He says in verse 10b, , *"...nor will you let your Holy One see decay."* David may have reasoned, "God cannot die. God doesn't have a body like me. For what purpose would God's 'Holy One' die, and yet not see decay in the grave?" Perhaps he then reasoned that God's *"Holy One"* must take on a body like his, yet be resurrected from the grave. Is it from this *"Holy One"* that he will receive an eternal inheritance? The answer is in Acts 2:29-32, where Peter addressed the crowd before him:

*"Brothers, I can tell you confidently that the patriarch David died and was buried, and his tomb is here to this day. But he was a prophet and knew that God had promised him on oath that he would place one of his descendants on his throne. Seeing what was ahead, he spoke of the resurrection of the Christ, that he was not abandoned to the grave, **nor did his body see decay.** God has raised this Jesus to life, and we are all witnesses of the fact."*

67. Jesus: The Crucified One
Psalm 22

I am poured out like water, and all my bones are out of joint. My heart has turned to wax; it has melted away within me. My strength is dried up like a potsherd, and my tongue sticks to the roof of my mouth; you lay me in the dust of death. Dogs have surrounded me; a band of evil men has encircled me, they have pierced my hands and my feet. I can count all my bones; people stare and gloat over me They divide my garments among them and cast lots for my clothing (Psalms 22:14-18).

The 22nd Psalm begins with what will ultimately be Jesus' words on the Cross as He gives His life for His Church: *"My God, my God, why have you forsaken me?"* (Psalm 22:1 and Matthew 27:46). Is He calling attention to the fact that this Psalm, written by David some one thousand years before, speaks so clearly of the death He would suffer? Perhaps, but only as a secondary motive. Jesus' desperate cry to His Father is in "real time," as we would say today. The Father had turned His face away from His Son, as Jesus took upon our sin Himself.

No other Psalm carries with it the sheer number of references to Jesus' life on earth as does this one. I've counted at least ten. Crucifixion as a means of capital punishment would not appear on the world scene for about five hundred years after David lived. Darius the Great is said to have used crucifixion in about 519 B.C. So how did David describe its torment so accurately? It would be impossible but for the Holy Spirit's leading.

Let's look at these prophesies one by one. (You'll need to open your Bible.) Verse 2 speaks of Jesus the night before His death, crying out to His Father, that the "cup" of His impending death be taken from Him (Matthew 26:37-44). In verse 6, we read that Jesus would be rejected and despised by the same people He came to save (Luke 23:21-24). The people and Romans mocked Jesus, (Matthew 27:39-40), a prediction that is stated in verse 7 of our text. In verse 8, the words that Jesus' executioners would say are recorded; *"He trusts in the Lord, let the Lord rescue him..."* (Matthew 27:43). Psalm 22:11b says *"...there is no one to help."* In the same way, we read in Mark 14:50 that Jesus' disciples had previously deserted Him.

Psalm 22:12 and 13 speak of Jesus being surrounded by the Romans and Jews who gathered around the Cross to watch the spectacle, taunting and mocking the Savior. The horrible torture of crucifixion is captured by verse 13 through 16 of our text. The gospels describe the agony Jesus suffered that corresponded with those verses. In John 20:25 we learn of the nails that were driven into His hands and feet (v. 16). In John 19:28, Jesus said, *"I am thirsty."* Compare His thirst with verse 15. Verses 14 and 17 of our text in Psalm 22 describe perfectly what crucifixion did to the human body, hanging there naked, the lungs suffocating by the downward pull of the body's own weight.

Verse 17a says, *"I can count all my bones."* None of Jesus' bones was broken just as John 19:32-33 states. Again, people stared and gloated over Him, as 17b reiterates. Verse 18 is particularly chilling. *"They divide my garments among them and cast lots for my clothing."* John 19:23-24 says, *"Let's not tear [Jesus' garment],... Let's decide by lot who will get it." This happened that the scripture might be fulfilled which said, "They divided my garments among them and cast lots for my clothing...."* The soldiers had free will and yet God's eternal decree was fulfilled by them.

The rest of Psalm 22 is more upbeat, and speaks of the salvation that awaits those who put their trust in the Crucified One. Verse 22 is quoted in Hebrews 2:12: *"I will declare your name to my brothers; in the congregation I will praise you."* Surely, as verse 24 says, *"[The Father] has not hidden his face from him but has listened to his cry for help."* Finally, the last verses of Psalm 22 speak wonderfully of Jesus: *"Posterity will serve him; future generations will be told about the Lord. They will proclaim his righteousness to a people yet unborn—for he has done it."* Praise His name!

68. JESUS: OUR GREAT AND GOOD SHEPHERD
Psalm 23

A psalm of David. The LORD is my shepherd, I shall not be in want. He makes me lie down in green pastures, he leads me beside quiet waters, he restores my soul. He guides me in paths of righteousness for his name's sake. Even though I walk through the valley of the shadow of death, I will fear no evil, for you are with me; your rod and your staff, they comfort me. You prepare a table before me in the presence of my enemies. You anoint my head with oil; my cup overflows. Surely goodness and love will follow me all the days of my life, and I will dwell in the house of the LORD forever.

In contrast to Psalm 22, Psalm 23 contains no prophesies that were specifically fulfilled in Jesus' life. Nevertheless, the Psalm points to Him like perhaps no other. Jesus said in John 10:14-15 *"I am the good shepherd; I know my sheep and my sheep know me—just as the Father knows me and I know the Father—and I lay down my life for the sheep."* Jesus is our Good Shepherd, and this beloved Psalm is the story of our relationship to Him.

Back in the 1970s and '80s, I used to recite Psalm 23 as I was going to bed, sometimes over and over, just so I could get some sleep. I had gone into the real estate development business and gotten myself into considerable financial difficulty. Other troubles haunted me as well. As a growing Christian, I found that our wonderful Shepherd is real. This Psalm helped me get to sleep each night, but, more importantly, helped me grow in Christ. Here is a verse-by-verse look at this wonderful Psalm.

"The LORD is my shepherd:" God is not an unknowable, ethereal being. He's a real Person in a real relationship with us.

"I shall not be in want:" As Paul says in Phil. 4:19, *"And my God will meet all your needs according to his glorious riches in Christ Jesus."*

"He makes me to lie down in green pastures:" Just as I was given sleep in my troubles, so also Jesus gives us rest (Matt. 11:28).

"He leads me beside quiet waters:" Still waters are peaceful places.

Jesus refreshes us with His perfect peace (John 14:27).

"He restores my soul:" Jesus heals our infirmities and gives us what we really need—eternal healing from sin and guilt (Matthew 8:17).

"He guides me in paths of righteousness:" Jesus' Spirit guides us on solid, straight paths, away from sin and worldly sorrow.

"For His name's sake:" Our life's purpose is to glorify His Name. He gives our lives purpose (1 Corinthians 10:31).

"Even though I walk through the valley of the shadow of death:" Jesus tests our faith in trials that purify us (1 Peter 4:12-13).

"I will fear no evil:" Jesus commanded, *"Fear not,"* more times than any other command. Why? Because He loves us and is in complete control of our circumstances (Rom. 8:28-29).

"For you are with me:" Jesus protects us always. God says, *"Never will I leave you, never will I forsake you"* (Heb. 13:5).

"Your rod and your staff they comfort me:" When we go astray, God disciplines us. Why? Because He loves us. (Hebrews 12:5-11). His rod and staff also speak of His willingness to shield our lives from the ravages of our enemies, and give us comfort.

"You prepare a table before me in the presence of my enemies:" Jesus gives us hope in the face of great difficulty and loss. He feeds us even as those who oppose us are closing in.

"You anoint my head with oil:" Anointing speaks of consecration to Him and also of His healing power (2 Corinthians 1:21 & Mark 6:13).

"My cup overflows:" Jesus said in John 10:10: *"...I have come that they may have life, and have it to the full."*

"Surely goodness and love [mercy - KJV] will follow me all the days of my life:" We who are in Christ are greatly blessed by His grace to us.

"And I will dwell in the house of the LORD:" We are firmly secure in the arms of our wonderful Shepherd (Matt. 18:12-13).

"Forever:" Secure not just for this life, but for all eternity.

69. Jesus: The One Betrayed by a Friend
Psalm 41

My enemies say of me in malice, "When will he die and his name perish?" Whenever one comes to see me, he speaks falsely, while his heart gathers slander; then he goes out and spreads it abroad. All my enemies whisper together against me; they imagine the worst for me, saying, "A vile disease has beset him; he will never get up from the place where he lies." **Even my close friend, whom I trusted, he who shared my bread, has lifted up his heel against me.** *But you, O LORD, have mercy on me; raise me up, that I may repay them* (Psalms 41:5-10).

On the evening before He was to go to the Cross, Jesus met with His disciples in the upper room for the Last Supper. Before they sat down to eat, Jesus washed the disciples' feet. In that context, we read these words in John 13:16ff:

"I tell you the truth, no servant is greater than his master, nor is a messenger greater than the one who sent him. Now that you know these things, you will be blessed if you do them. I am not referring to all of you; I know those I have chosen. **But this is to fulfill the scripture: 'He who shares my bread has lifted up his heel against me.'** *I am telling you now before it happens, so that when it does happen you will believe that I am He...After he had said this, Jesus was troubled in spirit and testified, "I tell you the truth, one of you is going to betray me." His disciples stared at one another, at a loss to know which of them he meant... Then, dipping the piece of bread, he gave it to Judas Iscariot, son of Simon.*

Psalm 41 is a Psalm of David. It ends the first division of Psalms, and is the third psalm that begins with a benediction. Here, the benediction is *"Blessed is he who has regard for the weak..."* (See 1:1 and 32:1). David also had a close friend who "raised up his heel" against him. Actually, Absalom was closer than a friend; he was David's son who tried to overthrow his father's reign in Israel (See 2 Samuel 13f). Of course, David was a type of the anti-type to come—Jesus. (See chapter 58.)

Judas is one of the most perplexing characters in Scripture. As He did the rest of His disciples, Jesus called Judas to follow Him (Matthew 10:1-4). Was Judas actually saved, and then later proved himself a traitor? Could it be possible for any saint of God to lose their salvation once truly converted? Jesus said in John 6:39: *"And this is the will of him who sent me, that I shall lose none of all that he has given me, but raise them up at the last day."* No. Another answer must be found.

The answer is that Judas was called to be a disciple, but Jesus knew all along who he really was and what he would do. He was never effectually called, nor was he converted. Judas acted of his own sinful, unconverted will, just as many who call themselves disciples today, yet refute the truth of the Word of God. Even though God knew from all eternity that Judas would sin in the way he did, God is not responsible for Judas' sin. The Westminster Confession of Faith puts it this way;

God, from all eternity, did, by the most wise and holy counsel of his own will, freely, and unchangeably ordain whatsoever comes to pass; yet so, as thereby neither is God the author of sin, nor is violence offered to the will of the creatures... (III, I).

In other words, God isn't the author of sin. He's not responsible for it in any way. Judas was responsible for his own actions, and acted according to his own sinful will. And yet, God ordained that he should act that way from all eternity. How does this work? It is a profound mystery, but not a contradiction. Theologically, the mystery is called "the doctrine of Concurrence." God is sovereign, but does not violate man's free will in causing him to sin.

Judas was never saved. As Dr. J. Vernon McGee used to say on his radio program, "I believe in the security of believers, but also in the insecurity of make-believers." Judas was a make-believer.

70. JESUS: OUR RIGHTEOUSNESS
Psalm 45:6-7

"Your throne, O God, will last for ever and ever; a scepter of justice will be the scepter of your kingdom. You love righteousness and hate wickedness; therefore God, your God, has set you above your companions by anointing you with the oil of joy."

The words above are reiterated by the writer to the Hebrews, in 1:6-9. He contrasts Jesus with angels, arguing that Jesus is much higher than angelic beings. He says:

In speaking of the angels he says, "He makes his angels winds, his servants flames of fire." But about the Son he says, "Your throne, O God, will last for ever and ever, and righteousness will be the scepter of your kingdom. You have loved righteousness and hated wickedness; therefore God, your God, has set you above your companions by anointing you with the oil of joy."

Notice he says, *"But about the Son he says..."* and then quotes our subject passage. There can be no doubt that the New Testament writer saw Jesus as the subject of the 45th Psalm.

Notice first that the Son is called *"God."* Jesus is not only a man. He is the God-Man. Jesus reigns from His throne, and His is an eternal, everlasting kingdom. The scepter (or rod) of Jesus' divine kingship is "righteousness" or "uprightness." What is "righteousness?" You will remember the vast gap that separates the "righteous" from the "wicked" in Psalm 1. Now we delve into the meaning of those words.

Someone might say, "Righteousness means following God's law," or "righteousness is living in a manner that is just and merciful and humble." Those would be reasonable answers. After all, in Micah 6:8, we read these words: *"He has showed you, O man, what is good. And what does the LORD require of you? To act justly and to love mercy and to walk humbly with your God."* But I believe those answers fall short of the mark. True righteousness is being in loving relationship with God. Wickedness is the opposite. Any righteousness that you or I have is ours only as we are "in Christ"—in relationship to Him as His sheep. In Matthew 5:17-20, Jesus says,

> *Do not think that I have come to abolish the Law or the Prophets; I have not come to abolish them but to fulfill them. I tell you the truth, until heaven and earth disappear, not the smallest letter, not the least stroke of a pen, will by any means disappear from the Law until everything is accomplished… For I tell you that unless your righteousness surpasses that of the Pharisees and the teachers of the law, you will certainly not enter the kingdom of heaven.*

The "righteousness" of the Pharisees and teachers of the law was thought to be by their own external observance of over 600 specific prohibitions which they had gleaned from the scriptures and Talmud. But as Paul says in Romans 9:32, *"[Israel pursued righteousness] not by faith but as if it were by works. They stumbled over the 'stumbling stone.'"*

Jesus says in Matthew 5:17 that it is He who will *"fulfill [the Law and the Prophets]."* When He says *"Law and Prophets"* here, He's speaking of the entire Old Testament. He came not only to fulfill the entire Old Testament by keeping all of its requirements perfectly, and fulfilling its portraits of Him perfectly, Jesus also fulfilled the Law for us—His Church. He lived, died, and rose again for His Church, so that *"[we] may have life, and have it to the full"* (John 10:10). Jesus IS the righteousness of the Old Testament. Only by trust in what Jesus has done for us—coming to Him in childlike faith—may we be clothed in His righteousness.

Our subject text concludes by saying that King Jesus was *"anointed with the oil of joy."* I cannot help but also conclude this chapter with these words from Hebrews 12:2: *"Let us fix our eyes on Jesus, the author and perfecter of our faith, who for the joy set before him endured the cross, scorning its shame, and sat down at the right hand of the throne of God."*

71. JESUS: THE ENDURING SAVIOR OF THE NATIONS
Psalm 72:11-17

All kings will bow down to him and all nations will serve him. For he will deliver the needy who cry out, the afflicted who have no one to help. He will take pity on the weak and the needy and save the needy from death. He will rescue them from oppression and violence, for precious is their blood in his sight. Long may he live! May gold from Sheba be given him. May people ever pray for him and bless him all day long. Let grain abound throughout the land; on the tops of the hills may it sway. Let its fruit flourish like Lebanon; let it thrive like the grass of the field. May his name endure forever; may it continue as long as the sun. All nations will be blessed through him, and they will call him blessed.

The author of this Psalm is Solomon, King David's son. Much of the Psalm reflects his reign in Israel, the wisdom he displayed in his just leadership of the people, and of the admiration and generous gifts of the nations. But the language here goes far beyond a mere mortal king and kingdom. Although Solomon did rule in justice for many years, this Psalm clearly refers to the Messiah to come—Jesus. All of the verbs Solomon uses in the Psalm are in the future tense. He points us ahead to the King who is to come.

Solomon, is of course, himself a type of Christ. He performed Christ's kingly role as the ordained leader of the temporal nation Israel. Jesus, however, is the ultimate King, who will rule eternally over all the nations of the world. Solomon ruled in wisdom. Jesus is *the* Wisdom from which Solomon was given his (1 Corinthians 1:24). The splendor of Solomon's reign was magnificent. Such splendor will pale into insignificance when compared to Jesus Christ's manifested glory. Solomon received gifts from the nations, but Jesus bestows gifts upon all nations of the world, and will ultimately receive their service and worship.

Notice also in verses 4 and 9 in your Bible that this King of which Solomon speaks will *"crush the oppressor."* And, *"His enemies will lick the dust.*" This is a clear reference to the verses we discussed in chapter 3, Genesis 3:14-15, where Adam and Eve received what is called the "proto-evangel"—the first glimpse of the Gospel:

> *So the LORD God said to the serpent, "Because you have done this,*
> *Cursed are you above all the livestock and all the wild animals! You will*
> *crawl on your belly and* **you will eat dust** *all the days of your life. And*
> *I will put enmity between you and the woman, and between*
> *your offspring and hers;* **he will crush your head,**
> *and you will strike his heel."*

Notice in verse 11 that worship and service by all the world's leaders will mark the eternal reign of the King of Kings. "*All kings will bow down to him and all nations will serve him.*" The coming King will also deliver from death those who cry out to Him. He will "*save the needy from death*" (v. 13). Later, Peter would say to Jesus, "*Lord, to whom shall we go? You have the words of eternal life.*" Only Jesus saves from death. Jesus said of Himself in Luke 19:10; "*For the Son of Man came to seek and to save what was lost.*"

The King to whom the Psalm points will live eternally. "*May his name endure forever; may it continue as long as the sun*" (v. 17). Certainly, Solomon wouldn't speak of his own "name" in this way. Why would this future King's name endure forever? Because of the next part of verse 17: "*All nations will be blessed through him, and they will call him blessed.*" This reminds us of the promises by God to Abraham back in Genesis 12:3, "*I will bless those who bless you, and whoever curses you I will curse; and all peoples on earth will be blessed through you.*" (See also Gen. 22:18 and 26:4).

Finally, in a wonderful doxology, Solomon concludes his Psalm with praise to the LORD God, "*who alone does marvellous deeds.*" The work of justice, righteousness, and salvation is by God alone, through the faithful work of our Savior—Jesus.

72. Jesus: The Faithful and Exalted King
Psalm 89:25-29

"I will set his hand over the sea, his right hand over the rivers. He will call out to me, 'You are my Father, my God, the Rock my Savior.' I will also appoint him my firstborn, the most exalted of the kings of the earth. I will maintain my love to him forever, and my covenant with him will never fail. I will establish his line forever, his throne as long as the heavens endure."

Three words dominate this Psalm of Ethan the Ezrahite: "forever" (used 8 times), "faithfulness" (7 times), and "covenant" (3 times). In poetic form, the Psalm is a restatement of God's covenant with David of 2 Samuel 7. In that text, David wanted to build a house for God—a temple for His dwelling place. But God, through the prophet Nathan, said that rather, God would build a house for David—a throne that would be established forever. That throne would ultimately be occupied by the coming Messiah—Jesus. God said, *"Your house and your kingdom will endure forever before me; your throne will be established forever."* Jesus is David's greater Son, whose throne is established eternally.

God's covenantal faithfulness is assured by His mighty power. In 89:8, the psalmist says, *"O LORD God Almighty, who is like you? You are mighty, O LORD, and your faithfulness surrounds you."* This power extends to the natural world. *"You rule over the surging sea; when its waves mount up, you still them"* (v. 9). How reminiscent this is of Jesus of whom His disciples said in Mark 4:41, *"Who is this? Even the wind and the waves obey him!"* How does He have this power? Because as verse 11 says, *"The heavens are yours, and yours also the earth; you founded the world and all that is in it."* (See John 1:3, 1 Corinthians 8:6, Colossians 1:16, and Hebrews 1:2 for statements that it is Jesus who is being referred to here.)

The foundation of God's eternal throne are *"righteousness and justice"* (v. 14). *"Love and faithfulness go before you."* That love and faithfulness has been manifested in our world through Jesus Christ. It is He who this passage now addresses.

Jesus is Lord of the seas and rivers (v. 25). He "*sustain[s] all things by his powerful word*" (Hebrews 1:3). He calls out to "*my Father*" 46 times in the New Testament, and to "*my God*" 10 times. Although Jesus doesn't specifically say "*my Savior*" in speaking of His Father, there can be no doubt that before His crucifixion He looked to His Father in faith for resurrection. Jesus prayed in John 17:5, "*And now, Father, glorify me in your presence with the glory I had with you before the world began.*"

Our subject Psalm goes on to say in verse 27: "*I will also appoint him my* **firstborn***, the most exalted of the kings of the earth.*" Not only is Jesus the "*only begotten*" of the Father (John 3:16, KJV), He is also the firstborn of God's new creation. Paul says in Romans 8:29, "*For those God foreknew he also predestined to be conformed to the likeness of his Son, that he might be the firstborn among many brothers.*" Jesus Christ is the faithful firstborn Son of Psalm 89. He is the faithful King ruling over the "*house*" that God promised David in 2 Samuel 7. The author of Hebrews says in 3:6; "*But Christ is faithful as a son over God's house. And we are his house, if we hold on to our courage and the hope of which we boast.*"

Finally, the psalmist, Ethan, speaks of God's covenantal loyalty in verses 28 and 29. The line of David's throne will never end, "*as long as the heavens endure.*" Again, God can make that promise and keep it because of His almighty power. God is the loving, faithful God who keeps His promises—His covenants with us. We make promises and break them all the time. Not intentionally, perhaps, but because we are fallen, ultimately powerless creatures. God never breaks His. Before creation, God the Father covenanted with the Son, and the Son with the Father, to bring salvation to their people. Over 4,000 years, several other covenants with men were instituted by God. Each was a subsequent unveiling of God's plan of redemption. Ultimately, the New Covenant was revealed in the person of Jesus Christ—the Savior promised as David's greater Son.

73. JESUS: OUR SCORNED & BETRAYED SAVIOR
Psalm 109

For the director of music. Of David. A psalm. "O God, whom I praise, do not remain silent, for wicked and deceitful men have opened their mouths against me; they have spoken against me with lying tongues. With words of hatred they surround me; they attack me without cause. In return for my friendship they accuse me, but I am a man of prayer. They repay me evil for good, and hatred for my friendship. Appoint an evil man to oppose him; let an accuser stand at his right hand. When he is tried, let him be found guilty, and may his prayers condemn him. May his days be few; may another take his place of leadership... I am an object of scorn to my accusers; when they see me, they shake their heads." (Psalm 109:1-8 and 25).

Several Psalms in the psalter are called "imprecatory" Psalms. That is, they call down curses upon the enemies of the writer, David, and hence, upon the enemies of God. Psalm 109 is the last of these imprecatory Psalms in the psalter, and the most virulent. These Psalms are difficult for Christians to understand in that Jesus has called us to love our enemies (Matthew 5:44, for instance). As sinners, we are to share the Gospel and treat with kindness the enemies of God, who we once were. But David is not just a private citizen, he is the King of Israel, anointed by God to rule God's chosen people in righteousness and justice. His enemies were numerous and vociferous.

As we have just seen in our discussion of Psalm 89, Jesus is David's greater Son, the One who will sit on his throne eternally. In Acts 1:20, we are given a specific application of verse 8 in our subject text to Judas, Jesus' betrayer. "'*For,' said Peter, 'it is written in the book of Psalms, 'May his place be deserted; let there be no one to dwell in it,' and, 'May another take his place of leadership.'*" The first quote is from Psalm 69:25, and the second from verse 8, above. Likewise, Psalm 109:25 is a Messianic prediction fulfilled in Matthew 27:37-39: "*Above his head they placed the written charge against him: THIS IS JESUS, THE KING OF THE JEWS...Those who passed by hurled insults at him, shaking their heads."* Jesus was scorned by those He came to save.

Have you ever noticed that hardly anyone today ever has a bad thing to say about Jesus? Yes, many take our Lord's name in vain by using it as a curse word, but, by and large, people say things like, "Jesus was a great teacher," or "Jesus was a great example for us." They scorn Him with faint praise. For Jesus claimed to be the very Son of God—God incarnate. He not only said as much directly to the Pharisees and teachers of the law, but our Lord also accepted the worship of His followers, and claimed the ability and power to forgive sins. Jesus also claimed eternality, or aseity (John 8:58). Other manifestations of His divine nature, such as His miracles, His transfiguration and resurrection, are also solid evidence of His deity.

As others have said, only three choices of who Jesus was and is remain to us. He is either "Lord, Liar, or Lunatic." No other options exist! By giving Him faint praise, *"They repay [Jesus] evil for good, and hatred for [His] friendship"* (Psalm 109:5). Jesus agonized over this. Even as people lined the streets of Jerusalem with palm branches, Jesus wept for them.

> *As he approached Jerusalem and saw the city, he wept over it and said, "If you, even you, had only known on this day what would bring you peace—but now it is hidden from your eyes. The days will come upon you when your enemies will build an embankment against you and encircle you and hem you in on every side. They will dash you to the ground, you and the children within your walls. They will not leave one stone on another, because you did not recognize the time of God's coming to you"* (Luke 19:41-44).

One final word about imprecatory Psalms. In the end, they overwhelmingly teach the awfulness of sin. Not just mild peccadillos of which we all are guilty. They teach the heinousness of unrepented sin against God and one's fellow man. They speak of the person who enjoys sin and wants to keep doing it. They warn such a person of his impending doom.

74. Jesus: Our Eternal King & Priest
Psalm 110

*The LORD says to my Lord: "Sit at my right hand until I make your enemies
a footstool for your feet." The LORD will extend your mighty scepter from
Zion; you will rule in the midst of your enemies. Your troops will be willing
on your day of battle. Arrayed in holy majesty, from the womb of the dawn
you will receive the dew of your youth. The LORD has sworn and will not
change his mind: "You are a priest forever, in the order of Melchizedek." The
Lord is at your right hand; he will crush kings on the day of his wrath. He
will judge the nations, heaping up the dead and crushing the rulers of the
whole earth. He will drink from a brook beside the way;
therefore he will lift up his head.*

This Psalm, from the pen of David as he was led by the Holy
Spirit, (Mark 12:36), is the most often quoted Psalm in the New
Testament. According to James Montgomery Boice, the Psalm is
quoted 27 times by the Apostles (p. 892 of Psalms, Volume III). He goes
on to say that the Psalm teaches "the doctrines of the divine Trinity, the
incarnation, sufferings, resurrection, ascension, and intercession of Jesus
Christ." (Page 893 quoting Edward Reynolds.) Boice devotes two chapters
to Psalm 110. Martin Luther wrote a 120-page commentary on it. How
can we possibly hope to handle it in a mere two pages?

Many of the Psalms that speak of kings speak of earthly kings,
(Psalm 89 for instance), who point to the eternal King—the Lord Jesus.
This Psalm is different. No earthly king is in view. It is a purely messianic
prophecy. One way we know this to be true because of Jesus' words in
Matthew 22:41-46 as the Pharisees were attempting to trap Him:

*While the Pharisees were gathered together, Jesus asked them, "What do
you think about the Christ? Whose son is he?" "The son of David," they
replied. He said to them, "How is it then that David, speaking by the
Spirit, calls him 'Lord'? For he says, "'The LORD said to my Lord: 'Sit at
my right hand until I put your enemies under your feet.' If then David
calls him 'Lord,' how can he be his son?" No one could say a word in*

reply, and from that day on no one dared to ask him any more questions.

Jesus applied Psalm 110 to Himself. When David says, "*The LORD said to my Lord,*" he's literally saying "*YHWH (Jehovah) said to my Adonai.*" Both of these names point to Someone greater than David. So how could David's son be greater than the great king himself? The Pharisees had no answer. The answer, as we have said previously, is that Jesus is *both* Son of David and Son of God (Romans 1:3-4).

Jesus is King, and He is also Priest. We examined Melchizedek back in chapter 8. He is a man who walks onto the biblical scene and then mysteriously walks off. He was both "*king of Salem and priest of God most High*" (Hebrews 7:1-2). He is one of the few men in Scripture who is said to hold more than one of the ancient offices of prophet, priest, or king. Much like the separation of powers in our government between the executive, legislative, and judicial branches, God separated the offices in the Old Testament in all but two cases, Moses and Melchizedek. We've seen Moses to be a type of Christ and so is Melchizedek.

To the ancient Jew, it must have been rather offensive to read in this Psalm that the Messiah was to be both a king and priest. They believed he would be a political savior, swooping down on their enemies to forever free their land of Palestine from oppression. They were blind to the Messiah's priestly role. The writer to the Hebrews explains what they missed: The old priestly order of Aaron was deficient in many ways. It sacrificed bulls and goats over and over again, which could never take away sin (Hebrews 10:11). Not only that, but priests were sinners, destined for the grave, who had also to sacrifice for themselves. But Jesus came in the "*order of Melchizedek*" to establish a permanent Priesthood, one that has no sin, one that doesn't die, and one that made an effectual atonement for sin, not just a preview of the real thing. Jesus is our eternal King and Priest!

75. Jesus: The Stone the Builders Rejected
Psalm 118:20-23

This is the gate of the LORD through which the righteous may enter. I will give you thanks, for you answered me; you have become my salvation. The stone the builders rejected has become the capstone; the LORD has done this, and it is marvelous in our eyes.

In Matthew 21:28 through 40, Jesus told a parable in the Temple courts to the chief priests and Pharisees. We know it as the Parable of the Vineyard. In the parable, Jesus describes a vineyard owned by an absentee landlord. He rented the vineyard to some tenant-farmers, but when he sent his servants to collect rent, the farmers beat them up, even killing one. More servants fared similarly. Finally, the landlord sent his son, whom the tenant farmers also murdered. When the Jews who heard the story agreed that the guilty farmers should be punished, Jesus said to them;

> *"Have you never read in the Scriptures: 'The stone the builders rejected has become the capstone; the Lord has done this, and it is marvelous in our eyes'? Therefore I tell you that the kingdom of God will be taken away from you and given to a people who will produce its fruit. He who falls on this stone will be broken to pieces, but he on whom it falls will be crushed."*

The entire Psalm 118 evokes the idea of the nation Israel being miraculously delivered from Egypt. In fact, the words of verse 14 are quoted by Moses' in Exodus 15:2, *"The LORD is my strength and my song; he has become my salvation."* It is a song of deliverance—of salvation. We have seen in Chapter 28, above, that the Exodus is a picture of the salvation that is ours in Christ. Israel is a picture of the *"stone the builders rejected,"* a nation rejected even today by the nations surrounding her.

But someone asks, "Why did the leaders of the Jews reject Jesus, and want Him executed?" The Jews were looking for a political savior, not a suffering servant. More than that, when they discovered that Jesus was from Galilee, they said "*Look into it, and you will find that a prophet does not come out of Galilee*" (John 7:22). That Jesus had been born in Bethlehem of Judah was unknown to them. Also, Jesus came on the scene as someone they might consider a "hick from the sticks." He was uneducated, at least in their schools and to their standards. Then, Jesus had the audacity to challenge the rules and regulations they had promulgated, like their many unbiblical restrictions on Sabbath day practices.

One of the central reasons the chief priests, (called Sadducees), and Pharisees hated Jesus was because he exposed their sin and made them feel guilty. Finally, the leaders of the Jews knew that they had a good thing going, and Jesus was threatening to rain on their parade. They were blinded by Satan, (2 Corinthians 4:4), and by their own sin, ambition, and arrogance. Today, Jesus is rejected by people for basically the same reasons.

We read in Acts 4:8-12, that Peter and John were jailed and then brought before the Jewish leaders. Peter then said this:

> "*Rulers and elders of the people! If we are being called to account today for an act of kindness shown to a cripple and are asked how he was healed, then know this, you and all the people of Israel: It is by the name of Jesus Christ of Nazareth, whom you crucified but whom God raised from the dead, that this man stands before you healed. He is* "**the stone you builders rejected, which has become the capstone.**' *Salvation is found in no one else, for there is no other name under heaven given to men by which we must be saved.*"

Notice that Peter changes the quote from Psalm 118. He says that "**you** *rejected*" the stone. But God has made the rejected stone the "*capstone*" by His resurrection from the dead. Have you rejected the "*capstone*??" There is still time to come to Him in simple childlike faith, "*for there is no other name under heaven given to men by which we must be saved.*"

76. JESUS: THE GOD WHO SAVES BY GRACE
Psalm 130

A song of ascents. Out of the depths I cry to you, O LORD; O Lord, hear my voice. Let your ears be attentive to my cry for mercy. If you, O LORD, kept a record of sins, O Lord, who could stand? **But with you there is forgiveness***; therefore you are feared. I wait for the LORD, my soul waits, and in his word I put my hope. My soul waits for the Lord more than watchmen wait for the morning, more than watchmen wait for the morning. O Israel, put your hope in the LORD,* **for with the LORD is unfailing love and with him is full redemption***. He himself will redeem Israel from all their sins.*

T his psalm is the eleventh of fifteen "songs of ascent" in the book of Psalms. They are sometimes said to have been sung by pilgrims on their way up to Jerusalem for the annual feasts. Jerusalem is situated in the mountains, and pilgrims would need to climb, or ascend, to get there. Another theory is that they were sung during the ascent from Babylon to Israel when the Jews were freed to return to their homeland. Others have speculated that the term "ascent," and the fifteen psalms, came from the fact that the Hebrew men would ascend the fifteen steps from the courtyard of the women to their upper courtyard next to the Temple. But we don't have to guess about this psalm. The "ascent" here is from the depths of despair about one's sin to the joy of one's salvation by the grace of God.

Psalm 130 is a clear and unambiguous statement that God's forgiveness and redemption are freely given, just as Jesus' Gospel declares. We know that the writer is crying out to God because of his sin and the guilt it has engendered, because he states in verse 3, "*If you, O LORD, kept a record of sins, O Lord, who could stand?*" He's asking for mercy, not justice, as he understands the abominable nature of his sin against an altogether holy and righteous God. He goes on to say, in verse 4, "*But with you there is forgiveness, therefore you are feared.*"

Many have rejected the true Gospel because they say free salvation by God's grace alone will only lead to lawlessness. "If I'm saved through no works of my own, then what difference will it make if I go on sinning?" Paul deals with this misconception in Romans 6:15. The point is that free salvation always is accompanied by *the fear of the Lord* (Proverbs 1:7).

Here's an acronym for godly fear: F*E*A*R. The "F" stands for "Faith" in Christ—trusting Him and His Word alone for salvation. The "E" stands for "Enjoyment." As the Westminster Shorter Catechism says in answer to "Q: What is man's chief end? A: Man's chief end is to glorify God and to enjoy Him forever." Enjoyment of God consists of being in right relationship with Him. "A" is for "Active obedience." If we are truly saved, we won't go around looking for ways to offend our all-merciful God. Rather, we want to obey Him, because He has put that desire in our hearts. Finally, "R" stands for "Reverential awe." We want to worship our all-powerful and benevolent God and Creator in spirit and in truth. I believe that this is perhaps what the writer of Psalm 130 meant when he said of God, *you are feared.*

James Boice draws four main points of God's forgiveness from a sermon on Psalm 130 by the great preacher, C. H. Spurgeon (Vol. III, p. 1141). First, God's forgiveness is all-inclusive. It has no limits. All sins are covered. Second, God's forgiveness is once and for all. It is for sins past, present, and future. Third, God's forgiveness is for those who ask for it. It is not universal. Fourth, God's forgiveness leads to godly living. I would humbly add one more point, which is not in the psalm, but which the Church has understood since Jesus finished His work on earth: God's forgiveness is based exclusively on the finished work of Christ, for *there is no other name under heaven given to men by which we must be saved*" (Acts 4:12).

We put our hope in the Lord, we wait for His appearing, for with Jesus and Jesus only is unfailing love and full redemption. What a wonderful Savior!

77. Jesus: The Eternal Wisdom of God
Proverbs 8

The LORD brought me forth as the first of his works, before his deeds of old; I was appointed from eternity, from the beginning, before the world began. When there were no oceans, I was given birth, when there were no springs abounding with water; before the mountains were settled in place, before the hills...I was there when he set the heavens in place, when he marked out the horizon on the face of the deep, when he established the clouds above and fixed securely the fountains of the deep, when he gave the sea its boundary so the waters would not overstep his command, and when he marked out the foundations of the earth. Then I was the craftsman at his side. I was filled with delight day after day, rejoicing always in his presence, rejoicing in his whole world and delighting in mankind (Proverbs 8:22-31).

Proverbs is one of the "wisdom" books of the Bible. In the Old Testament, the wisdom books are Job, Psalms, Proverbs, Ecclesiastes, and Song of Songs. James is the only wisdom book in the New Testament. The *Evangelical Dictionary of Theology* says this about godly wisdom:

> *In contrast with this human wisdom...there is a divine wisdom, given by God, which enables man to lead a good and true and satisfying life. Such divine wisdom keeps the commandments of God (Prov.4:11), is characterized by prudence (Prov. 8:12), discernment (Prov. 14:8), humility (Prov. 10:8), is based on the fear of the Lord (Job 28:28; Prov. 9:10), and is of inestimable value (Job 28:13ff). Only God, of course, possesses this wisdom in its absolute sense (Job 12:13)* (p. 1174).

Of course, all the books of the Bible contain great wisdom for us, but these books are focused upon it. In the passage quoted above, wisdom has been personalized, as it is often in these first passages of Proverbs. This personified wisdom speaks of its institution by Yahweh—(the LORD Jesus)—in eternity, and its role in the design and creation of the world.

A great debate is being carried on in America today between those who would teach only Darwinian evolution in our public schools, and those who argue for the inclusion of intelligent design into biology curriculums. The Darwinists say that to teach a Designer is to allow religion in the classroom. They champion "science" as the only real source of truth, and relegate the notion of design to superstition. If you think about it for two seconds, you'll see the error in their logic. First, they too presuppose a religion. It's called atheism, or agnosticism. Just like the theist, they assume their basic position by faith. Second, it is evident that the world is the creation of a very wise Designer (Romans 1:18-20). His name is Jesus. (See also John 1;3, 1 Cor. 8:6, Eph. 3:9, and Heb. 1:2.)

In the first chapter of 1 Corinthians, Paul speaks of the wisdom of God in a truly personalized human form—our Lord Jesus Christ. Beginning in verse 20, he says,

> *Where is the wise man? Where is the scholar? Where is the philosopher of this age? Has not God made foolish the wisdom of the world? For since in the wisdom of God the world through its wisdom did not know him, God was pleased through the foolishness of what was preached to save those who believe. Jews demand miraculous signs and Greeks look for wisdom, but we preach Christ crucified: a stumbling block to Jews and foolishness to Gentiles, but to those whom God has called, both Jews and Greeks, Christ the power of God and* **the wisdom of God** (1 Cor. 1:20-24).

Where indeed is the "scholar of this age?"? He spouts utter foolishness! Beloved, we will win the battle for the classroom. The evidence for design is overwhelming and is becoming more acknowledged every day. (See www.icr.org, and www.reasons.org.)

Paul goes on to say in verse 30: "*It is because of [God] that you are in Christ Jesus,* **who has become for us wisdom from God**—*that is, our righteousness, holiness and redemption.*" Jesus Christ is our eternal wisdom of God. His wisdom shouts from the heavens, (Psalm 19:1-2), and from His revealed Word—our Bible.

78. JESUS: SON OF THE HOLY ONE
Proverbs 30:1-5

The sayings of Agur son of Jakeh—an oracle: This man declared to Ithiel, to Ithiel and to Ucal: "I am the most ignorant of men; I do not have a man's understanding. I have not learned wisdom, nor have I knowledge of the Holy One. Who has gone up to heaven and come down? Who has gathered up the wind in the hollow of his hands? Who has wrapped up the waters in his cloak? Who has established all the ends of the earth? What is his name, and the name of his son? Tell me if you know! Every word of God is flawless; he is a shield to those who take refuge in him."

Not long ago a book entitled "The Prayer of Jabez" was on the Christian bestseller charts. Agur, in Proverbs 30, also prayed a wonderful prayer in Proverbs 30:7-9:

Two things I ask of you, O LORD; do not refuse me before I die: Keep falsehood and lies far from me; give me neither poverty nor riches, but give me only my daily bread. Otherwise, I may have too much and disown you and say, "Who is the LORD?" Or I may become poor and steal, and so dishonor the name of my God.

Sad to say, but I doubt if a book on Agur's prayer would sell many copies in Christendom today.

Agur says that he's an ignorant man. Don't believe it for a second. He's like a law professor engaged in Socratic dialogue with his class. He claims that he has no knowledge of the "Holy One"—the Lord God. Then Agur begins to ask a series of questions to his class that make clear he knows a lot about the "Holy One."

Who has gone up to heaven and come down? (v. 4)Remember the stairway to heaven in Genesis 28 (Our Chapter 13) that pointed to the One who had come down from heaven and gone up again—our Lord Jesus. Jesus said, *"No one has ever gone into heaven except the one who came from heaven—the Son of Man"* (John 3:13). In the same way, Paul says this about Jesus in Ephesians 4:7-9:

> *But to each one of us grace has been given as Christ apportioned it. This is why it says: "When he ascended on high, he led captives in his train and gave gifts to men." (What does "he ascended" mean except that he also descended to the lower, earthly regions? He who descended is the very one who ascended higher than all the heavens, in order to fill the whole universe.*

Agur is referring to the Lord Jesus Christ.

Agur then asks, *"Who has gathered up the wind in the hollow of his hands? Who has wrapped up the waters in his cloak?"* Who but the Lord Jesus Christ has control of the natural elements of this world? He proved Himself by quieting the tempest and walking on the waters, among many other miraculous deeds. Jesus is the One who *"sustain[s] all things by his powerful word"* (Hebrews 1:3).

Agur knows the Creator of the universe and makes an allusion to the Trinity when he says, *"Who has established all the ends of the earth? What is his name, and the name of his son? Tell me if you know!"* Jesus Christ is truly the only begotten Son of God. He has not only established the universe, Jesus has established its "ends"—its past and its future.

Finally, Agur concludes his questioning with these words in Proverbs 30:5-6: *"Every word of God is flawless; he is a shield to those who take refuge in him. Do not add to his words, or he will rebuke you and prove you a liar."* John begins his gospel this way: *"In the beginning was the Word, and the Word was with God, and the Word was God."* John speaks of the living Word—our Lord Jesus Christ. Jesus is the revelation of the true God in both His flawless physical manifestation, and in the flawless manifestation of His written Word—our Bible. The entire Bible points to Jesus, and speaks of His love for His Church, and of His strategy for bringing eternal life for all who would simply believe in Him, trusting in His Word.

79. Jesus: Our Virgin-Born Immanuel
Isaiah 7:13-14

Then Isaiah said, "Hear now, you house of David! Is it not enough to try the patience of men? Will you try the patience of my God also? Therefore the Lord himself will give you a sign: The virgin will be with child and will give birth to a son, and will call him Immanuel."

We now leave the wisdom books, and enter the final portion of the Old Testament, that of the prophets. We've seen other prophesies of Christ in earlier books, but now we will focus almost entirely on specific prophesies that have had their fulfillment in the life of one Man—the Lord Jesus.

One of the first books I purchased when I was a young Christian many years ago was Josh McDowell's popular work on Christian apologetics, *Evidence That Demands A Verdict*. On page 147, he speaks of the Messianic prophesies contained in the ancient biblical texts, all written at least 250 years before Christ. The Hebrew text was translated into the Greek Septuagint at about that time. Many of the original Hebrew texts were probably finished much earlier. Nevertheless, McDowell writes that over 300 Old Testament references to the Messiah were fulfilled in Jesus' life on earth.

Josh quotes Peter Stoner in *Science Speaks* (Moody Press, 1963), who calculated some probabilities regarding Old Testament prophesies being fulfilled in the life of just one man (Page 175 of my copy). Using only eight of the many prophesies that speak of Christ, Stoner says, *"We find that the chance that any man might have lived down to the present time and fulfilled all eight prophesies is one in 10^{17}."* (That's 1 in 100,000,000,000,000,000, or 1 followed by 17 zeros.) Stoner illustrates the incredible odds of this happening by supposing that if:

"...we take 10^{17} silver dollars and lay them on the face of Texas[, t]hey will cover all of the state two feet deep. Now mark one of those silver

dollars and stir the whole mass thoroughly, all over the state. Blindfold a man and tell him that he can travel as far as he wishes, but he must pick up one silver dollar and say that this is the right one. What chance would he have of getting the right one? Just the same chance that the prophets would have had of writing those eight prophecies and having them all come true in any one man, from their day to the present time, providing they wrote in their own wisdom."

But they all came true in Christ.

Those eight prophesies concerned our Savior's (1) being born in Bethlehem (Micah 5:2); (2) being preceded by a messenger (Isaiah 40:3); (3) entering Jerusalem on a donkey (Zechariah 9:9); (4) being betrayed by a friend (Psalms 41:9); (5) for 30 pieces of silver (Zechariah 11:12); (6) which were then thrown into God's house (Zechariah 11:13b); (7) being silent before His accusers; and (Isaiah 53:7); and (8) being crucified with His hands and feet pierced (Psalms 22:16). In a court of law in America, prosecutors only have to prove the guilt of a defendant beyond a reasonable doubt. Jesus' case has been proven far beyond that! And, many more such prophesies exist! One of those is that He be born of a virgin.

The word translated "virgin" in our subject text—*"ha-almah"*—may also be translated, "young woman." Therefore, many modern scholars have suggested that the virgin birth was a myth, and that Jesus' birth wasn't supernatural. While lots of young unmarried women get pregnant in our day, in Jesus' day it was unspeakable and rare. The reason the word is translated either way is because both "young woman" and virgin" (or "maiden") had the same meaning to the Jewish mind.

Read Matthew 1:18 through 25. These verses confirm that these words in Isaiah 7 point to the One who would be born without the taint of original sin. If our Lord had been born already tainted with sin, He would not have been able to save Himself, much less you and me. This is why Mary conceived by the Holy Spirit.

80. Jesus: Our Wisdom, Power, Love, & Peace
Isaiah 9:6-7

For to us a child is born, to us a son is given, and the government will be on his shoulders. And he will be called **Wonderful Counselor, Mighty God, Everlasting Father, Prince of Peace.** *Of the increase of his government and peace there will be no end. He will reign on David's throne and over his kingdom, establishing and upholding it with justice and righteousness from that time on and forever.*

Our church has two banners employed behind the pulpit throughout much of the year. Together, they recite verse 2 of Isaiah 9, above, *"The people walking in darkness have seen a great light."* That *"light"* is Jesus, the child who was to be in Bethlehem, where the angels announced, *"Today in the town of David a Savior has been born to you; he is Christ the Lord"* (Luke 2:11). Jesus came to this earth in very humble circumstances that belied His eternality and exaltation. For Jesus is the *"Wonderful Counselor, Mighty God, Everlasting Father, and Prince of Peace"* of Isaiah 9:6.

His name *"Wonderful Counselor"* speaks of Jesus' wisdom. Paul says in 1 Corinthians 1:24 that Jesus is the *"wisdom of God."* In Colossians 2:2-3, Paul again speaks of Jesus' wisdom:

My purpose is that they may be encouraged in heart and united in love, so that they may have the full riches of complete understanding, in order that they may know the mystery of God, namely, Christ, **in whom are hidden all the treasures of wisdom and knowledge.**

The Old Testament wisdom books all point to Jesus who is our wisdom. Because of His wisdom, we can trust in His leadership, and His Gospel.

I have heard it said by some that Jesus never really claimed to be the *"Mighty God"* of Isaiah 6. Nothing could be further from the truth. When He appeared before Caiphas, the high priest as recorded in Matthew 26:63-64, *"...Jesus remained silent. The high priest said to him, 'I charge you under oath by the living God: Tell us if you are the Christ, the Son of God.' 'Yes, it is as you say,' Jesus replied...'* That's just one example of many. Merely by accepting worship, or claiming the authority to forgive sin, Jesus was stating that He was the Mighty God. But Jesus did not exhibit all His power while on earth. He claimed then that His power was from His Father. (John 10:32). Now, He rules the universe at God's right hand. We are encouraged in our struggles because the all-wise Jesus is also the Mighty God who has the power to keep His promises.

It might seem strange that Jesus is called *"Everlasting Father"* in Isaiah 9, but it shouldn't. (It doesn't mean some **ontological** confusion between Father and Son.) After all, Jesus created the world and each of us (John 1:3). His Spirit guides us through the Word that is His Word, and calls us unto Himself. He is our caring, loving Father, who providentially knows what we need before we ask Him. Providence is a word that has been dropped from many vocabularies today. It comes from the Latin words "pro," which means "before," and "video," which as you can guess, means "to see." Jesus, our great High Priest, hears our prayers, and sees our needs before they arise in us. What great joy it is to know that Jesus cares for us, and provides us with exactly what we need.

Finally, Jesus is also our *"Prince of Peace."* Wonderfully, He brings peace between His people and their God. Paul writes in Romans 5:1, *"Therefore, since we have been justified through faith, we have peace with God through our Lord Jesus Christ..."* We who were enemies of God (Romans 5:10), have been brought near by Jesus' blood (Ephesians 2:13). Jesus is also the Prince of Peace in our relationships with others. My wife Amy and I have been active in Christian peacemaking—mediating disputes between believers. Jesus is at the center of all we try to do. Jesus brings healing to our many relationships.

Jesus will reign eternally on David's throne, *"establishing it and upholding it with justice and righteousness...The zeal of the Lord Almighty will accomplish this"* (Isaiah 9:7). To Him be power and glory forever!

81. JESUS: THE BRANCH FROM THE ROOT OF JESSE
Isaiah 11:1-5

A shoot will come up from the stump of Jesse; from his roots a Branch will bear fruit. The Spirit of the LORD will rest on him—the Spirit of **wisdom** *and of* **understanding,** *the Spirit of* **counsel** *and of* **power**, *the Spirit of* **knowledge** *and of the* **fear of the LORD**—*and he will delight in the fear of the LORD. He will not judge by what he sees with his eyes, or decide by what he hears with his ears; but with righteousness he will judge the needy, with justice he will give decisions for the poor of the earth. He will strike the earth with the rod of his mouth; with the breath of his lips he will slay the wicked. Righteousness will be his belt and faithfulness the sash around his waist.*

In the mountains of North Carolina, one of our most common deciduous trees is the poplar. They are difficult to kill. If you fell a poplar tree so that just the stump remains, a good possibility exists that a shoot will rise up from the stump to keep the tree alive. In these verses, however, the root and stump of David's line of Judaean kings had been dead for 600 years before these words of Isaiah are fulfilled in Jesus. Isaiah 10:33-34 sets the context for our subject verses as Isaiah predicts, *"The lofty trees [the proud] will be felled, the tall ones will be brought low."*

Just as He can make dead bones come to life (Ezekiel 37), and Aaron's rod to bud and bring forth fruit, (See chapter 52), so God can make the stump of a dead kingly line burst forth with branches, flowers, and a bumper crop. Way back in Genesis 49:8-12 (Chapter 23), we saw how the Messiah was to come to earth through the tribe of Judah. Jesse, of course, was David's father, and part of that line. Why does Isaiah mention Jesse here and not David? Perhaps it was because he was testifying to the humility of our Lord. David was far more famous than his dad.

In verses 2 and 3 of our text, we are given insight into who this "Branch" from the "stump" is: *"The Spirit of the LORD will rest on him— the Spirit of wisdom and of understanding, the Spirit of counsel and of power, the Spirit of knowledge and of the fear of the LORD—and he will delight in the fear of the LORD."* Seven characteristics of the Spirit of the Lord are invested in the Branch—the Lord Jesus in His earthly ministry.

First of all, we are told that it is the Holy Spirit—the Spirit of the Lord. Quoting from another verse in Isaiah, Jesus began His earthly ministry with the words, *"The Spirit of the Lord is on me, because he has anointed me to preach good news to the poor..."* (Luke 4:18). This Spirit was not the evil spirit that Jesus' accusers falsely claimed that He had.

The second of the Spirit's characteristics mentioned, as we saw in chapter 80, it is the Spirit of wisdom. Jesus is *"the wisdom of God"* (1 Corinthians1:24).

Third, The Holy Spirit is the Spirit of understanding. Jesus understands His brothers and sisters completely. Hebrews 4:15 says, *"For we do not have a high priest [Jesus] who is unable to sympathize with our weaknesses, but we have one who has been tempted in every way, just as we are—yet was without sin."* Jesus understands all things.

The fourth characteristic of the Holy Spirit is that of counsel. Jesus, as we have seen, is the *"Wonderful Counselor"* of Isaiah 9:6. He brings both wisdom and understanding to the benefit of His people.

The Spirit of power is the fifth characteristic. In Romans 1:4, Paul says, *"[Jesus], through the Spirit of holiness was declared with power to be the Son of God by his resurrection from the dead..."* Jesus is our all-powerful Savior and Lord.

Sixth, the Holy Spirit bestowed upon Jesus all knowledge. Jesus is the omniscient One who knew the thoughts of His opponents, as well as the past and the future. His knowledge is without error or lack.

Finally, in the seventh characteristic, (seven being a number of completeness), the Spirit bestowed upon the Branch of Jesse *"delight in the fear of the LORD."* The righteousness of Jesus was principally exhibited in His delighting to do the Father's will, even to go to His death on the Cross. Seven characteristics, all blended perfectly into One person—Jesus, the *"one whom...God [gave] the Spirit without limit"* (John 3:34).

82. Jesus: Our Living Cornerstone
Isaiah 28:16-18

So this is what the Sovereign LORD says: "See, I lay a stone in Zion, a tested stone, a **precious cornerstone** *for a sure foundation; the one who trusts will never be dismayed. I will make justice the measuring line and righteousness the plumb line; hail will sweep away your refuge, the lie, and water will overflow your hiding place. Your covenant with death will be annulled; your agreement with the grave will not stand. When the overwhelming scourge sweeps by, you will be beaten down by it."*

My dad was in the building business in San Diego for many years. When the company he worked for built the public library downtown, the city held a ceremony laying the "cornerstone." I recall that it was a rather small piece of marble upon which was engraved the date and the names of the mayor and other dignitaries. But in ancient times, the cornerstone of a building was a very large block of stone cut and laid precisely so that the rest of the building was measured and constructed based upon it.

The New Testament speaks of Jesus as the "chief cornerstone" of His building known as the Church. In Ephesians 2:19-22 Paul says:

Consequently, you are no longer foreigners and aliens, but fellow citizens with God's people and members of God's household, built on the foundation of the apostles and prophets, **with Christ Jesus himself as the chief cornerstone.** *In him the whole building is joined together and rises to become a holy temple in the Lord. And in him you too are being built together to become a dwelling in which God lives by his Spirit.*

The cornerstone of the foundation reflected the shape and purpose of the entire building. In the Church, our Cornerstone is the Lord Jesus. He provides the shape and future of our hope, with His apostles and prophets as the "*sure foundation*" (Eph. 2:20).

When I think of a "chief cornerstone," the one I think of is at the top of the building, and not in its foundation. The shape of this corner-stone, or "capstone" is exactly the shape of the building that it rests atop. Can you imagine such a cornerstone? How about the pyramids of Egypt? They each had a stone at their summits that reflected the shape of the entire structure. So also the Church of Jesus Christ is to reflect His image. We read these words from 1 Peter 2:4-9:

As you come to him, the living Stone—rejected by men but chosen by God and precious to him—you also, like living stones, are being built into a spiritual house to be a holy priesthood, offering spiritual sacrifices acceptable to God through Jesus Christ. For in Scripture it says: "See, I lay a stone in Zion, a chosen and precious cornerstone, and the one who trusts in him will never be put to shame." Now to you who believe, this stone is precious. But to those who do not believe, "The stone the build-ers rejected has become the capstone," and, "A stone that causes men to stumble and a rock that makes them fall." They stumble because they disobey the message—which is also what they were destined for. But you are a chosen people, a royal priesthood, a holy nation, a people belonging to God, that you may declare the praises of him who called you out of darkness into his wonderful light.

Men reject the "capstone" because, even though their deeds are evil in God's sight, they think that they've done enough good works to make them acceptable to Him. It's the most common theological fantasy of our day. Men think that all one has to do to be saved is to die! Peter speaks of this type of thinking in verses 7 and 8 of the above quote: *"The stone the builders rejected has become the capstone," and, "A stone that causes men to stumble and a rock that makes them fall."* Those who stumble on the Gospel of God's grace alone through faith alone in Christ alone, receive the curses of the latter portion of our subject verses from Isaiah: *"...hail will sweep away your refuge, the lie, and water will overflow your hiding place. Your covenant with death will be annulled; your agreement with the grave will not stand. When the overwhelming scourge sweeps by, you will be beaten down by it."*

83. JESUS: A LIGHT FOR THE GENTILES
Isaiah 49:5-6

And now the LORD says—he who formed me in the womb to be his servant to bring Jacob back to him and gather Israel to himself, for I am honored in the eyes of the LORD and my God has been my strength—he says: "It is too small a thing for you to be my servant to restore the tribes of Jacob and bring back those of Israel I have kept. I will also make you a **light for the Gentiles***, that you may bring my salvation to the ends of the earth."*

Shortly after Jesus was born, Mary and Joseph took Him to the Temple in Jerusalem. There, He was circumcised and brought before the priests to be consecrated. An old, devout Jew named Simeon was led by the Spirit into the Temple courts, took Jesus in his arms and prayed, saying:

"Sovereign Lord, as you have promised, you now dismiss your servant in peace. For my eyes have seen your salvation, which you have prepared in the sight of all people, a light for revelation to the Gentiles and for glory to your people Israel." (Luke 2:29-32).

The nation Israel was the object of God's affection. God said to Israel in Deuteronomy 7:7-8, *"The LORD did not set his affection on you and choose you because you were more numerous than other peoples, for you were the fewest of all peoples. But it was because the LORD loved you and kept the oath he swore to your forefathers..."* Israel is the Church of the Old Testament. The chosen nation was to lay a foundation in redemptive history out of which would arise the promised Messiah. The Messiah—the Christ—would not come merely for the nation Israel. He would come to be *"a light for the Gentiles"* as well. Israel was a conduit for the salvation of the whole world.

That Jesus would be a light for the Gentiles was revealed very early in His life. In the east, beyond the borders of Israel, a bright light—a brilliant star—shone in the heavens. Wise men, who also were Gentiles, saw the bright light of the star and traveled to Bethlehem, where they knew the Christ was to be born. When they found Jesus and Joseph and Mary, they presented their gifts of gold, frankincense, and myrrh (Luke 2:1-12).

They brought the child gold because He who had been born was the King of the Jews. Indeed, the Messiah of Israel would be King of Kings and Lord of Lords. They brought precious incense which speaks of deity and of man's duty to worship the true God with obedience and prayers. And, they brought myrrh, which was an ointment commonly used in embalming the dead. Myrrh spoke of the Messiah's impending death to save His people from their sins. Thus were Gentiles brought to Jesus by the light of the star, and were among the first to worship Him.

In the Book of Acts, the apostles preached the good news to both Jews and Gentiles. In Acts 13:44-49 we read these words:

> On the next Sabbath almost the whole city gathered to hear the word of the Lord. When the Jews saw the crowds, they were filled with jealousy and talked abusively against what Paul was saying. Then Paul and Barnabas answered them boldly: "We had to speak the word of God to you first. Since you reject it and do not consider yourselves worthy of eternal life, we now turn to the Gentiles. **For this is what the Lord has commanded us: "I have made you a light for the Gentiles, that you may bring salvation to the ends of the earth."** When the Gentiles heard this, they were glad and honored the word of the Lord; and all who were appointed for eternal life believed. The word of the Lord spread through the whole region.

That the majority of Jews did not believe is discussed by Paul in Romans 9 through 11. In 11:25-26a he says this: *"...Israel has experienced a hardening in part until the full number of the Gentiles has come in. And so all Israel will be saved..."* The Gentiles would flock to Jesus in droves, becoming the "New Israel," the Church of the Living God—our Lord Jesus Christ.

84. Jesus: The Man of Sorrows
Isaiah 53:1-3

Who has believed our message and to whom has the arm of the LORD been revealed? He grew up before him like a tender shoot, and like a root out of dry ground. He had no beauty or majesty to attract us to him, nothing in his appearance that we should desire him. He was despised and rejected by men, a man of sorrows, and familiar with suffering. Like one from whom men hide their faces he was despised, and we esteemed him not.

The next three portraits in our study deal with this one chapter in the Hebrew scriptures: Isaiah 53. For those of us who have come to know Jesus as Savior and Lord, Isaiah 53 gives us perhaps our most comprehensive portrait of Jesus in the entire Old Testament. Others cannot see Him here. They see the prophecies contained in Isaiah 53 as dealing with the nation Israel, or some other figure in history, not God's Suffering Servant—Jesus.

The Jews of Jesus' day thought the Messiah would be a political savior, ushering in a new day for Israel, where they would be free from oppression and suffering. Actually, they were right in that at His Second Coming, the true Messiah—Jesus—will come in great power and might to bring righteousness and renewal to the earth. As the Jews looked from the mountaintop of prophecy to the mountaintop of the Messiah's coming in power and glory, they failed to see the little mountain called Calvary.

The portrait of Christ in Isaiah 53 actually begins in Chapter 52, verse 13. *"See, my servant will act wisely; he will be raised and lifted up and highly exalted."* Who is wiser than Jesus? Who of all men in history has been raised, and then lifted up and more highly exalted? If not Jesus, then who? Israel? Hardly. Isaiah goes on, describing Jesus' disfigurement at the hands of His executioners, then says in 52:15, *"so will he sprinkle many nations, and kings will shut their mouths because of him. For what they were not told, they will see, and what they have not heard, they will understand."* Sprinkling speaks of blessing—the Suffering Servant will bless the nations.

He will rule over kings. What the Gentiles had never been taught, they will now understand. Let's move now to chapter 53.

"*Who has believed our message and to whom has the arm of the LORD been revealed?*" (v. 1). This is the unbelievers' problem. They have not believed the message of God's Gospel. It has not been revealed to them in the faith that follows regeneration.

"*He grew up before him like a tender shoot, and like a root out of dry ground*" (v. 2a). Jesus is often described as part of a tree. He is the root of Jesse and the Branch of Isaiah 11:1. We saw in the Tabernacle and elsewhere that wood signified His humanity. He entered this world out of "*dry ground,*" an Israel that had long since left its heritage of the Patriarchs.

"*He had no beauty or majesty to attract us to him, nothing in his appearance that we should desire him*" (v.2b). Men judge on outward appearances, but God looks upon the heart (1 Samuel 16:7). Jesus came as an ordinary man (Philippians 2:7-8). He wasn't a great beauty like David's son, Absalom, that men would gravitate to His side (2 Samuel 14:25).

"*He was despised and rejected by men, a man of sorrows, and familiar with suffering*" (v. 3a). Jesus' following grew large. But people were attracted to Him by what He could do for them, like feed them or heal their diseases. The minute Jesus was arrested, they despised and rejected Him and shouted "*Crucify Him! Crucify Him!*" (Luke 23:21). Jesus was also a "*man of sorrows, and familiar with suffering.*" We are familiar with Jesus' suffering at Calvary, but we often forget what it must have been like for the holy God to live in a sinful world for more than 30 years. We may see His anguish in what He said: "*O unbelieving generation... how long shall I stay with you? How long shall I put up with you?*" (Mark 9:19).

"*Like one from whom men hide their faces he was despised, and we esteemed him not*" (v. 3b). Were it not for God's grace in quickening us from our dead condition, we, too, would despise the Savior. We would hide our faces from Him, and esteem Him not.

85. JESUS: CRUSHED FOR OUR INIQUITIES
Isaiah 53:4-6

Surely he took up our infirmities and carried our sorrows, yet we considered him stricken by God, smitten by him, and afflicted. But he was pierced for our transgressions, he was crushed for our iniquities; the punishment that brought us peace was upon him, and by his wounds we are healed. We all, like sheep, have gone astray, each of us has turned to his own way; and the LORD has laid on him the iniquity of us all.

We turn again to Isaiah 53, this time to verses 4 through 6. Unbelievers cannot see Jesus in these verses. They are blinded. It is as Paul says in 2 Corinthians 4:4; "*The god of this age has blinded the minds of unbelievers, so that they cannot see the light of the gospel of the glory of Christ, who is the image of God.*" But to us who have believed, the portrait of Jesus literally jumps out of the verses.

"*Surely he took up our infirmities and carried our sorrows...*" (v.4a). The sufferings of Jesus have been discussed in the last chapter. Here we are told another reason why He suffered while on earth. He took upon Himself our burdens of illness and sorrow. For example, when His friend Lazarus died, "*Jesus wept*" (John 11:35).

"*...yet we considered him stricken by God, smitten by him, and afflicted*" (v. 4b). In John 10:20, after hearing Jesus, "*Many of [the Jews] said, 'He is demon-possessed and raving mad. Why listen to him?*'" Rather than seeing who Jesus really was, the Pharisees and teachers of the Law accused Him of being demon-possessed. They spoke against the Holy Spirit.

"*But he was pierced for our transgressions, he was crushed for our iniquities; the punishment that brought us peace was upon him, and by his wounds we are healed*" (v. 5). Who else or what else in the history of humanity could this verse be referring to if not the Lord Jesus? The verse clearly teaches the principle of vicarious atonement—that one person might die to atone for the sins of another.

For the natural man, this is pure foolishness. Paul tells us in 1 Corinthians 1:22-24;

Jews demand miraculous signs and Greeks look for wisdom, but we preach Christ crucified: a stumbling block to Jews and foolishness to Gentiles, but to those whom God has called, both Jews and Greeks, Christ the power of God and the wisdom of God.

"*We all, like sheep, have gone astray, each of us has turned to his own way; and the LORD has laid on him the iniquity of us all*" (v. 6). One of the things that angers the natural, unsaved man is the Bible's referring to his sinfulness. Frankly, some "Christians" are offended as well. "We're good, honest citizens," someone says, "not evil, like others." But the Bible "tells it like it is," as the late sports announcer Howard Cosell used to say, proud of his own brutal honesty.

Most bad theology has bad anthropology at its foundation. We think too highly of ourselves and, therefore, too poorly of God. But Isaiah says, "*Each of us has turned to our own way.*" Left on our own, we don't want God. We want be autonomous—a law unto ourselves. Only by the grace of God in His saving mercy can we do anything good.

One other word about verse 6. Isaiah says, "*The Lord has laid on him the iniquity of us all.*" This is the Gospel, pure and uncluttered. Why did Jesus come to earth? "*...To save His people from their sins*" (Matthew 1:21b). "*For the Son of Man came to seek and to save what was lost*" (Luke 19:10). His victory on the Cross actually saved His people. It didn't just make it possible for some to be saved. His atoning sacrifice was totally effective! Then, in the course of the centuries, the Holy Spirit has been applying His work to individuals like you and me.

Christ died for the whole world without distinction—Jews as well as Gentiles. Jesus didn't die for everyone. Jesus died for His Church—the elect of God. How do we know the difference between who's elect and who is not? We don't. We are to call everyone to repentance. Why? Because Jesus commands it (Matthew 28:18-20 with Acts 17:30).

86. JESUS: OUR GUILT OFFERING
Isaiah 53:7-10

*He was oppressed and afflicted, yet he did not open his mouth; he was led
like a lamb to the slaughter, and as a sheep before her shearers is silent, so
he did not open his mouth. By oppression and judgment he was taken away.
And who can speak of his descendants? For he was cut off from the land of
the living; for the transgression of my people he was stricken. He was assigned a grave with the wicked, and with the rich in his death, though he
had done no violence, nor was any deceit in his mouth. Yet it was the Lord's
will to crush him and cause him to suffer, and though the LORD makes his
life a guilt offering, he will see his offspring and prolong his
days, and the will of the LORD will prosper in his hand.*

We return to Isaiah 53, which portrays our Savior as the Suf-
fering Servant who came to bear the iniquities of His people.
These verses speak so clearly of Jesus, yet many refuse to see
Him at all. Perhaps these four verses will help to convince some:

"*He was oppressed and afflicted, yet he did not open his mouth; he
was led like a lamb to the slaughter, and as a sheep before her shearers is silent,
so he did not open his mouth*" (v. 7). In Matthew 27:12-14, we read of the
Lamb of God remaining silent while being prosecuted before the Jewish
priests and Pontius Pilate:

> *When [Jesus] was accused by the chief priests and the elders, he gave
> no answer. Then Pilate asked him, 'Don't you hear the testimony they
> are bringing against you?' But Jesus made no reply, not even to a single
> charge—to the great amazement of the governor.*

"*By oppression and judgment he was taken away. And who can speak
of his descendants? For he was cut off from the land of the living; for the transgression of my people he was stricken*" (v. 8). Notice that Isaiah prophesies
that Jesus will be taken away and "*cut off*"—executed. (Actually, the Lord
Himself is speaking. See Isaiah 52:5.)

Notice also that the Lord also gives the reason why Jesus was stricken: for the transgressions of the Lord's people! A distinct group.

"*He was assigned a grave with the wicked, and with the rich in his death, though he had done no violence, nor was any deceit in his mouth*" (v. 9). In Matthew 27:57-60 we see the fulfillment of these words that Jesus would be buried in a rich man's grave. Joseph of Arimathea asked Pilate for Jesus' body and he laid it in his own tomb. Also notice that the injustice of the Lord's death is noted, as is a hint of His absolute sinlessness.

"*Yet it was the LORD's will to crush him and cause him to suffer, and though the LORD makes his life a guilt offering*" (v. 10a). Even though great injustice was done to an innocent Jesus, we read here that it was all in the Lord's will. Jesus' death was not only voluntary, (Philippians 2:8; John 10:17), it had been decreed from the very beginning (Genesis 3:15). Jesus' death was a guilt offering. Remember the sin and guilt offerings in the wilderness of Sinai. Hebrews compares them to Jesus' sacrifice of Himself: "*The high priest carries the blood of animals into the Most Holy Place as a sin offering, but the bodies are burned outside the camp. And so Jesus also suffered outside the city gate to make the people holy through his own blood*" (Hebrews 13:11-12). Jesus is our guilt offering, just as Isaiah has written.

"*...he will see his offspring and prolong his days, and the will of the LORD will prosper in his hand*" (v. 10b). Although "*cut off,*" Jesus would "*see his offspring, and prolong his days.*" The Messiah was resurrected to a glorified body on the third day. You and I are His offspring. "*But Christ has indeed been raised from the dead, the firstfruits of those who have fallen asleep*" (1 Cor. 15:20). And, Jesus always did the will of the Father, just as Isaiah said: "*the will of the LORD will prosper in his hand.*

Finally, we roam out of our subject verses to the last half of verse 12: "*...because he poured out his life unto death, and was numbered with the transgressors. For he bore the sin of many, and made intercession for the transgressors.*" Jesus was not only crucified between two transgressors, He also bore the sins of many transgressors, and is today making intercession for us in heaven.

87. Jesus: Good News for the Poor
Isaiah 61:1-3

The Spirit of the Sovereign LORD is on me, because the LORD has anointed me to preach good news to the poor. He has sent me to bind up the broken-hearted, to proclaim freedom for the captives and release from darkness for the prisoners, to proclaim the year of the Lord's favor and the day of vengeance of our God, to comfort all who mourn, and provide for those who grieve in Zion—to bestow on them a crown of beauty instead of ashes, the oil of gladness instead of mourning, and a garment of praise instead of a spirit of despair. They will be called oaks of righteousness, a planting of the LORD for the display of his splendor.

At the beginning of His public ministry, Jesus returned to Nazareth, where He had lived as a youth (See Luke 4:16-30). He entered the synagogue on the Sabbath day, and then stood up to read. The scroll containing the words of the prophet Isaiah was handed to Him. Jesus unrolled the scroll until He found our subject verses, and read them to the assembly. "*The Spirit of the Sovereign Lord is on me,*" Jesus began. He read the first 3 verses, ending with the words, "*to proclaim the year of the Lord's favor...*" He stopped. "*Then he rolled up the scroll, gave it back to the attendant and sat down. The eyes of everyone in the synagogue were fastened on him, and he began by saying to them, 'Today this scripture is fulfilled in your hearing'*" (Luke 4:20-21).

The men in the synagogue were amazed at the words of Jesus, a fellow who had grown up among them. "*Isn't this Joseph's son? they asked.*" Jesus rebuked the assembly with examples of how God had gone to the aid of the Gentiles in the time of Elijah and Elisha, while overlooking Israel's need. The men became furious. "*They got up, drove him out of the town, and took him to the brow of the hill on which the town was built, in order to throw him down the cliff. But he walked right through the crowd and went on his way*" (Luke 4:29-30).

Notice first where Jesus stopped reading. He didn't read, "*and the day of vengeance of our God.*" That day would come later. He had now come to bring *"good news to the poor"*—the Gospel of salvation by faith in His blood. Notice what Jesus claims when He says, *"Today this scripture is fulfilled in your hearing."* First, Jesus claims to be anointed by God. He doesn't stand up on His own, but has been called by God and claims God's Spirit is upon Him. These were blasphemous claims to Jewish ears!

Jesus then says that God had sent Him to do five things: He was to evangelize the poor. He was to bring them the good news. Jesus uses the Greek word *"euangelisthai."* We get our word "evangelical" from it, meaning "Gospel," or "good news."

Second, by the good news, captives would be released. Released from what? I submit that they would be released from their fear of death, (Hebrews 2:15), and subsequent judgment.

Third, those who had been blinded to the truth of God would be able to see it clearly. The Lord Jesus himself would manifest truth.

Fourth, Jesus said that God had sent Him to free the oppressed. The people of Israel were oppressed by a overwhelming system of works righteousness that they hoped would ingratiate themselves to God. The Pharisees and teachers of the law promulgated this phony system. The Jewish leaders were looking for another kind of Messiah who would release them from the political oppression of the Romans.

Lastly, Jesus says that He had come to announce the *"acceptable"* year of the Lord, or year of the Lord's favor. A new day had dawned, a new covenant had arrived. Jesus made in these verses the amazing claim that Isaiah spoke of Him approximately 700 years earlier. No wonder His hearers that day were shocked and amazed!

Finally, let's look briefly at the verses that Jesus did not recite. Look at some of the words: *"comfort," "beauty," "gladness," "praise," "righteousness,"* and *"splendor."* They describe His Church, established by His Gospel in all nations of the world. No more ashes, mourning, or despair. God would plant *"oaks of righteousness"*—His saints—for the praise of His glory.

88. JESUS: RIDICULED FOR SPEAKING THE TRUTH
Jeremiah 20:7-9

O LORD, you deceived me, and I was deceived; you overpowered me and prevailed. I am ridiculed all day long; everyone mocks me. Whenever I speak, I cry out proclaiming violence and destruction. So the word of the LORD has brought me insult and reproach all day long. But if I say, "I will not mention him or speak any more in his name," his word is in my heart like a fire, a fire shut up in my bones. I am weary of holding it in; indeed, I cannot.

Jeremiah lived at a time when Israel had turned far away from God. They had fallen into much sexual immorality and debauchery, preferring to worship idols of their own making instead of the God of their fathers. They wouldn't listen to God's message of the Gospel of the coming Savior, so Jeremiah preached condemnation. It was a very unpopular message. Jeremiah was thrown into prison and even into a well for speaking God's truth. We see him in these verses praying fervently to Yahweh—the LORD God—about his predicament.

Matthew Henry and others would comment that verse 7, above, which introduces our subject verses, may be translated in this way: "O, LORD, *Thou hast persuaded me, and I was persuaded. Thou wast stronger than I; and didst overpower me by the influence of thy Spirit upon me.*" After all, it is contrary to God's character that He would deceive anyone, much less His prophet. God's words are always true words. His Word is truth (John 17:17). Jeremiah complained to God that by merely speaking God's truth, he had become the object of ridicule and insult. But he realized that if he did not speak God's truth, it burned in his chest like a fire.

Jesus, too, suffered ridicule and reproach because of God's truth. "*In fact,*" Paul says, "*everyone who wants to live a godly life in Christ Jesus will be persecuted...*"(2 Timothy 3:12). But few of us have had to shed our blood for the truth of God's Word, or be nailed to a cross. Jesus was ridiculed and oppressed everywhere He went, because He not only spoke

God's Word, He *was* God's incarnate Word (John 1:1). The Israelite leaders and the people following them didn't want to hear it.

After Jesus had healed the man born blind, the Jewish leaders questioned the man about his healing. The man said that they ought to speak to Jesus, not him. They replied, "*We know that God spoke to Moses, but as for this fellow, we don't even know where he comes from*" (John 9:29). Can you feel their demeaning, contemptuous disrespect for the Lord in their words, "*this fellow*"? In Matthew 11:18-19, Jesus said; "*For John came neither eating nor drinking, and they say, 'He has a demon.' The Son of Man came eating and drinking, and they say, 'Here is a glutton and a drunkard, a friend of tax collectors and "sinners."*" The Pharisees and teachers of the law slandered and attacked our Lord at every turn.

In Matthew 21:33-40, Jesus told the parable of the Vineyard:

> Listen to another parable: "There was a landowner who planted a vineyard. He put a wall around it, dug a winepress in it and built a watchtower. Then he rented the vineyard to some farmers and went away on a journey. When the harvest time approached, he sent his servants to the tenants to collect his fruit. The tenants seized his servants; they beat one, killed another, and stoned a third. Then he sent other servants to them, more than the first time, and the tenants treated them the same way. Last of all, he sent his son to them. 'They will respect my son,' he said. But when the tenants saw the son, they said to each other, 'This is the heir. Come, let's kill him and take his inheritance.' So they took him and threw him out of the vineyard and killed him. "Therefore, when the owner of the vineyard comes, what will he do to those tenants?"

Jesus spoke of Himself, of course, as the Son, and the prophets of God who were persecuted and assassinated before Him. Jeremiah could not but speak God's truth; So too the incarnation of God's truth told the truth. Seventy-eight times in seventy-eight verses in the gospels, Jesus said, "*I tell you the truth.*" Because He did, we have life in His name.

89. Jesus: The Mediator of a New Covenant
Jeremiah 31:31-33

*"The time is coming," declares the LORD, "when I will make a **new covenant** with the house of Israel and with the house of Judah. It will not be like the covenant I made with their forefathers when I took them by the hand to lead them out of Egypt, because they broke my covenant, though I was a husband to them," declares the LORD. "This is the covenant I will make with the house of Israel after that time," declares the LORD. "I will put my law in their minds and write it on their hearts. I will be their God, and they will be my people."*

In Luke 22, we have the account of Jesus and His disciples at the Last Supper, the evening before His betrayal. We read these words in verses 19 and 20:

*And he took bread, gave thanks and broke it, and gave it to them, saying, 'This is my body given for you; do this in remembrance of me.' In the same way, after the supper he took the cup, saying, 'This cup is the **new covenant** in my blood, which is poured out for you.*

If there is a "New Covenant," there must be an "Old Covenant" to compare it to. In verse 32b of our text, the Lord makes it clear that the old covenant was the Mosaic covenant, given to Israel at Sinai. It contained three types of law: moral (ten commandments), ceremonial (sacrificial system), and civil (governmental).

The moral law of Moses was given for three reasons, or uses: 1) To show the Israelites that their God was a righteous and holy God, and that they could not live up to God's law, thereby forcing them to come to Him for mercy. 2) The law was given to restrain sin in Israel, and in all societies. 3). Finally, the moral law was given as a blessing to God's people—to show them wonderful *"paths of righteousness"* (Psalms 23:3). As Psalm 119:32 says, *"I run in the path of your commands, for you have set my heart free."*

The whole Mosaic moral code of the Old Covenant boiled down to Jesus' quote of Matthew 22:37-40: "'...*Love the Lord your God with all your heart and with all your soul and with all your mind.' This is the first and greatest commandment. And the second is like it: 'Love your neighbor as yourself.'* But Israel, "*broke my covenant, though I was a husband to them, declares the LORD*" (Jeremiah 31:32b). The Old Covenant of Moses was a two-party, conditional covenant. Israel broke it, so another Covenant—a unilateral Covenant—had to be instituted by God.

"Instituted" may be the wrong word, because the Abrahamic covenant of God's grace had never been abrogated. Remember, back in Chapter 9, we quoted Genesis 15:6: "*Abram believed the LORD, and [the LORD] credited it to him as righteousness.*" If a person was saved in Old Testament days, he was saved by faith in God's promises. No one was ever saved by keeping the Mosaic law (Romans 3:20). What is "new" about the New Covenant, is that the New Covenant was established for the redemption of sins through the shed blood of Jesus.

But, someone argues, Jeremiah 31b and 33a say that the New Covenant will be made with the houses of Israel and Judah. It says nothing about Gentiles. But the Church *is* the new Israel. We Gentiles been grafted in to the "root" that is the LORD. Paul says this in Romans 11:17-20:

> *If some of the branches have been broken off, and you, though a wild olive shoot, have been grafted in among the others and now share in the nourishing sap from the olive root, do not boast over those branches. If you do, consider this: You do not support the root, but the root sup- ports you. You will say then, "Branches were broken off so that I could be grafted in." Granted. But they were broken off because of unbelief, and you stand by faith. Do not be arrogant, but be afraid.*

We who have been saved by faith alone in Jesus' blood have been brought into His Church, which is under the New Covenant, of which Christ is the Mediator (Hebrews 9:15; 1 Timothy 2:5).

90. Jesus: Bringing Life Out of Death
Ezekiel 37:1-14

The hand of the LORD was upon me, and he brought me out by the Spirit of the LORD and set me in the middle of a valley; it was full of bones. He led me back and forth among them, and I saw a great many bones on the floor of the valley, bones that were very dry. He asked me, "Son of man, can these bones live?" I said, "O Sovereign LORD, you alone know." Then he said to me, "Prophesy to these bones and say to them, 'Dry bones, hear the word of the LORD! This is what the Sovereign LORD says to these bones: I will make breath enter you, and you will come to life. I will attach tendons to you and make flesh come upon you and cover you with skin; I will put breath in you, and you will come to life. Then you will know that I am the LORD.'"... So I prophesied as he commanded me, and breath entered them; they came to life and stood up on their feet—
a vast army (Ezekiel 37:1-6 & 10).

Ezekiel's vision of the Valley of Dry Bones is one of the most famous in the Old Testament. I suppose much of its fame comes from the old spiritual that our family used to sing when I was a boy. Remember the lyrics? "Them bones, them bones, gonna walk around." It was upbeat and syncopated, and made me want to dance and shout for joy!

The bones that Ezekiel sees are not only disjointed human bones, they are dry. They've been lying out in the sun for a long time. No life remains in them. The Lord asked Ezekiel, "*Son of man, can these bones live?*" (v.3). Ezekiel responded, "*O Sovereign LORD, you alone know..*" The term "Sovereign LORD" is used three times in our subject verses of Ezekiel 37:1-14. God is addressed or referred to as the "Sovereign LORD" 217 times in Ezekiel, 74% of the times it is used in the entire Old Testament. The phrase is important.

God's "omnipotence" describes His power. "Omni" means "all" and "potence" means "power." God is all-powerful. God's sovereignty, on the other hand, speaks of His willingness to use His great power. The God of the Bible isn't the god of the deists who wound things up, and then sits back in his La-Z-Boy to watch how everything turns out. Not at all! God is intimately involved in His creation. He sovereignly provides for the needs of His creatures, *"for, [as Paul said, quoting a pagan philosopher], in him we live and move and have our being"* (Acts 17:28).

The dry bones of Ezekiel's vision represent the Church universal. (As we have seen, Israel is a type of the Church.) But is a Church of dry bones even possible? Ezekiel is ordered to, *"Prophesy to these bones and say to them, 'Dry bones, hear the word of the LORD!'"* (v. 4). The prophet is to preach the Word of God to the dry bones! Preaching is the way that God brings life out of death. *"Consequently, faith comes from hearing the message, and the message is heard through the word of Christ"* (Romans 10:17). The prophet, or preacher, cannot bring life out of death. Only the Word of God can bring resurrection. And resurrection is possible only through the finished work of our Lord Jesus Christ.

As the Apostle said in 1 Corinthians 8:6; *"...yet for us there is but one God, the Father, from whom all things came and for whom we live; and there is but one Lord, Jesus Christ, through whom all things came and* **through whom we live.**" Jesus said in John 5:24: *"I tell you the truth, whoever hears my word and believes him who sent me has eternal life and will not be condemned; he has crossed over from death to life."* Because Jesus lives, we, too, shall live.

Ezekiel preached and the bones came to life. *"So I prophesied as he commanded me, and breath entered them; they came to life and stood up on their feet—a vast army"* (v. 10). The metaphor is unmistakable. The bones aren't sick or near death. The bones are dead and dried out! The bones are a picture of you and me before Jesus brought us *"from death to life."* Jesus declared to Nicodemus in John 3:3. *"I tell you the truth, no one can see the kingdom of God unless he is born again."* Our faith in Christ is a gift of God (Ephesians 2:9), that follows immediately upon our new birth. Our God is the God who makes dead men live.

91. JESUS: OUR SAVIOR FROM THE FIRES
Daniel 3

The king's command was so urgent and the furnace so hot that the flames of the fire killed the soldiers who took up Shadrach, Meshach and Abednego, and these three men, firmly tied, fell into the blazing furnace. Then King Nebuchadnezzar leaped to his feet in amazement and asked his advisers, "Weren't there three men that we tied up and threw into the fire?" They replied, "Certainly, O king." He said, "Look! I see four men walking around in the fire, unbound and unharmed, and the fourth looks like a son of the gods" (Daniel 3:22-25).

Shadrach, Meshach, and Abednego were Jews who had been carried off into exile in Babylon in the 6th century B.C.. Babylon's King Nebuchadnezzar had set up a golden image of himself and ordered all his subjects to worship it whenever they heard a certain music being played. He commanded that whoever did not fall down and worship the image would be thrown into a blazing furnace. But the three Hebrew youths defied the word of the king and refused to worship the image. They said,

"O Nebuchadnezzar, we do not need to defend ourselves before you in this matter. If we are thrown into the blazing furnace, the God we serve is able to save us from it, and he will rescue us from your hand, O king. But even if he does not, we want you to know, O king, that we will not serve your gods or worship the image of gold you have set up" (Daniel 3:16).

They were ready to face death rather than bow to the golden image.

The king was furious. As in our subject verses, above, he cast the three into a super-hot furnace. The soldiers who cast them in even perished in the flames! Looking in to the furnace, the king and his men were shocked to see Shadrach, Meshach, and Abednego walking around. They were alive and another man was with them—one who looked *"like a son of the gods."*

We have discussed "theophanies" earlier, and also what we termed a "Christophany"—a physical manifestation of the pre-incarnate Christ. Here we see a Christophany—the fourth man in the furnace. How do we know this to be true? First, the fact that our three brave and faithful young men survived the fire is a miracle. The Bible says that not a hair on their head was singed (v. 27). Only God can interfere with the natural laws of His created order. Second, the figure was that of a man. What other man could it have been? Even the soldiers who tossed the three young men into the fire died in doing so. This "man who resembled a son of the gods," was indeed the God of the universe—the pre-incarnate Jesus.

Third, we know it was the pre-incarnate Christ because the effect His appearance and miracle had upon the Gentiles present and their king. Nebuchadnezzar said in verse 29, "*no other god can save in this way.*" Miracles always testify to the true God's work and Word. We use the term too loosely today, saying even the most common of all God's extraordinary providence to us is a "miracle." Finally, we know the fourth man was Jesus because it is Jesus who saves His people from the fires of hell.

The Bible rarely speaks of hell. The term "hell" only occurs 14 times in the New Testament, and 12 of those times it comes from the lips of Jesus. For instance, He said in Matthew 18:9: "*And if your eye causes you to sin, gouge it out and throw it away. It is better for you to enter life with one eye than to have two eyes and be thrown into the fire of hell.*" In Mark 9:43 these words of Jesus are recorded: "*If your hand causes you to sin, cut it off. It is better for you to enter life maimed than with two hands to go into hell, where the fire never goes out.*" Hell is, of course, represented by other terms. In Revelation 20:14 we read, "*Then death and Hades were thrown into the lake of fire. The lake of fire is the second death.*" Just as Shadrach, Meshach, and Abednego were saved from Nebuchadnezzar's fire by their faith in God's deliverance, so also we who have come to Jesus by faith in His blood, shall be saved from the fire that burns forever.

92. Jesus: The "Cut Off" Anointed One
Daniel 9:25-26

"Know and understand this: From the issuing of the decree to restore and rebuild Jerusalem until the Anointed One, the ruler, comes, there will be seven 'sevens,' and sixty-two 'sevens.' It will be rebuilt with streets and a trench, but in times of trouble. After the sixty-two 'sevens,' **the Anointed One will be cut off** *and will have nothing. The people of the ruler who will come will destroy the city and the sanctuary. The end will come like a flood: War will continue until the end, and desolations have been decreed."*

T he angel Gabriel appeared to Daniel and gave him the prophecy we have before us (vv. 20-23). Gabriel began by saying, *"Seventy 'sevens' are decreed for your people and your holy city to finish transgression, to put an end to sin, to atone for wickedness, to bring in everlasting righteousness, to seal up vision and prophecy and to anoint the most holy"* (Daniel 9:24). What does the angel mean when He spoke of *"seventy sevens."*? While we think in tens, (i.e. decimals), the Hebrew mind thought in terms of sevens. There are 7 days in a week beginning on the Sabbath day, and every seven years was a Sabbath year—a year-long vacation of allowing the fields to lie dormant. Seven times seven years—every 49 years—the Jews celebrated the year of Jubilee, a time when debts were forgiven and indentured servants set free (Leviticus 25:10).

The Hebrews were also used to days coming to mean years. In Numbers 14:34, we're told that 40 days of the spies' visitation of the land would be equivalent to the 40 years the people would wander in the desert. So, Gabriel's "seventy sevens" are seen to be seventy weeks of years, or 490 years. The angel continued to say in verse 24 that six things would happen within the time span of 490 years. First, *"transgression"* would be finished. Second, that time would be needed *"to put an end to sin."* Third, *"atonement for wickedness"* would be made. Fourth, *"everlasting righteousness"* would be brought in, and, fifth, *"vision and prophecy"* would be sealed up.

Finally, the *"most holy"* would be anointed. The beginning of the

490 years would be triggered by a decree to rebuild Jerusalem (v. 25a).

In Ezra 7:11-28, we have a decree by Artaxerxes in approximately 457 B.C. allowing the Jews to return to Jerusalem and restore the city. Counting 483 years from that date, we arrive at the approximate time that Jesus began His earthly ministry. (See verse 25 where only 69 weeks, or 483 years, are counted.) In that ministry, Jesus would work *"to finish transgression, to put an end to sin, to atone for wickedness, [and] to bring in everlasting righteousness..."* Prophecy would be *"seal[ed] up"* at the coming of the anointed *"most holy,"* because it dealt with Him. Jesus is the fulfillment of Old Testament prophecy concerning the coming Messiah.

In Daniel 9:25, we are told who this *"most holy"* one is. He is the Messiah—the Christ. In verse 26, we are told that the Messiah will be *"cut off"* —He would be slain or executed. These words were unthinkable to the Hebrew mind, in that the Messiah they expected would come as a great political deliverer, in power and great glory. Again, they looked from the mountaintop of prophecy to the mountaintop of Christ's Second Coming, never seeing the small hill called "Calvary."

In the latter part of verse 26, Gabriel spoke of *"the people of the ruler who will come."* This ruler and his people would destroy Jerusalem and the Temple, which had been rebuilt during the 483 years since Nebuchadnezzar had destroyed it during Daniel's lifetime. This destruction of Jerusalem and the Temple was literally fulfilled in 70 A.D. when Titus and the Roman legions took the city by siege. Jesus spoke of the destruction of the Temple in Luke 21:6: *"As for [the Temple], the time will come when not one stone will be left on another; every one of them will be thrown down."* The Temple's *"sacrifice and offering"* of verse 27 was ended and has never been reinstituted for almost 2,000 years.

But that's not exactly accurate. Fifty days after the Passover when Jesus was "cut off," a new, eternal, "Temple" was erected in Jerusalem. That Temple is Christ's Church, of which He is the Chief Cornerstone.

93. JESUS: OUR FAITHFUL HUSBAND
The Book of Hosea

*I will plant her for myself in the land; I will show my love to the one I
called "Not my loved one." I will say to those called "Not my people," "You
are my people": and they will say, "You are my God." The LORD said to me,
"Go, show your love to your wife again, though she is loved by another and
is an adulteress. Love her as the LORD loves the Israelites, though
they turn to other gods..." (Hosea 2:23 - 3:1).*

Beginning very early in the Old Testament, the Lord instituted marriage between a man and a woman. *"The LORD God said, 'It is not
good for the man to be alone. I will make a helper suitable for him'"*
(Genesis 2:18). So God created a partner for Adam to procreate a race of
human beings and to assist him in his tasks of managing God's creation.

In Genesis 11, we have the record of Abraham's marriage to Sarah.
Their son Isaac would marry Rebekah, and so on. Jesus would also take
a Bride. The former runaway best-seller and film, "The DaVinci Code,"
had as the basis to its plot the Gnostic invention that Jesus married Mary
Magdalene and sired children by her. Of course this is nonsense. A far
greater Bride is being prepared for Jesus—His Church, or chosen ones.

The book of Hosea begins a section of the Bible we call "The
Minor Prophets." They are not minor in the quality of what they write
to us, but in quantity. They are short. The book deals with an order that
Hosea received from God:

*When the LORD began to speak through Hosea, the LORD said to him,
"Go, take to yourself an adulterous wife and children of unfaithfulness,
because the land is guilty of the vilest adultery in departing from the
LORD." So he married Gomer daughter of Diblaim, and she
conceived and bore him a son (Hosea 1:2-3).*

The marriage was ordered by God to symbolize and to make clear to the
nation Israel Hosea's message to God's chosen people. They were a sinful,

186 • 101 PORTRAITS OF JESUS IN THE HEBREW SCRIPTURES

unfaithful people, prone to wander. But throughout all their unfaithfulness, the Lord would remain faithful. The book also has the message for
us: Our justification is the monergistic work of God. "Mono" means
"one," as in Disneyland's monorail. "Erg" is the measuring unit of work,
and is found in words such as "energy." Salvation is God's sole work. The
Reformers termed this concept in their five "Solas." "Sola Gratia" or Grace
Alone, captures the essence of Hosea. We are saved by God's grace alone,
through faith alone, in Christ alone.

One of my favorite stories is of the young man who was being
interviewed for church membership. The elders asked him to give a short
rendition of his Christian experience—the circumstances surrounding his
salvation. The young man said, "It was a joint effort between God and
me." The elders were taken aback by his response, and asked, "How was
this so?" The young man replied, "God did the saving and I did the run-
ning away." Our entire salvation, from the new birth to our glorification
is the work of God's Spirit working in us: "...*for it is God who works in you
to will and to act according to his good purpose*" (Philippians 2:13).

In Revelation 19-22, we are given glimpses of the wedding supper
of the Lamb to His Bride—the saints of God—His Church. "...*the wedding
of the Lamb has come, and his bride has made herself ready. Fine linen, bright
and clean, was given her to wear.*"... *Then the angel said to me, 'Write: "Blessed
are those who are invited to the wedding supper of the Lamb!"'* (Revelation
19:7-9). Then, in Revelation 21:9 we read this, "*One of the seven angels...
said to me, 'Come, I will show you the bride, the wife of the Lamb.'*" We, the
Church of Jesus Christ, are formally engaged to Him now by His grace in
regeneration and the faith He gives us. One day we will attend that supper
in heaven and will declare in tumultuous shouts as the Bride of the living
God, "*Hallelujah! For our Lord God Almighty reigns. Let us rejoice and be
glad and give him glory!*" (Revelation 19:6-7).

94. JESUS: OUR RESURRECTED LORD
Hosea 6:1-3

Come, let us return to the LORD. He has torn us to pieces but he will heal us; he has injured us but he will bind up our wounds. After two days he will revive us; **on the third day he will restore us,** *that we may live in his presence. Let us acknowledge the LORD; let us press on to acknowledge him. As surely as the sun rises, he will appear; he will come to us like the winter rains, like the spring rains that water the earth.*

Notice the phrase in the above verses, "*on the third day he will restore us, so that we may live in his presence.*" Hosea was written in the 8th century B.C., over 700 years before these words of Hosea would be fulfilled in the resurrection of our Lord Jesus Christ. Yes, Jesus was the One who was "restored" on the third day. But make no mistake, His resurrection guaranteed our own—we who have come to Him, by faith, as Lord and Savior.

The 15th chapter of Paul's first letter to the church in Corinth is one of the most wonderful in the Word of God. Its theme is the Resurrection of Jesus and of those who trust in Him. He says in verses 20-23,

But Christ has indeed been raised from the dead, the firstfruits of those who have fallen asleep. For since death came through a man, the resurrection of the dead comes also through a man. For as in Adam all die, so in Christ all will be made alive. But each in his own turn: Christ, the firstfruits; then, when he comes, those who belong to him.

The resurrection of Jesus is one of the most firmly documented events in human history. In verses 5 through 8 of 1 Corinthians 15, Paul presents a host of witnesses who actually saw the risen Lord. In a court of law, one or two witnesses may bring an appropriate verdict that is "beyond a reasonable doubt." Paul can bring in over 500 witnesses! In his book, *Evidence That Demands a Verdict: Volume 1,* (page 185f in my 1972 version), Josh McDowell offers copious arguments through quotes of experts and other biblical and extra-biblical evidence, affirming that the resurrection of Jesus cannot be denied by reasonable men. Some have tried to deny it by offering spurious theories such as Jesus didn't really die on the Cross—He merely "swooned." Others have said that the disciples stole the body. Still others claim that the witnesses of Jesus' resurrection body were merely hallucinating, and so on. Josh answers all of these arguments with facts. I highly recommend the book to you, whether you are already a Christian, or are seeking the truth.

When I was in the commercial real estate business in San Diego, one of the first statements of real estate jargon I learned was, "Done deal!" That meant that the deal was closed, the transaction was finished, completed, accomplished. A friend of mine in our office bought a large fishing vessel he named, "Done Deal." One day while fishing off of the Coronado Islands in Mexican waters, he mistakenly steered the boat onto a submerged rock. The boat sank in minutes. Later, on the Coast Guard boat that rescued him and those with him, my friend took the keys of the sunken boat and threw them over the stern, shouting, "It's official!" Likewise, my friends, the resurrection of Jesus is a "done deal." It is "official!"

Verse 3 of our subject text from Hosea reads, "*As surely as the sun rises, he will appear; he will come to us like the winter rains, like the spring rains that water the earth.*" Our resurrection with Jesus is also a "done deal." It is "official!" Because He rose from the dead in a physical body, our bodies, too, will be resurrected when He appears. It is as certain as the sun rising tomorrow, yet we see it now only through the eye of faith. In Romans 8:30 we have these words of Paul: "*And those [God] predestined, he also called; those he called, he also justified; those he justified, he also glorified.*" Have you ever noticed that Paul's verbs are all in the past tense? That's because our resurrection with Jesus has been assured since Jesus rose up on the third day, almost two thousand years ago. It is a "done deal."

95. Jesus: Foreshadowed in Jonah's Life
Jonah 1:17 - 2:10

*But the LORD provided a great fish to swallow Jonah, and Jonah was inside
the fish three days and three nights. From inside the fish Jonah prayed to the
LORD his God. He said: "In my distress I called to the LORD, and he answered me. From the depths of the grave I called for help, and you listened
to my cry"... And the LORD commanded the fish,
and it vomited Jonah onto dry land.*

Once again, we see Jesus foreshadowed by an Old Testament
character. Like Joseph, Samson, David, Elijah, Elisha and
others before him, Jonah was just a man, a sinner, yet whose
life pointed to the One who would be our sinless Savior. You know the
story. Jonah was ordered by God to go and preach to Nineveh, a wicked
Gentile city of the Assyrians, hated enemies of Israel. Rather than obey
God, Jonah ran the other way, and caught a boat bound for Tarshish.
They ran into a storm and Jonah was thrown overboard after he told the
sailors his story.

We spoke in an earlier chapter of water being either a type of judgment or of blessing. Here, the waters of the Mediterranean Sea point to
judgment, as Jonah was judged to have caused the violent storm and was
thrown into the churning waters. God brought discipline to bear upon
His unfaithful prophet. His actions were so unlike the Lord's. Whereas
Jonah ran away from his duty to God, Jesus ran *toward* His ordained duty
and appointment with the Cross.

But God would not leave Jonah in the waters of judgment. "*The
Lord provided a great fish to swallow Jonah, and Jonah was inside the fish
three days and three nights*" (v. 17, above). Here, the pattern of our Lord's
death and resurrection may be clearly seen. As our Lord spoke of His own
death and resurrection in Matthew 12:40: "*For as Jonah was three days
and three nights in the belly of a huge fish, so the Son of Man will be three*

days and three nights in the heart of the earth." In the fish's bowels, Jonah prayed this prayer:

> He said: "In my distress I called to the LORD, and he answered me. From the depths of the grave I called for help, and you listened to my cry. You hurled me into the deep, into the very heart of the seas, and the currents swirled about me; all your waves and breakers swept over me. I said, 'I have been banished from your sight; yet I will look again toward your holy temple.' The engulfing waters threatened me, the deep surrounded me; seaweed was wrapped around my head. To the roots of the mountains I sank down; the earth beneath barred me in forever. But you brought my life up from the pit, O LORD my God. "When my life was ebbing away, I remembered you, LORD, and my prayer rose to you, to your holy temple" (Jonah 2:2-7).

Notice in the middle of Jonah's prayer, he cried out, *"I have been banished from your sight; yet I will look again toward your holy temple."* How like Jesus who said on the Cross, *"My God, my God, why have you forsaken me"* (Matthew 27:46). Jesus, too, knew that His Father would raise Him from the grave, just as Jonah did while in the fish. Our Lord, like Jonah, could say, *"But you [Father] brought my life up from the pit."*

I believe that either Jonah actually died in the fish or God kept him alive miraculously, as he sloshed around breathless in the fish's potent digestive juices. Either way, Jonah's faith was in his Lord. He said in Chapter 2, verses 8 and 9; *"Those who cling to worthless idols forfeit the grace that could be theirs. But I, with a song of thanksgiving, will sacrifice to you. What I have vowed I will make good. Salvation comes from the LORD."*

The fish could not hold the prophet, just as the grave could not hold Jesus. Jonah got up and went to Nineveh, and there preached repentance to the Assyrians. Our Lord also commanded that we do the same, saying, *"Therefore go and make disciples of all nations..."* (Matthew 28:19).

96. Jesus: The Ruler from Bethlehem
Micah 5:2

But you, Bethlehem Ephrathah, though you are small among the clans of Judah, out of you will come for me one who will be ruler over Israel, whose origins are from of old, from ancient times.

We have already seen in Genesis 49:10, as well as other places, that the Messiah would come from the line of Judah. The land originally given to the tribe of Judah surrounded Jerusalem and included nearby Bethlehem. (See Joshua 15.) The New Testament makes it abundantly clear that Bethlehem is precisely the place where Jesus was born to Mary.

So Joseph also went up from the town of Nazareth in Galilee to Judea, to Bethlehem the town of David, because he belonged to the house and line of David. He went there to register [for the census] with Mary, who was pledged to be married to him and was expecting a child. While they were there, the time came for the baby to be born... (Luke 2:4-6).

As further testimony, we have seen in Chapter 83 that the Gentile Magi from the east knew from Micah's prophecy that Bethlehem in Judah was indeed the prophesied place (Matthew 2:1-2). So, Micah, writing approximately 700 years before Jesus' birth, pinpointed the exact town where His delivery into this world would take place.

Some critics have argued that Micah 5:2 does not refer to the town of Bethlehem as Messiah's birthplace. They say that Bethlehem Ephrathah refers to the descendants of a man by that name. But the Bible refutes their claim. For instance, in Genesis 35:19 we read, *"So Rachel died and was buried on the way to Ephrath (that is, Bethlehem)."* Again, in 1 Samuel 17:12, we have these words that speak of Israel's great king; *"Now David was the son of an Ephrathite named Jesse, who was from Bethlehem in Judah."* The place referred to by Micah is clearly Bethlehem in Judah.

What else did Micah have to say about this "ruler?" Notice he continues in verse 2: "...*whose origins are from of old, from ancient times.*" Micah speaks of the pre-existent Christ, the Creator of the universe. Jesus is also the Ruler of the universe He created. In Hebrews 1:2 we read; "...*but in these last days [God] has spoken to us by his Son, whom he appointed heir of all things, and through whom he made the universe.*" Speaking of Jesus, Paul writes in Ephesians 1:22 "*And God placed all things under his feet and appointed him to be head over everything for the church...*" Jesus "*is King of Kings and Lord of Lords*" (Rev. 19:16).

In verses 4 and 5a, Micah states of this coming One: "*He will stand and shepherd his flock in the strength of the LORD, in the majesty of the name of the LORD his God. And they will live securely, for then his greatness will reach to the ends of the earth. And he will be their peace.*" This Shepherd will clearly not just be a Deliverer or Shepherd to the nation Israel alone. "*His greatness will reach to the ends of the earth...*" His blessing and rule will be for the whole world.

One last word before we leave Micah's prophecy. In chapter 6, verse 8, these words appear: "*He has showed you, O man, what is good. And what does the LORD require of you? To act justly and to love mercy and to walk humbly with your God.*" In His earthly ministry, Jesus was continually challenged and harassed by the leaders of the Jewish people—the Pharisees and teachers of the law. They had cast this verse aside and had tried to establish their own righteousness by attempting to keep every little detail of the Mosaic law, and more. Jesus condemned their selfish attempts at righteousness, saying, "*Woe to you, teachers of the law and Pharisees, you hypocrites! You give a tenth of your spices—mint, dill and cummin. But you have neglected the more important matters of the law—**justice, mercy and faithfulness.** You should have practiced the latter, without neglecting the former*" (Matthew 23:23). Ultimately, these men would send Jesus to His death. We are the same way. We neglect justice, mercy, and faithfulness. We need the Ruler from Bethlehem to rule in our hearts by faith.

97. Jesus: The God of Grace
Zechariah 3:1-5

Then he showed me Joshua the high priest standing before the angel of the LORD, and Satan standing at his right side to accuse him. The LORD said to Satan, 'The LORD rebuke you, Satan! The LORD, who has chosen Jerusalem, rebuke you! Is not this man a burning stick snatched from the fire?' Now Joshua was dressed in filthy clothes as he stood before the angel. The angel said to those who were standing before him, "Take off his filthy clothes." Then he said to Joshua, "See, I have taken away your sin, and I will put rich garments on you." Then I said, "Put a clean turban on his head." So they put a clean turban on his head and clothed him, while the angel of the LORD stood by.

When I was a new Christian, one of the most difficult words for me to get my arms around was the word "grace," as in God's saving grace. I was told that God's saving grace was "unmerited favor." Somehow, that definition didn't quite make sense to me, because all "favor" is essentially unmerited. If I do a favor for someone, it's done not because the person has done something meritorious to deserve my favor. Favors are always unmerited. It had to mean more.

I struggled with the meaning of God's saving grace for nineteen years. Ultimately, I discovered what I had really misunderstood was the radical depravity of my own heart. I had been dead spiritually, an enemy of God. Once I got that right, the meaning of "God's saving grace" fell into place. I found that God's saving grace means that I didn't get the hell I deserved. Instead, by God's grace, *"He lifted me out of the slimy pit, out of the mud and mire; he set my feet on a rock and gave me a firm place to stand"* (Psalms 40:2). Paul says it this way: *"For God did not appoint us to suffer wrath but to receive salvation through our Lord Jesus Christ"* (1 Thessalonians 5:9). By God's grace alone, this foul sinner was appointed from eternity to reign forever with Christ Jesus. That's God's saving grace.

I know this may be difficult for some of you, but God's saving grace and His election of the saints are two sides of the same coin. You can't have one without the other. Paul says,

> *"For* **he chose us** *in him before the creation of the world to be holy and blameless in his sight. In love* **he predestined us** *to be adopted as his sons through Jesus Christ, in accordance with his pleasure and will—to* **the praise of his glorious grace***, which he has freely given us in the One he loves"* (Ephesians 1:4-6).

Good theology needs good anthropology at its foundation. That is, an inaccurate understanding of God is usually preceded by an inaccurate understanding of man. Meditate on Romans 3:9-18 and upon the words of Ephesians 1 above. None of us seeks the true and living God, because our clothes—our works—like Joshua's in our subject verses from Jeremiah, are filthy rags. Only by grace can we be like Joshua, "*a burning stick, snatched from the fire.*" A decision for Jesus can only come after the new birth.

Notice in our subject verses that Joshua is the high priest. He's not some vagabond out lying in the street in a drunken stupor. He's a highly respected man in the community. He stands between the Angel of the Lord—the pre-existent Jesus—and his accuser—Satan. The Lord, (Notice that the "*Angel*" now becomes "*the LORD*"), rebuked Satan and commanded those who were standing before him, "*Take off [Joshua's] filthy clothes.*" Joshua is standing there filthy before the Lord. He doesn't say a word. This is all the Lord's doing. He has been "*snatched from [Satan's] fire*" only by the Lord's hand. He is saved only by the Lord's grace.

Now the Lord says, "*See, I have taken away your sin, and I will put rich garments on you.*" Joshua's "filthy clothes" represent his sin. The Lord unilaterally takes his sin away, and then replaces Joshua's sin with "rich garments"—the righteous robe of Christ. That's God's saving grace! He takes sinners from the depths of depravity, gives them a new birth, and elevates them to the heights of glory! What a Savior! What grace!

98. Jesus: The King of Jerusalem
Zechariah 9:9

Rejoice greatly, O Daughter of Zion! Shout, Daughter of Jerusalem! See, your king comes to you, righteous and having salvation, gentle and riding on a donkey, on a colt, the foal of a donkey.

This verse is the one I quoted in a banner I made many years ago. It pictures what literally occurred some 500 years after it was written. Matthew 21:1-9 tells the story for us:

As they approached Jerusalem and came to Bethphage on the Mount of Olives, Jesus sent two disciples, saying to them, "Go to the village ahead of you, and at once you will find a donkey tied there, with her colt by her. Untie them and bring them to me. If anyone says anything to you, tell him that the Lord needs them, and he will send them right away." This took place to fulfill what was spoken through the prophet: "Say to the Daughter of Zion, 'See, your king comes to you, gentle and riding on a donkey, on a colt, the foal of a donkey.'"

These words send chills up my spine!

The disciples went and did as Jesus had instructed them. They brought the donkey and the colt, placed their cloaks on them, and Jesus sat on them. A very large crowd spread their cloaks on the road, while others cut branches from the trees and spread them on the road. The crowds that went ahead of him and those that followed shouted, "Hosanna to the Son of David!" "Blessed is he who comes in the name of the Lord!" "Hosanna in the highest!"

We celebrate this event as "Palm Sunday," but it was actually on a Thursday. The very next day, the day before the Passover, Jesus would be crucified to the cheers of the same people who had shouted "*Hosanna.*"

For royalty to ride into Jerusalem on a donkey meant to the populace that the rider was coming in peace. Conquering generals or kings rode into the cities they conquered on the backs of strong, sleek stallions—war horses. But Jesus was entering the city to bring a peace that *"transcends all understanding"* (Philippians 4:7). He came to bring all peoples peace with God through His shed blood.

Jesus, following Zechariah's prophecy, specified which animal He would ride. It was to be *"on a donkey, on a colt, the foal of a donkey."* This was no ordinary donkey. John tells us that Jesus rode not on the mother, but on the foal (John 12:14-15). Jewish custom may have interpreted the words *"on a donkey, on a colt, the foal of a donkey"* to indicate that it was a purebred donkey—one especially prepared for the Messiah.

Notice that Jesus quotes Zechariah and applies it to Himself. He calls Himself a King. Later, Jesus would confirm this in His conversation with Pilate as recorded in Luke 23:3: *"So Pilate asked Jesus, 'Are you the king of the Jews?' 'Yes, it is as you say,' Jesus replied.'"* Often, we hear someone say that Jesus never claimed to be the Jewish Messiah—never claimed to be God incarnate. In this instance, however, and in many others, His claim is unmistakable.

Following this striking prophecy of the Messiah's triumphant entry into Jerusalem, Zechariah turns to our Lord's Second Coming. He says in 9:10-11,

> *I will take away the chariots from Ephraim and the war-horses from Jerusalem, and the battle bow will be broken. He will proclaim peace to the nations. His rule will extend from sea to sea and from the River to the ends of the earth. As for you, because of the blood of my covenant with you, I will free your prisoners from the waterless pit.*

This Ruler's kingdom will extend over the entire earth. Prisoners will be released from prisons of dry cisterns, because of the *"blood of my covenant."* Much animal blood was shed over the years at the Tabernacle and in the Temple in Jerusalem. But the blood of animals could never take sin away (Hebrews 10:4). Their blood pointed to the blood of the One who would shed His in Jerusalem the day following His triumphant entry. His blood would be effectual for the salvation of many.

99. JESUS: SOLD FOR THIRTY PIECES OF SILVER
Zechariah 11:12-13

I told them, "If you think it best, give me my pay; but if not, keep it." So they paid me thirty pieces of silver. And the LORD said to me, "Throw it to the potter"—the handsome price at which they priced me! So I took the thirty pieces of silver and threw them into the house of the LORD to the potter.

Back in the books of Moses, God gave the people many specific, every day applications of the Ten Commandments. In one such application, we are told in Exodus 21:32, "*If [a] bull gores a male or female slave, the owner must pay thirty shekels of silver to the master of the slave, and the bull must be stoned.*" What irony that the Lord of the universe was sold for the same price an owner received for a slave who was gored to death by someone's bull! Thirty shekels of silver...*the handsome price at which they priced me! (v. 12b).* Matthew gives us the fulfillment of Zechariah's words:

Then one of the Twelve—the one called Judas Iscariot—went to the chief priests and asked, "What are you willing to give me if I hand [Jesus] over to you?" So they counted out for him thirty silver coins. (Matthew 26:14-16).

The chief priests needed a precise identification of Jesus. Judas was just the traitor they needed. Later, after the dark deed was accomplished, and Jesus had been arrested, we read these words:

Early in the morning, all the chief priests and the elders of the people came to the decision to put Jesus to death. They bound him, led him away and handed him over to Pilate, the governor. When Judas, who had betrayed him, saw that Jesus was condemned, he was seized with remorse and returned the thirty silver coins to the chief priests and the elders. "I have sinned," he said, "for I have betrayed innocent blood." "What is that to us?" they replied. "That's your responsibility." So Judas threw the money

*into the temple and left. Then he went away and hanged himself. The
chief priests picked up the coins and said, "It is against the law to put
this into the treasury, since it is blood money." So they decided to use the
money to buy the potter's field as a burial place for foreigners.*
(Matt. 27:1-7).

Judas' conscience began to overwhelm him, so he threw the thirty
coins into the Temple treasury. Then he went off and hanged himself. But
the chief priests agreed that the money should not stay in the Temple. Think
about this. They had just paid this money for a traitorous act against an
innocent man. They now self-righteously concern themselves with extra-
biblical statutes about where the shekels should go! What an incredible
display of hypocrisy!

More irony is here. Zechariah said in 11:13, "...*I took the thirty
pieces of silver, and cast them to the potter in the house of the LORD*" (KJV).
The potter worked in the Valley of Ben Hinnom, a polluted valley, but
where clay was plentiful. The silver coins then went from the Temple to the
potter's field. We are reminded of Peter's words at Pentecost in Acts 2:23:
"*This [Jesus] was handed over to you by God's set purpose and foreknowledge;
and you, with the help of wicked men, put him to death by nailing him to
the cross.*" The chief priests revealed themselves to be lumps of clay under
wrath:

> *Does not the potter have the right to make out of the same lump of clay
> some pottery for noble purposes and some for common use? What if God,
> choosing to show his wrath and make his power known, bore with great
> patience the objects of his wrath—prepared
> for destruction?* (Romans 9:20-21).

Even in their two-faced scheming, the chief priests carried out what had
been planned by the Potter since the beginning of time. Evil men plot
"*against the Lord and against His Anointed One,*" but "*the Lord scoffs at
them.*" He "*will dash them to pieces like pottery*" (Psalm 2:1, 4, & 9).

100. Jesus: Forsaken by His Disciples
Zechariah 13:6-7

If someone asks him, "What are these wounds on your body?" he will answer, "The wounds I was given at the house of my friends. Awake, O sword, against my shepherd, against the man who is close to me!" declares the LORD Almighty. "Strike the shepherd, and the sheep will be scattered, and I will turn my hand against the little ones."

On the night He was betrayed by Judas, Jesus shared a meal with His disciples in an upper room. The event has become known as the Last Supper, where Jesus gave instructions regarding His sacrament of the Lord's Supper. After they ate, they sang a hymn and then walked over to the Mount of Olives. Matthew gives us this detail in 26:31-32: *Then Jesus told them, "This very night you will all fall away on account of me, for it is written: 'I will strike the shepherd, and the sheep of the flock will be scattered.' But after I have risen, I will go ahead of you into Galilee."*

Jesus applied the above words of the prophet Zechariah to what was about to occur on Calvary. Peter was livid. He said, *"Even if all fall away on account of you, I never will." "I tell you the truth,"* Jesus answered, *"this very night, before the rooster crows, you will disown me three times"* (Matthew 26:33). Doubtless the rest of the disciples were also offended by Jesus' words to them. But you know the rest of the story. When the soldiers came to arrest Jesus, His disciples feared for their lives and ran away.

Why did they run away? Someone says, "I wouldn't have run! I would have stuck by Jesus' side!" It's easy to speculate on our own heroism, but we must remember some facts about the timing of Jesus' arrest and the disciples spiritual condition. Like us, the disciples were sinful people. Jesus had chosen simple, everyday human beings from the lakes and byways of Palestine to follow Him. Unlike us, however—those of us who have put our trust in Jesus—the disciples had not yet received the Holy Spirit.

They were attempting to rely on the strength of their own flesh, which had none. Another fifty-three days would pass before the Holy Spirit would come upon them with power, and give them the strength they needed to overcome their fear of death, and the enemies of God who would rise up against them.

Following the resurrection;

> *On the evening of that first day of the week, when the disciples were* *together,* **with the doors locked for fear of the Jews,** *Jesus came and stood among them and said, "Peace be with you!" After he said this, he showed them his hands and side. The disciples were overjoyed when they saw the Lord* (John 20:19-20).

Notice that the disciples were still trembling in their boots for fear of the Jewish leaders. Several days later, *"On one occasion, while [Jesus] was eating with them, he gave them this command: 'Do not leave Jerusalem, but wait for the gift my Father promised, which you have heard me speak about'"* (Acts 1:4). The gift, of course, was the gift of the Holy Spirit which they received at Pentecost. After that event, the disciples were greatly encouraged—given courage—to stick with their Lord even if it meant persecution and even execution. Their new-found courage would lead almost all of them to die for Christ.

Many followers of Christ since that time have forfeited their lives on this earth to stick with their Lord. Just as their Shepherd was struck down, men and women around the world today stand ready to be struck down carrying His message of hope in the Gospel to a lost and dying world. But, for many of us in America, the question is not, "Will we die for Christ, or will we cut and run?" The real question is, "Will we **live** for Christ, or will we cut and run?" The answer is up to each of us. May we pray that through the strength and courage of Christ's Spirit, we will live for the honor and glory of Jesus our Lord and Savior (1 Corinthians 10:30).

101. Jesus: The Messenger of the Covenant
Malachi 3:1-3a

See, I will send my messenger, who will prepare the way before me. Then suddenly the Lord you are seeking will come to his temple; the **messenger of the covenant***, whom you desire, will come,' says the LORD Almighty. But who can endure the day of his coming? Who can stand when he appears? For he will be like a refiner's fire or a launderer's soap. He will sit as a refiner and purifier of silver; he will purify the Levites and refine them like gold and silver.*

You may hear someone ask the question, "Who was the greatest Old Testament prophet"? It's kind of a trick question, because the answer is John the Baptizer, who appears in the New Testament, not the Old. Jesus said of him, "*I tell you the truth: Among those born of women there has not risen anyone greater than John the Baptist; yet he who is least in the kingdom of heaven is greater than he*" (Matthew 11:11).

Isaiah spoke of John when he said, "*A voice of one calling: 'In the desert prepare the way for the LORD; make straight in the wilderness a highway for our God.'*" (Isaiah 40:3). Malachi seems to base his prophecy on those words, when he reports Yahweh as saying, "*See, I will send my messenger, who will prepare the way before me.*" John comes out of Old Testament days, preaching sin, repentance, and salvation—the great themes of the Old Testament prophets before him. He preached in the desert wilderness, decrying the moribund state of the nation Israel at that time.

But Malachi's prophecy in 3:1-3a, above, also speaks of another messenger—the Messenger of the Covenant—the Lord Jesus Christ. Interwoven in the text are prophecies of Christ's first and second coming. Ironically, the Jews of Jesus' day did not desire Him. They were not seeking Him, as Malachi says they would, except for a remnant who did, like Simeon and Anna in Luke 2:25-38. The many were seeking a political Messiah who would free them from the grip of the Romans. Many now are seeking Jesus to return in great power, to redeem our bodies from the earth and grave (1 Cor. 15:51-54). He will come "*suddenly*," as the KJV rightly translates the Hebrew word *pithom* in Malachi 3:1. Speaking of the *parousia*—His Second Coming—Jesus says of Himself in Mark 13:36-37: "*If he comes suddenly, do not let him find you sleeping. What I say to you, I say to everyone: 'Watch!'*"

Jesus is said by Malachi to come to His Temple. In His first coming, our Lord taught in the Temple in Jerusalem, and cleansed it of money changers. Soon, He will come for the living Temple—His Church. "*Who can endure the day of his coming?, Who can stand when he appears?,*" Malachi asks. The answer is: We who have been given grace to stand before Him. We now are tried as in a "*refiner's fire or a launderer's soap.*" By His Spirit, we are being cleansed—sanctified by His Word and through fiery trials.

Someone asks, if Jesus is referred to as the "*Messenger of the Covenant*" here, which covenant is Malachi speaking of? The answer is, of course, **all** of the covenants of God, both in the Old Testament and the New. He fulfilled them all! Jesus is the fulfillment of Adam's Covenant of Works. Our Lord executed Abraham's Covenant of Grace through faith alone. He achieved the righteousness of the Mosaic Covenant of Law, and is the antitype of the ceremonial priesthood and sacrificial system of that Covenant. Our Lord is of Jesse, and fulfills the Davidic Covenant as well. Jesus and only Jesus is the fulfillment of the New Covenant of Jeremiah 31:31, "*Behold, the days are coming, says the LORD, when I will make a new covenant with the house of Israel and with the house of Judah...*" Jesus is Lord of all the covenants!

This brings to an end our study of Jesus in the Hebrew Scriptures. I pray that it is not the end of your study of these marvelous truths, but that it has merely opened to you a lifelong study about our precious Savior from the pages of the Old Testament. Can you find Him on every page?

BIBLIOGRAPHY

Alexander, William, *The Witness of the Psalms to Christ and Christianity*; John Murray, London:1877.

Baron, David, *Rays of Messiah's Glory: Christ in the Old Testament*; Wipf and Stock, Eugene, OR: 2001.

Barrett, Michael P., *Beginning at Moses: A Guide to Finding Christ in the Old Testament*; Ambassador-Emerald Int'l., Greenville: 1999.

Boice, James Montgomery, *Genesis, Volume 1, Creation and Fall*; Baker Books, Grand Rapids: 2000.

Boice, James Montgomery, *Genesis, Volume 2, A New Beginning*; Baker Books, Grand Rapids: 1999.

Boice, James Montgomery, *Genesis, Volume 3, Living by Faith*; Baker Books, Grand Rapids: 1999.

Boice, James Montgomery, *Psalms, Volume 1: Psalms 1 - 41;* Baker Books, Grand Rapids: 1994.

Boice, James Montgomery, *Psalms, Volume 2: Psalms 42 - 106;* Baker Books, Grand Rapids: 1996.

Boice, James Montgomery, *Psalms, Volume 3: Psalms 107 - 150;* Baker Books, Grand Rapids: 1998.

Clowney, Edmund P., *Christ in the Old Testament*; Lectures at Westminster Theological Seminary, Philadelphia: 1987

Clowney, Edmund P., *The Unfolding Mystery: Discovering Christ in the Old Testament*; NavPress, Colorado Springs:1988.

Clowney, Edmund P., *Preaching Christ in All of Scripture*; Crossway, Wheaton: 2003.

Drew, Charles D., *The Ancient Love Song: Finding Christ in the Old Testament*; P&R, Phillipsburg: 2000.

Elwell, Walter A., Ed., *Evangelical Dictionary of Theology*; Baker Book House, Grand Rapids:1989.

Epp, Theodore H., *Portraits of Christ in the Tabernacle*; Back to the Bible, Lincoln: 1976.

Erdman, Charles R., *The Book of Leviticus: An Exposition*; Baker Book House, Grand Rapids: 1951.

Erdman, Charles R., *The Book of Deuteronomy: An Exposition*; Baker Book House, Grand Rapids: 1953.

France, R.T., *Jesus and the Old Testament*; Regent College Publishing, Vancouver: 1998.

Hodgkin, A.M., *Christ in All the Scriptures*; Christian Heritage, Great Britain: 2004. (Originally published in 1909.)

Johnson, Dennis E., *Him We Proclaim: Preaching Christ in All the Scriptures*, P&R, Phillipsburg, NJ: 2007.

Kaiser, Walter C., Jr., *The Messiah in the Old Testament*; Zondervan, Grand Rapids: 1995.

McDowell, Josh, *Evidence That Demands a Verdict: Historical Evidences for the Christian Faith*; Campus Crusade for Christ: 1982.

Pink, Arthur W., *Gleanings in Genesis*; Moody Press, Chicago: 1981.

Pink, Arthur W., *Gleanings in Exodus*; Moody Press, Chicago: 1981.

Poythress, Vern S., *The Shadow of Christ in the Law of Moses*; P&R, Phillipsburg, NJ: 1991.

Robertson, O. Palmer, *The Christ of the Covenants*; P&R, Phillipsburg, NJ: 1980.

Robertson, O. Palmer, *The Christ of the Prophets*; P&R, Phillipsburg, NJ: 2004.

Silvano, Dr. Rita, *Seeking Jesus in the Old Testament*; Our Sunday Visitor Publishing, Huntington, IN: 2006.

Spurgeon, C. H., *Christ in the Old Testament*; AMG Publishers, Chattanooga: 1994.

Wright, Christopher J. H., *Knowing Jesus Through the Old Testament*; InterVarsity, Downer's Grove: 1992.

Scripture Index

2:13 - *186*
3:9 - *84*
4:19 - *135*

Colossians

1:16 - *143*
2:2-3 - *159*

1 Thessalonians

4:16-17 - *124*
5:9 - *193*

1 Timothy

2:5 - *178*

2 Timothy

3:12 - *175*

Titus

3:4-5 - *84*

Hebrews

1:1 - *1*
1:2 - *143, 154, 192*
1:2 & 8 - *127*
1:3 - *107, 108, 144, 156*
1:5 - *127*
1:6-9 - *139*
1:14 - *25, 106*
2:5-9 - *130*
2:12 - *134*
2:14 - *6*
2:15 - *103, 174*
2:17 - *112, 130*
3:2 - *89*
3:4-6 - *48*
3:6 - *144*
4:12 - *58*
4:15 - *162*
5:4 - 101
6:17-18 - *18, 103*
7:1-3 - *15, 148*
7:11-16 - *15*
7:23-27 - *66*
7:26 - *38, 62*
8:5 - *67*
8:5-6 - *102*
9:4 - *72*
9:5 - **73**
9:7 - *83*
9:11-12 - *67, 68, 82*
9:15 - *178*
9:17 - *132*
9:20-22 - *96*

9:23-24 - *68*
9:25-28 - *98*
10:4 - *196*
10:11 - *148*
10:11-14 - *10*
10:17 - *94*
10:19-22 - *84*
11:10 - *60*
11:17-19 - *24*
11:24-26 - *89*
11:32 - *110*
12:1 - *86*
12:2 - *140*
12:5-11 - *136*
12:22 - *25*
13:5 - *58, 76, 136*
13:11-12 - *172*
13:12-13 - *94*

1 Peter

1:11 - *57*
1:18-19 - *80*
1:20 - *90*
1:23 - *88*
2:4-9 - *164*
2:5 - *69*
2:23 - *90*
3:22 - *38*
4:12-13 - *136*
5:8 - *110*

1 John

1:7 - *96*
2:2 - *85*
2:8 - *4*
2:22 - *6*
3:2-3 - *124*
3:8b - *52*
5:3 - *66*

Revelation

2:7 - *11*
2:27 - *128*
5:5 - *46, 69*
7:14 - *79*
8:7 - *52*
8:8 - *52*
9:15 - *52*
9:20-21 - *52*
11:3-6 - *52*
12:5 - *128*
13:13-16 - *52*
16:2 - *52*
16:4-5 - *52*
16:10 - *52*
16:13 - *52*
19:6-7 - *186*
19:7-9 - *186*

19:11-16 - *122*
19:16 - *192*
20:10 - *51*
20:14 - *182*
21:2 - *39*
21:3 - *68*
21:9 - *186*
22:2 - *11*
22:14 - *11*
22:19 - *11*